D0394056

Praise for *Straight Talk on Leadership*

"It is clearly time for Canadian business leaders to confront our national leadership dilemma. Williamson lays out a compelling agenda for leaders to act on to prepare us for a successful tomorrow."

—**Warren Bell**, Executive Vice President &
Chief Human Resources Officer, OMERS
(Ontario Municipal Employees Retirement System)

"Williamson's approach is effective and real-world: confront truths, wear them, and move forward quickly with accountable action. This book is an invaluable recipe as to the how and why leadership is critical to Canada's economic future."

—**Rupert Duchesne**, Group Chief Executive, Aimia Inc.
(Formerly Group Aeroplan Inc.)

"This book is for leaders who aspire to make a difference by transforming their organizations for global competitiveness. It is for those who approach leadership as a privilege to be re-earned each and every day, rather than a reward for past successes. Doug covers the landscape of issues facing leaders today in a compelling, insightful manner, and always with the frankness for which he is respected in the business community."

—**Eric Siegel**, President & Chief Executive Officer (Retired),
Export Development Canada

"The turbulent fast changing times we live in pose great leadership challenges. There are no easy leadership recipes. Doug Williamson's unvarnished straight talk puts the environment in global perspective and provides leaders with a competency framework suited to the times we live in. A must read."

—**Naseem Somani**, President & C.E.O.,
Gamma-Dynacare Medical Laboratories

"Succeeding in global markets requires an aggressive and competitive style. Doug has created a must-read blueprint for Canadian companies to succeed in domestically and internationally. Open communications and high transparency are the hallmarks of the best-run companies, and *Straight Talk on Leadership* makes a no-nonsense, patriotic plea for pragmatic leadership in the boardroom."

—**Robert Corteau**, Chief Executive Officer, Altus Group Limited

"Doug Williamson's book recognizes the unique position occupied by Canada in a changing global economy. He reinforces the need for Canadians to take advantage of that perspective by demonstrating a new type of leadership better suited to building not only highly profitable but also sustainable business organizations in this changing world. Rightfully, he sounds a warning in the event we do not heed the call to action."

—**Mark Young**, Managing Partner, Cassels Brock & Blackwell LLP

"If you are currently a leader in Canada, or aspire to be a successful one someday, this is a must-read book. From the title of the Introduction—'Moving Backward at the Speed of Light'—Doug's book has forced me to stop, think and plan action to change."
—**Johanne R. Bélanger**, President, AVW-TELAV
Audio Visual Solutions

"Doug Williamson understands the fabric of Canada. Strategy has been his forte and his book brings this to life. He sees the need for new leadership in business so that Canada itself can become a truly global leader. This is lofty, but necessary, thinking. I would hope that not only business leaders, but that many of our political leaders would read and follow Doug's teachings. He has hit the nail on the head!"
—**John Martin**, Retired Chairman and Chief Executive Officer,
Maxxam Analytics Inc.

"This book takes us out of our comfort zone. Doug challenges us to not accept the established norms and lets us know the consequences if we do. A mandatory read for all those who realize that businesses and institutions lacking in visionary leadership won't reach their potential and often will actually fail."
—**Judson Whiteside**, Former Chairman and Chief Executive Officer,
Miller Thomson LLP

"Motivating employees is the key to successful growth, both in Canada and elsewhere. The challenge for managers of international growth is the tailoring of management and incentive tools to reflect the cultural differences of employees in different countries. Doug's years of experience in assisting managers to identify and resolve these business issues are now available for all to read."
—**Nick Orlando**, President & Chief Executive Officer,
Martinrea International Inc.

"The world is now, more than ever, a changing landscape. *Straight Talk on Leadership* is an excellent and thoughtful read that extends the knowledge base of leadership and provides valuable insights. It clearly defines the challenges facing the modern business leader. This book rises like Everest, above all other leadership books."
—**Mary Ellen Carlyle**, Senior Vice President &
General Manager, Dome Productions

"It is refreshing to find a uniquely Canadian perspective on leadership, the business challenges we face and the opportunities afforded us. This is what Doug delivers best—straight talk—without pulling any punches."
—**David Harris**, President & Chief Executive Officer, Kinectrics Inc.

"This book is a must read for all current and future Canadian leaders. As a country, Doug's call for greater leadership and transformational leadership is timely and well warranted."
Douglas Harrison, President & Chief Executive Officer,
VersaCold Logistics Services

Straight Talk on Leadership

Straight Talk on Leadership

SOLVING CANADA'S BUSINESS
CRISIS

R. DOUGLAS WILLIAMSON

WILEY

Library and Archives Canada Cataloguing in Publication Data:

Williamson, R. Douglas, 1952-, author
    Straight talk on leadership : solving Canada's business crisis
/ R. Douglas Williamson.

Includes bibliographical references and index.
Issued in print and electronic formats.
ISBN 978-1-118-58168-1 (bound).—ISBN 978-1-118-858293-0 (pdf).—
ISBN 978-1-118-858301-2 (epub).—ISBN 978-1-118-858300-5(mobi)

    1. Leadership.   2. Industrial management—Canada.   I. Title.
HD57.7.W54 2013   658.4'092   C2013-903371-8
                                                     C2013-903372-6

Production Credits
Managing Editor: Alison Maclean
Executive Editor: Don Loney
Production Editor: Pauline Ricablanca
Cover Design: Adrian So
Composition: Thomson Digital
Printer: Courier

Printed in Canada

1 2 3 4 5 CR 17 16 15 14 13

This book is dedicated to all of the proud, hard-working men and women of Canada, including my grandfathers, Cyril Edward Williamson (1906–1988) and Maxwell Harvey Gifford (1900–1969). They represent the everyday people from small towns, farms and fishing villages across this country who, with nothing other than their dreams, big hearts and calloused hands, built this country one brick at a time. We owe them a huge debt of gratitude, not only for their efforts and commitment to building Canada, but also for promoting Canadian values and for their unwavering faith in the basic good and positive intentions of people everywhere in the world.

This book is my humble effort to honour our past by providing fresh ideas and constructive solutions that can assist Canada in realizing its full potential in a rapidly changing, more complex and far more competitive global environment.

CONTENTS

Contents

Contents

Contents

A NOTE TO THE READER

This book has been written for all concerned Canadian citizens, business leaders in every sector, politicians and government officials at all levels as well as professors and their students. This book aspires to provide a voice of hope for every Canadian worker, future business leader or entrepreneur who believes:

- Canadians can and should do more than we have, on both the domestic and international stages. This requires us to build businesses that can offer uniquely Canadian services, solutions and expertise to the rest of the world while creating the basis for a prosperous economy at home, offering quality jobs, training and promising career opportunities for everyone.
- Canadians must urgently improve the quality of our business leadership talent pool by developing new mindsets, attitudes, beliefs and behaviours. This includes the development of a new set of transformational leadership competencies capable of helping us carve a bold new path to growth, sustainable success and an outward-facing, global sense of purpose and commitment.

In this book, I will:

- Profile eight transformational leadership competencies required for business success in the future. They will be presented as individual forms of leadership "intelligence" that must work together, in a complementary fashion, to provide a balanced set of capabilities.
- Highlight several successful Canadian organizations and their leaders, who have followed a transformational path and represent actual "Case Studies in Canadian Business" that we can all learn from and apply.
- Review some of the less successful Canadian organizations and business leaders from the past to learn what we can from their failures in strategy development, leadership effectiveness, organizational performance and execution.

- Summarize a series of practical steps leaders can take to put their organizations on the road to transformation.

I hope this book will serve to create a vigorous national dialogue about Canada's economic future and the role business leaders should play in ensuring that Canada remains relevant in the midst of a rapidly changing world order.

FOREWORD

Straight talk is Doug Williamson's speciality. I have worked with nobody better at the scarce skill of having courageous conversations with managers who need to hear the unvarnished truth about their performance. Sometimes that requires a combative spirit, sometimes a soft word that "turneth away wrath." Doug can do both, which requires him to curb his natural desire to just get on with it.

It's that practical approach I have admired and valued in the 10 years that Doug and his Beacon Group consultancy have worked with *The Globe and Mail* management team. Early on he deduced that we were not fans of textbook solutions, or prone to endless patience, so he adjusted his style to military-march pace. That sense of urgency and willingness to challenge the status quo are ever more appropriate today, as the world of media goes through a period of startlingly fast change that is disrupting business models all over the world.

Doug's book, with its emphasis on taking ownership of difficult situations and not flinching from risk, is relevant to *The Globe*, as it is to much of corporate Canada, with its tendency to cautiously take the middle of the road.

Preaching resolute confidence stemming from a thorough under-standing of the requisite competencies is what Doug Williamson does best. His message is not for the faint-hearted, who rapidly slip down his rigorous ratings ladder.

To follow the Beacon way implicitly assumes courage to confront the challenges and manage through them with gritty determination. Sometimes managers find that too hard to handle—the tendency to back off and revert to the status quo should never be underestimated. If this book doesn't deliver the stiffening of the backbone needed to make the difference, none will.

Transformational change begins with big ambition and courage. It's questionable if those qualities can be learned, but the tool kit to build conviction of purpose and commitment to team success is what Doug's book delivers. It's a step-by-step, methodical pursuit of big objectives and small wins that make it possible. This is how managers can create the self-belief that enables them to communicate a compelling story to staff, without whose support all else fails.

At *The Globe*, Doug has been the coach in our corner for the last decade, so we can vouch for his pragmatic wisdom. Now, sit up and pay attention!

Phillip Crawley
Publisher and CEO of *The Globe and Mail*

Introduction

Moving Backward at the Speed of Light

I have always had a fascination with the special, rugged and romantic role the lighthouse had in shaping Canada's national fabric. This is, no doubt, born out of the fact my grandfather Cyril Williamson was a lightkeeper for 25 years (1945–1970). While I was growing up, I had the good fortune to work as his "assistant" during the summers. Every day we watched giant ocean-going vessels from all corners of the world pass no more than 50 metres away from the house in which we lived. I remember how my eyes would strain to read the exotic names of their home ports written on the stern just below their national flag. It never ceased to amaze me how the crew on board, from countries all around the world, could look toward shore and see the red ensign, and later the maple leaf, flying proudly from the flagpole mounted just in front of the giant light tower.

Those summers taught me not just about the joy and dreams of adventure, but also a great deal about life, hard work, character and respect for working men and women everywhere. People like my grandfather, who have always relied on others to guide the ships of businesses, both large and small, to responsibly manage the companies for whom he worked in order to provide honourable employment and to lead on many different levels. In return, these everyday Canadians have been happy to toil in more routine work and less glamorous roles with the simple desire of earning a decent living for their families and hope for their communities.

In a working lighthouse, the light serves to guide ships when the night is clear and the passage calm. However, of far more interest to me was the second important piece of navigational guidance equipment, the foghorn. The haunting, dark, rumbling tones of the horn help to guide and orient ships on those occasions when their visibility is impaired by fog, mist, snow or heavy rain. Captains of ocean-going vessels have known for centuries that when conditions change, they have to alter their perspective and modify their dependencies, in this case, moving from the power of sight to the comfort of sound.

Adaptation is the basis for all forms of human survival. It is the willingness, ability and confidence to adjust to circumstances as they change, and to allow other tools or senses to guide us when conditions shift and our existing repertoire is no longer sufficient or relevant. So it is in business. When conditions change, we need to alter the methods we use to make sense of the environment around us and then adjust our course. If we don't, we will sail straight onto the rocky reef hidden by the thick wall of fog.

Throughout history, the great leaders have known when and how to adapt or pivot. They seem to have a sixth sense and know exactly the right moment at which to abandon what is no longer working and comfortably embrace new tools more suited to the conditions they find themselves in. It is part experience, part intuition and part luck, but successfully identifying and then navigating these crucial inflection points is the responsibility of our leaders. The average leader can perhaps do a respectable enough job when conditions are normal, but it takes an exceptional leader to navigate confidently in uncertain, uncharted and turbulent waters.

It seems as though these dangerous, pivotal moments have been presenting themselves with increasing frequency in recent years. The more interconnected global economy, rapid technological advances and constantly evolving social, political and demographic changes have all come together to alter the once reliable maps we used to guide us in the post-WWII period. The question that should concern and even haunt us is why, in the face of these changes, so many leaders, organizations and nations have not been brave enough, vigilant enough or just plain smart enough to switch tack from what may have been right and relevant in one set of circumstances to a new course, better suited to the changing conditions of the future.

Which brings me to the heart of this book—Canada.

* * *

Canada is a country of great wealth, whether measured in terms of our ample natural resources, our outstanding agricultural good fortune or our abundant maritime gifts. We who live here have been granted easy fortune in a world where many are far less privileged and less well endowed than we are. In the old economy, Canada's physical assets were a source of unique economic value creation and placed us in demand as an exporter of products sought by others to feed their people and fuel their own economies. Canada was a good partner with whom to trade. We were reasonable, respected and fair. We had no natural enemies or historical foes and, as a result, we were regularly called upon to be a peacekeeper in situations where others were not so welcome or trusted.

Slowly, our international role began to diminish as Canada stepped back from not only its traditional role as a recognized and well-regarded international peacekeeper but also as a primary source of traditional raw material exports. Unfortunately, this happened at about the same time the global economy matured to a point where goods, services and intellectual capital were replacing wheat, ore, fish and other natural resources as the primary engines of economic prosperity.

According to a recent study undertaken by the International Finance Corporation and the World Bank, Canada seems to have lost its way more than many appreciate. We are currently ranked 17th in the world in terms of our "ease of doing business with." This means we are well behind countries such as Singapore at number one, the United Kingdom at number seven and Australia at number 10. To add salt to the wound, it means we are also ranked behind a collection of countries not normally considered to be in our "tier," such as Georgia, Malaysia, Korea and Taiwan. We cannot allow this perception of our "brand" to continue.

An even more damning set of numbers comes from the CIA World Factbook and its report on GDP growth from 2010 to 2011 (as of December 10, 2012). Canada ranks 140th globally, with a year-over-year improvement of only 2.4%, compared to the world average of 3.7%. While we may be able to understand the reasons our low growth rate puts us behind such fast-charging notables as China in 9th place at 9.2% or India in 35th place at 6.8%, we still rank behind others with whom we share a similar profile, such as Sweden who is in 100th place at 4.0%.

3

It appears Canada has gone from being a virile, confident and enthusiastic teenager to a much slower-moving, tentative middle-aged adult in a relatively short period of only 50 years. We have failed to pivot when we should have. We have failed to understand what has been changing around us and appreciate that it is not what we have that matters, it's what we do with what we have, and we have not done enough. It is not too late, though. We have an outstanding platform on which to build a modern, globally focused economy, but we are not using it wisely, and any number of global indices and benchmarks tell us this.

On the positive side of the ledger:

- We continue to be widely seen around the world as a place of tolerance and freedom, with the Reputation Institute ranking Canada first in the world, ahead of the Nordic countries and well ahead of the United States, who ranks 23rd.
- The *Wall Street Journal*'s Market Watch Report for 2012 ranks Canada first in the world when it comes to educated adults. In Canada, 51% of the population have post-secondary degrees, ahead of Japan at 45%, the United States at 42% and Australia at 38%.

On the not-so-positive side of things, there is other data that should deeply concern us in a changing world.

- The Legatum Prosperity Index ranks Canada 16th in terms of entrepreneurship.
- The International Living Quality of Life Index ranks Canada 29th, well down the list and well below where we have been in the past and where we think we should be.

There is no doubt these indictments will sound harsh, and even unfair, to those who want to believe that the merits of our noble past afford us the guarantee of future success. Unfortunately, that would be like a ship's captain failing to heed the warnings of the foghorn and choosing to maintain the same course, even though the conditions have changed so fundamentally that full speed ahead will only bring the rocky shore closer at greater speed.

FACTS ARE FACTS

Let's just call it like it is. We are moving backward for a number of pretty basic and easy-to-understand reasons. We must be more willing than we have been to face the facts as they are, not as we wish them to be.

- First, others are simply running faster than we are. Whether they are fitter, better trained, better coached or more motivated does not really matter. The fact is, they are already well ahead of us in the race and opening up even more of a lead every day.
- Second, they are running in a new and different direction. Somewhere along the way, it seems we forgot to take a turn and, while we are expending decent energy, solid effort and ample sweat, we are simply on the wrong path and will inevitably have to circle back and start all over again.

It's becoming more than a little embarrassing. It is as though we are playing the modern game with the same old equipment we used 20 years ago, while others have the latest in new technology, fitness and development and have totally reinvented the way in which the game is played. Have we become the other guys? Have we become the guys we played in the 1972 hockey Summit Series? The guys with ill-fitting helmets, old skates and wooden sticks who dared challenge us at our national game and who put the fear of failure and disgrace into all of us until Paul Henderson scored late in the final game. These were the guys we didn't take seriously until Vladislav Tretiak and Alexander Yakushev showed us that those from outside Canada could be just as good as we are at our own game. Do we have to wait until the final few minutes of the game in order to pull out a victory?

Sure, we are strong and safe as a nation. Sure, we did not suffer from the forces of financial greed and rampant speculation that infected our American neighbours and almost brought them, and the rest of us, to our knees. Sure, we have been far more fiscally responsible than some of our European cousins, but so what? Without doubt, the cold, hard facts indicate we were able to weather the global economic storm in better shape than most. However, it is not just about survival and stability for the sake of survival and stability. It is about making wise use of the foundation we have in order to build for the future. It's not about conserving what we have, it's about using what we have to drive opportunity, expand relevance and support our social infrastructure.

Instead of playing to win, we are playing a safe, defensive game. As a result, we are losing our relative share of opportunity and not putting ourselves in a position to actually win the game. We have not taken anything near the advantage we could have, given our relative financial position and our respected national brand. Our national preference for comfort and our predisposition toward complacency have lured us into a lazy slumber. We seem better suited to an afternoon nap on the dock by the lake, rather than the cut, thrust and effort needed to participate in the shaping of the future global space. To quote Gary Hamel and C. K. Prahalad, *"in the race to the future there are drivers, passengers and road kill."* It is as though we made a choice, but have conveniently disregarded the inevitable consequences.

INTO THE STIFF WIND

There is an old saying in the field of organizational behaviour that we tend to "acquire our bad habits in good times and our good habits in bad times." Well, things have been pretty good in Canada for quite a while now, so it's not surprising that we have developed some fairly bad habits. We should be concerned about one of these habits in particular, which is our tendency to think that we are doing better than we really are. In this regard, it looks to many as though Canada is suffering from a severely dislocated shoulder, which has, no doubt, been brought about by patting ourselves on the back too hard.

It's time to check our navigational aids, realistically assess the environment and make the necessary changes in course, speed and direction, before it's too late. The fundamentals have changed and, as a result, we need to acquire some critical new leadership competencies in order help navigate the future. We need imaginative, inspired and transformational leaders to shape the opportunities that lie just over the horizon, but which are fading fast. We need businesses, in every sector of the economy, to do a better job of developing transformational leaders. We need leaders equipped for the times in which we live and, even more importantly, leaders equipped for the future that is coming our way, whether we are ready or not. We need leaders with new capabilities, fresh mindsets and passion for building the hypercompetitive Canada of the future, not those who are content with the comfortable Canada of the past. We need transformational leaders, not caretaker managers.

It is not about avoiding choices or postponing the inevitable. It's about character, credibility and the courage of conviction. It is about a clarity of purpose and a willingness to tackle opportunity to the ground with fierce resolve and total commitment. It's about transformational leadership.

LEADING FOR A BETTER FUTURE

There are two contrasting ways in which to lead an organization (or a country) to a new and radically different place. One way is to lead by map, and the other is to lead by compass. In the first instance, the leader provides a very detailed map to the organization and asks people to follow it. In the second instance, the leader chooses a general direction, points people in that direction and has confidence in their ability to follow the compass setting. Both approaches can work well enough, although the optimal one depends on the situation. As a result, the leader has to know which one will work best, given the circumstances.

Maps are fine on land, where the road has been surveyed and travelled by others, and where convenient signposts have been erected along the way by previous travellers. Maps are fine in a certain, predictable and known environment where progress can be measured in small increments with little or no deviation permitted by the leader.

On the other hand, as any good sailor from well before the time of Christopher Columbus would tell you, it is quite different in the frothy, uncharted waters of the open sea where, out of necessity, a good compass replaces the map as the primary means of navigation.

Today, we are being asked to lead under conditions that look much more like those of the stormy, unpredictable North Atlantic than the well-paved routes of the Trans-Canada Highway. As a result, we need leaders who are comfortable, confident and capable of navigating by celestial compass, not locked into the rigid, dependable, well-travelled roads shown on a map.

Those leaders are different. They are built with a certain confident sense of themselves and others. They are not handcuffed by memories of the past or fears of the future. They are not dependent upon the tried, the tested and the true. They are adventurers, driven and motivated by the thrill of discovery, not the comforts of home. They know a ship moored at harbour is not the safest place to ride out a major storm. They know their ship is much better off being at sea when a hurricane blows through. The choices are up to the captain, and the outcome will be the direct result of the choices he or she makes.

THE IMPORTANCE OF PERSPECTIVE

Award-winning photojournalist Dewitt Jones arrived at some valuable conclusions for business leaders based on his experience with *National Geographic* magazine over the past 20 years. His professional career choice has required him to master the same skills as those needed by business leaders today. They include not just a spirit of adventure, but also a mindset that allows him to unveil the possibilities that others do not readily see. He is constantly challenged with finding just the right set of conditions, the best possible position and the optimal angle to frame the picture he wants to shoot. His mission is to capture our imagination and, in his own words, "to make the ordinary, extraordinary."

Although Jones is not a business leader, or even someone with direct experience in the corporate world, he has wise insight. He knows that when it comes to facing the unknown and trying to make sense of something unfamiliar, it is the process of putting the picture in proper focus and ensuring that it appeals to our emotions that, in turn, makes the impossible possible and the improbable more likely.

STRAIGHT TALK FIRST STEPS

The lessons from the field of photography are summarized in the book that Jones co-wrote with Stephen Covey and Roger Merrill, *The Nature of Leadership*. They can readily be adopted by the transformational business leaders we need in Canada as

---

a starting point to help guide us through the wild and uncertain conditions we face.

Step 1: Switch to a Wide-Angle Lens

Many of us look at the world, and its opportunities, through too narrow a lens. We allow our personal fears and professional insecurities to block our ability to frame the picture correctly and then, to make matters even worse, we combine that with our traditional Canadian risk aversion. Together, these traits lead us to believe that it is only by shrinking the size of the challenge that we will be able to make it more understandable and digestible.

Unfortunately, the very premise of that argument is false. In fact, it is the exact opposite of what we need to do. In the face of the unpredictable and the unknown, we actually have to change to a wide lens. The wider we frame the picture, the more of the picture we see. The more we see, the more we understand. The more we understand, the lower our fear and trepidation.

Switching to a wider lens has several benefits:

- It prevents us from falling into the easy trap of assuming there is only one right answer to a problem, rather than multiple right answers. If all we do is start to chase the first right answer when it appears in our lens, we deprive ourselves of finding even better right answers, which are possible if we can just learn to shift our vantage point and be patient.
- It affords us a much better chance of identifying the place of greatest long-term opportunity, rather than the place of most short-term convenience. We need to see the vantage point that provides the best overall perspective from which to view the challenge.
- It frees us from the terrifying disappointment of failure that comes from not capturing the perfect result on our first attempt. When we search for multiple right answers rather than seeing an initial setback as a failure, we can begin to see it

(continued)

9

as a necessary rite of passage on the journey toward excellence. We can begin to see the first right answer as a sure sign that we are headed in the right direction and that the next right answer is hidden just out of view around the corner.

There is a deeply embedded tendency in corporate life to do just the opposite of these three things. We often seek the easiest, quickest, cheapest answer, the one closest to perfection, and then stop, saying it is good enough.

The better choice would be to widen the lens setting, back away to gain better perspective and then force ourselves to discover multiple right answers before we lock ourselves down too early to a fixed and readily obvious path.

Step 2: Change Your Filter

Bias is a dangerous thing, especially when you are not aware it exists. While it is a normal part of the human condition, it does not have to be the fatal flaw it often becomes. The puncturing of worn beliefs, the debunking of old myths and the elimination of institutional and personal bias should be amongst the top priorities of the modern transformational leader.

The leaders we need must have the patience, objectivity and discipline to look at problems from multiple perspectives when faced with chaos, uncertainty and the unknown. We need leaders who combine that ability with the courage to suspend their judgment and understand that problems take on different shapes in different lights. Putting the correct filter on the camera can make the situation look entirely different than it may have initially appeared.

In the crazy, fast-paced, high-pressure world we live in today, it might seem counterintuitive to suggest we consciously slow down when faced with a challenging situation we have not experienced before. However, continuing down the first road you find, at reckless speed and with careless abandon, can simply put you on a quicker path to eventual disaster. The better option is to pause, step back, calibrate and then define the challenge or opportunity in more depth by altering the filter through which you examine the issue. In so doing, you'll conserve energy and refocus your mission, and then you can deploy, at speed and with confidence, when it comes to execution and implementation.

In the current environment, the cognitive and interpretive skills of the leader will be put to the test like never before. The old approach, previously tried and tested, is not likely to be the best approach to use in solving new challenges where there is no precedent to call upon. The leader of the future must learn how to pressure test the underlying premise upon which assumptions are based, rather than gloss over the logic in the rush to find an answer.

Step 3: Adjust Your Vantage Point

If all else fails, if there is no wider lens to be had and no new filter through which to view the situation, then the very least that leaders can do is take purposeful and intentional steps to raise the level of their own curiosity. Great leaders know that chief amongst their curiosity skills is the ability to pose fresh new questions that, in turn, lead to new and fresh insight. Learning how to ask the wicked questions, those penetrating, deeply insightful questions rooted in curiosity, is a master competency required by leaders when facing the unknown or the unexpected.

It is not easy to be the constantly questioning provocateur, because the inevitable by-product of enhanced curiosity can be increased discord and anxiety. Deep questioning, by its very nature, means you are disrupting convention. Therefore, you need to be able to understand and embrace the inherent tension that comes from passionate debate and vigorous dialogue. Avoiding conflict, believing that consensus is always best and striving for superficial harmony are not the answers to excellence or breakthrough thinking.

The best way to gain a new, unique and clear perspective is to get away from the immediate task at hand, elevate your vantage point and put yourself in the place of greatest tension

(continued)

11

or discomfort. In other words, walk toward the fire, rather than away from it. In the case of business leaders, this inevitably means getting out into the real world of your customers, and your customers' customers, to see what they are feeling and experiencing. Leaders must be like anthropologists, willing to visit the gritty front lines of their businesses and get as close as they can to the "tribes" who work right at the coal face, where life can get tough. It is only there that they will be able to sharpen their perspective, awaken their senses and find the right questions to ask when they return to the boardroom table.

Final Thoughts

Every organization faces obstacles, barriers and excuses that get in the way of striving for the optimal outcome or of finding the next right answer and not just defaulting to the most easily identified and convenient one. In most cases, the bad trade-offs and poor choices made by the organization are well known and obvious to everyone except the senior leaders. All too often, the senior leaders are protected and cocooned from the unsightly realities experienced down the chain of command.

The leader at the top needs to defend against the lure of comfort and complacency by remaining vigilant, curious and active, even when it does not appear to be necessary. The current climate, in which the swamp has been drained, provides the perfect opportunity for leaders to see the rocks that had previously been hidden just under the surface. When they do so, they then have to deal firmly and convincingly with what are now the obvious risks and impediments to sustainable high performance.

Canadians are used to the regular changes of the seasons, and they understand that each new season has its charms and inconveniences. The global economic season has changed, and now you need to dress accordingly, based upon whether you believe we are approaching the promise of spring or the dark night of autumn.

PART I

Leveraging Our National Brand through Bold Leadership

Business leaders and politicians have notoriously short and convenient memories. Each time we hit yet another predictable cyclical economic downturn, we endlessly debate the reasons, are quick to point the finger of blame and then we conveniently use the excuse of external market forces as a means to justify our short-sighted overreaction. This recurring pattern of behaviour does no more than reveal the inherent weaknesses of our leadership acumen, and yet we allow the pattern to continue rather than learn, adjust and compensate accordingly.

In Part I, we suggest this recidivist pattern of misguided leadership behaviour has had an even worse impact on Canada than it has had on other countries whose leaders act in the same way. It has caused us to lose valuable competitive ground at the very time we should have been accelerating out of the global downturn with confidence. Canadians need to take a new stand, and our business leaders and politicians cannot be allowed to squander the tremendous hidden value of our national brand.

As Canadians, we need to find the courage and conviction to transform our economy through the restructuring of our historical business models and the rapid development of a new generation of leaders equipped to compete with a modern set of leadership competencies. These competencies of the future and the mindset of global competitiveness will allow us to remain relevant in the long term rather than shelter behind the short-sighted naïveté and complacency that have lured us into believing we are doing better than we really are.

1

Crimes of Leadership Malfeasance

Leadership is never easy, even in the best of times. So when you add the extra stresses associated with the deep economic downturn we have experienced since the fall of 2007, the competence of business leaders has been pressure tested like never before. Rising financial uncertainty, market instability and the enormous destruction of wealth we have witnessed across the global economy mean that every sector, household and organization has been touched in some negative way.

The loss of financial value in the stock markets, the depressed employment markets and reduced levels of industrial performance and productivity are the issues that most often make the headlines. They are the most visible of the consequences because they are the most easily measured. Harder to measure is the human toll, also a tragic consequence of a system gone wrong.

The global financial crisis has put the world into the worst economic and social tailspin since the Great Depression. The lingering effects of this inconvenient reality will be felt for years to come and, unfortunately, there are not likely to be any quick turnarounds. While there were a number of converging factors fuelling the crisis—many of them cloaked by complex financial market chicanery—the real underlying causes were behavioural in nature.

Whether it was greed on the part of financial institutions, speculators and market traders, or whether it was simple self-serving human behaviour on a more basic level, the fact of the matter is that too many people in the United States accumulated too high a level of personal debt to maintain a lifestyle they could not afford. It is like they were cheating and chasing the American dream on the backs of their credit cards or mortgage debt with the belief that rising property values in the long term would forgive the sins of overextending themselves in the short term.

In an environment of steadily decreasing interest rates and large inflows of foreign capital, which began as we entered the new millennium, the easy availability of credit fuelled a housing construction boom in the United States. As banks began to provide more credit, housing prices began to rise and wealth accumulation looked like an effortless, guaranteed ride for all Americans, many of whom were looking for a shortcut to prosperity.

With the tacit encouragement of both the government and the banks, Americans who could not afford to purchase a house willingly jumped on the bandwagon for fear of being left behind. Between 1997 and 2006, the price of the average American house increased by 124%. However, we now know it was not real value appreciation underpinned by sound fundamentals, but more like a sophisticated Ponzi scheme.

Observing what was going on, large foreign and domestic investors wanted a piece of the action, and so a series of financial agreements called mortgage-backed securities (MBS) and collateralized debt obligations (CDO) were created to allow those investors to indirectly invest in the housing boom. Between the intense competition for market share and a limited supply of creditworthy borrowers, mortgage lenders began to significantly relax their underwriting standards. They took on riskier and riskier loans, the so-called subprime mortgages, which grew rapidly to become 20% of all mortgages written by 2004 and remained at that high level for the next three years.

As we know, this all came to a head when average U.S. housing prices quickly declined by over 20%. Those people with adjustable-rate mortgages simply could not refinance their debt or afford to pay higher monthly payments. Instead, they began to default. The American attitude, which some would see as a sense of entitlement, allowed people to think they could just walk away from these contractual obligations regardless of societal morality, personal pride or basic financial responsibility. As a result, during 2007, lenders foreclosed on 1.3 million properties, and the number increased to 2.3 million by 2008. In August 2008, 9.2% of all U.S. mortgages were delinquent or in foreclosure, and a year later, the bad debt portfolio had risen to 14.4%.

There was a corresponding negative response in the stock market. It had peaked in October 2007 with the Dow Jones Industrial Average exceeding 14,000 points, but by March 2009, it had reached a low of 6,600, falling more than 50% over just 17 months.

In August 2007, a large French bank, BNP Paribas, became concerned and blocked withdrawals from three large hedge funds due to what it saw as an evaporation of market liquidity. This led to panic as investors tried to liquidate assets held in the more highly leveraged financial institutions. Companies dealing in mortgages could no longer obtain financing, ultimately resulting in more than 100 mortgage lenders going bankrupt between 2007 and 2008. During one week in September 2008, $144.5 billion was withdrawn from the money markets compared to $7.1 billion the week prior.

The personal price paid and pain experienced by Americans between June 2007 and November 2008 was astonishing. They lost an average of 25% of their net worth between declines in home equity, retirement assets, savings, investment assets and pensions. Americans lost $8.3 trillion in total, the result of what turned out to be no more than a false belief in a strange form of financial black magic.

Most definitions of exemplary leadership would include something about how, in moments of crisis, leaders are expected to rise to the occasion, offer incisive insight and take bold, courageous action. We saw just the opposite. The hesitation, distortion, evasion and blame were almost too much to bear. Politicians and business leaders, especially those in the United States, did nothing to distinguish themselves as leaders deserving of our admiration. In Canada, we performed marginally better on the leadership ledger, but we failed to seize the day and use our comparative strength, candour and realism to good advantage. In that regard, Canadian leaders also failed, just in a different way than those south of the border or in Italy, Greece, Ireland and Portugal.

2

Lessons from the Recent Past

In the bleak economic crisis of the 1930s, the economist Joseph Schumpeter coined the phrase "creative destruction" to explain the natural cycle of economic cleansing that is necessary to ensure long-term sustainable growth and economic health. In recent times there have been several of these cleansings, or recessions, particularly in the United States. Almost all were triggered by some type of financial market event far removed from the day-to-day lives of those on Main Street and their ability to understand either the substance or the nuance of what it all meant behind the scenes. We in Canada have not been as strongly impacted as those south of the border. However, while our financial system and practices are healthier and we did not hit the same low lows, we still need to think long and hard about the dark side of short-term, lustful, get-rich-quick capitalism. In Canada, we have long known both the advantages and disadvantages of our close relationship with the United States. It has always been the case that "when the United States sneezes, we catch a cold."

Free markets are undoubtedly the best way to create economic prosperity; there is no question about that. However, when things are taken to wild extremes of speculation, poor judgment and bad behaviour, the trickle-down pain caused to innocent families and small businesses can be devastating. Defined as a general slowdown in economic activity, a recession occurs when there is a sudden widespread drop in spending, triggered by any number of events. The first to feel it are the middle class and businesses that depend on their spending.

The 1981 to 1982 recession was caused by ill-considered monetary policy, specifically actions taken by the U.S. Federal Reserve to reduce the size of the monetary supply in an attempt to control high inflation in the wake of the 1973 oil crisis and the 1979 energy crisis. Interest rates rose and, as a result, industries such as housing, steel manufacturing and automobile production were hit hard. Consequently, high levels of unemployment followed and wallets dried up.

The 1987 decline was attributable to the collapse of the U.S. Savings and Loan industry, which created widespread panic due to rising financial uncertainty for millions of Americans.

The seeds of the 1990 to 1991 recession were sown on the infamous Black Monday of October 1987, when the Dow Jones fell by 22.6% in one day. The drop was bigger than the one in 1929, which triggered the Great Depression. The 1990 Gulf War added fuel to the fire and resulted in a spike in oil prices, making matters even worse.

The 2001 recession was the inevitable downside of the dot-com boom of the mid to late 1990s in which an extraordinarily large number of Internet and technology companies emerged from nowhere. Those companies, which were speculative in nature, were able to raise rather large amounts of short-term capital with relative ease to cover start-up costs intended to get them to a point of long-term sustainability.

Unfortunately, far too many never made enough or even any profit, and were either acquired at bargain basement prices or simply liquidated. The crash between 2000 and 2002 caused the loss of almost $5 trillion in the market value of traded companies. The terrorist attacks of September 11, 2001, compounded the large financial losses with the even more tragic loss of human life. While al Qaeda did not bring the U.S. economy to its knees, as it hoped, the Dow Jones did suffer its worst one-day point loss and the biggest one-week loss in history up to that point.

LESSONS FROM CANADIAN BUSINESS

While history may not be a very good, or accurate, predictor of the future, it is still instructive to look back at some of the bigger and more dramatic business failures in Canada. Not only can they help us gain perspective, but they may also help us to avoid such disasters in the future.

(*continued*)

Campeau Corporation (1953–1990)

Campeau was a major real estate development and investment company founded by Robert Campeau to exploit the growth in the Ottawa area commercial and residential property market, which had been fuelled by the expanding civil service industry. In the 1980s, emboldened by its success in Ottawa, Campeau began purchasing larger businesses outside of Canada and outside of its real estate development expertise. The acquisitions included high-risk retail property propositions, such as Allied Stores and Federated Department Stores, the owner of Bloomingdale's. At the end of the day, Campeau's debt obligations were too high and both acquisitions ended in bankruptcy, bringing the Campeau Corporation to an inglorious end.

CanWest (1974–2009)

CanWest was a diversified media company founded by Israel Asper in Winnipeg. In 1997, it bought the privately owned CBC affiliate in Quebec City. It eventually rebranded to become the Global Television Network, and over time it expanded its coverage in the West. In 2007, it partnered with Goldman Sachs to acquire Alliance Atlantis Communications and, in the process, assumed large amounts of debt, which had grown to $4 billion by 2009. The company eventually had no choice but to separate its empire into parts and sell those parts off. In February 2010, Shaw Communications bought significant parts of CanWest's assets, excluding the newspaper holdings, which were sold to the Postmedia Network.

Olympia and York (1952–1993)

O&Y, as it was best known, was an international property development firm that built a series of major office complexes, including Canary Wharf in London, the World Financial Center in New York and First Canadian Place in Toronto. Founded by brothers Paul, Albert and Ralph Reichmann in the 1950s, it would become the largest property development firm in the world by the 1980s. Along the way, the brothers expanded their sights and purchased a number of different businesses, including Gulf Canada Resources, Brinco Inc., Abitibi-Price, Royal Trust Company and English Property Corporation. After the collapse of Olympia and York, which resulted from a combination of too much debt and an addiction to growth for the sake of growth, the brothers began to rebuild again and eventually sold their new company to Brookfield Properties in 2005 for $2.1 billion.

These three examples of failed leadership and failed business are worth remembering, both because of their size and impact, as well as the fact that when the final chapter was written, the verdict was the same.

- They stretched themselves too far, too fast and allowed themselves to wander away from their roots and their core competencies.
- They allowed greed, ego and bravado to replace common sense and good business practice and, in the process, saw themselves as immune from bad judgment.
- With the support and encouragement of the big banks in Canada and overseas, they assumed levels of debt that were not sustainable, and they believed they could "rent" other people's money in order to grow quickly.

3

Hidden Costs of the Current Crisis

While we all tend to focus on the conventional data sets that tell us we are in the midst of a perfect economic storm, things like GDP growth, debt levels, bankruptcies, stock market trends and trade flows, those metrics only reveal the symptoms of something much deeper. No one seems to want to talk about the important root causes and the other less obvious ways in which value has been eroded, even though the impact, both financial and otherwise, has arguably been just as great.

Specifically, I am referring to the loss of value, on many different levels, as a result of bad leadership. It is something that simply does not get enough press. It is almost as though we don't want to address the fault lines in our business leadership foundation, and would rather expend our energy griping about the symptoms, rather than focusing on the disease. The things we should be looking at include the cost of

- poor strategic foresight, which can cause a business to underestimate or inadequately anticipate a competitive threat and get hammered as a result;
- an acquisition gone wrong, due to a failure to fully integrate cultures or harmonize production capacity in order to ensure economic synergies;
- habitual, shortsighted underinvestment in research and development, which results in products and/or services that fail to keep pace with consumer demand;
- an ill-equipped workforce, resulting from a failure to upgrade skill sets through proper training; and

- lost business opportunity and its corresponding revenue potential when poor leadership and bad human capital management result in unresolved tensions, frictions, dysfunctions and barriers to success.

It somehow seems easier for people to point the finger of blame at the external factors we cannot control, rather than look in the mirror and accept responsibility for the things we can.

4

Confronting Our Complacency

It is the responsibility of every leader, especially in times like these, to challenge conventional wisdom at every turn and to seek out the truth, no matter where it takes them. Senior leaders are expected to ensure their organizations avoid the sin of complacency and are challenged, every day, to raise the bar of expectations and performance. Leaders must maintain the very delicate balance between fostering a culture of superficial congeniality and tolerating a culture of harmful discord and dysfunction. They simply cannot be passive when it comes to fuelling the energy level and metabolism of the organization, and they must be prepared to infuse energy when it is required. It is the responsibility of the leader to maintain the overall cultural and emotional fitness level of the organization and ensure that everyone lives up to their true potential, rather than just a passable level of mediocre performance.

Leadership requires high levels of personal commitment, tenacity and fierce resolve. You cannot lead a business to the future from behind a control panel, tinkering with dials and buttons and occupying your day reading sanitized reports presented by managers who feel they have little to gain from identifying cracks in the hull of the ship. Leaders need to be out in the field, out where the action is taking place, not behind their desks. A leader needs to feel and sense what is happening. You can't lead a business in fast-changing, hypercompetitive times by focusing on the clinical analysis of cold data that is geared to explaining the retrospective results of the previous month or quarter. You need to capture the nuance, which can only present itself in the light of day.

Management is about the present. Leadership is about the future. The metrics used to gauge relative performance are changing as quickly as the weather, yet too few leaders have recognized the full magnitude of this shift, and many have failed to develop the future-oriented predictive metrics that really matter. Leaders are responsible for the future, and there is little to be gained by driving to the future with one eye on the rear-view mirror. Leaders must lean into the business, lift their own game, harness their own energy and focus their own efforts by making decisions about the future, decisions that matter, that create new opportunity and that offer promise.

These are times for truly transformational leaders, not bookkeepers, analysts and organizational mechanics whose skills are limited to maintaining the status quo. Transformational leaders, by their very nature, are wired and motivated differently; they operate according to a different agenda. Their core leadership philosophy is deeply rooted in a complex combination of their chronic dissatisfaction with the way things are and a fervent belief that things can be better.

Transformational leaders read the situation quite differently than conventional leaders, who typically see business as a series of transactions over which they must maintain strict control and total order. Transactional leaders manage by enforcing compliance to a set of standard operating practices, policies and procedures with the belief that strict adherence and conformity are the answers to success.

Transformational leaders, on the other hand, don't believe in the constraining rationale of building stronger and higher fences in a futile effort to keep things under control. Instead, they believe in the benefits, merits and opportunities only found on the open range, where there are no fences, just miles and miles of endless rolling prairie. The transformational leader does not see himself as the chief organizer of tasks and processes, but rather as the chief disorganizer of mindsets and beliefs. The transformational leader sees himself as the "agitator in chief," the purposeful but quirky deviant who demands fresh, new and different, not big, beige and boring.

5

Mastering Transformational Tension

In order to lead any meaningful and significant organizational transformation, you first need to understand that the inevitable result will be a much higher level of tension and stress within the organization. It will be the kind of tension and anxiety that comes from operating at the very outer edge of performance expectations, where the adrenalin is high, the senses are heightened and the fast-paced thrill of the pursuit is the elixir that keeps people going, even when they want to give up and cruise on autopilot for a while. The question the leader must know the answer to is, "How much tension is enough tension to keep things sharp and moving forward at pace?"

It would be a fundamental misunderstanding of human nature, and the economic value creation equation, to believe eliminating conflict and reducing tension is a good thing. It's quite the opposite. Maximum value is not created in periods of stability, but rather in periods of disruption, when innovation is high, disequilibrium is at its peak and healthy paranoia is an accepted state of mind. In such an environment, there is bound to be conflict and tension, so the leader's job is not to eliminate it, but rather to tap into it and use it as a source of purposeful energy to drive the organization forward at maximum speed.

Someone once said, in a far less strenuous and troublesome time, that if you are not moving ahead, you are falling behind. In today's turbocharged, hypercompetitive, increasingly flat and virtually connected 24/7 world, the sentiment captured in that simple phrase is not only true, but the failure to heed its advice even more perilous. The real challenge for leaders today is not how to contain what they already have by making their organization leaner and more compliant, but how to keep their organization sharp, hungry and relevant for the future. As many young Canadians know, when you want to play pond hockey in the early spring or late fall, it is best to "skate fast over thin ice" rather than dawdle too long making up your mind. This advice is equally well directed to transformational leaders who need to move quickly in order to get their organization to the safety of the future shore.

Transformation, by its very nature, is an unleashing, an opening of the safety valve to let the steam out. It offers leaders the opportunity to shake things up, refresh their own thinking and challenge the organization to do likewise. To quote economist Paul Romer, "ideas are inexhaustible resources," and they are the one sure renewable resource leaders must tap into to harness the energy embedded in conflict and tension and to use it to constructive advantage. This is a particularly important competency for modern leaders to develop in themselves and their teams. It is an essential requirement if we are going to keep asking high-performance teams and business units to work together more collaboratively and charging them with finding bold, new break-through solutions for the future value creation that customers demand.

6

The Canada Brand—An Inexhaustible Natural Resource

Canada occupies a unique space in the minds of people around the world. We enjoy a positive, fresh and fair image on the international stage, quite distinct from the brash bravado of the Americans, the taciturn reserve of the British and the stiff formality of the Germans. This image should give us a natural advantage over most others, especially when it comes to applying transformational leadership techniques to boost our global business profile and leverage our brand internationally.

When people elsewhere think of Canada, they generally imagine snowcapped mountain ranges, fresh lakes and ice hockey. The sad news is they probably don't see us for much more than those majestic scenes of nature captured in the posters hung in the windows of travel agencies around the world. This is only made worse by the fact that there is a very good chance they actually have a relative living here, someone who took the plunge and emigrated from Treviso or Tel Aviv, Athens or Addis Ababa, Bangalore or Beijing. It is very unlikely they know that the subway cars used in Barcelona were made by a Canadian company based in Montreal or that their BlackBerry is the result of breakthrough work by engineers in Waterloo.

At a time like this, when the old answers don't work because the game has changed so radically and the new questions leave us perplexed, there is a unique window of opportunity for "Made in Canada" solutions. Solutions framed here, by Canadians, through our own unique social lens and our distinctive national experience as a multicultural, tolerant, immigrant society and based on our own intellectual property and know-how. We need a new breed of business leader, one that reflects the essential elements of our national brand

and our core values as a balanced, considerate, open-minded, fair and inclusive people, people you would want to do business with because of who they are and what they stand for.

Canada has a great deal to offer the world when it comes to business leadership and Canadian ideas, but we have not worked hard enough at defining, packaging and exporting our unique point of view. Sadly, it seems we have been more than willing to outsource our leadership thinking, operating models and guiding principles to the Americans, and that is not in our future best interests.

7

Leveraging the Maple Leaf

The brand called Canada is seriously underleveraged. If we do not make it an urgent priority to breathe new life into it, we will miss the opportunity to seize the business leadership baton from the hands of our shaken American and European cousins. We are all going to live in the future, whether we want to or not, and we can't afford to allow the future to happen by accident or be shaped by others to suit their own ambitions. We have to be deliberate, thoughtful and intentional. We need a strategic plan for the future of our national brand, but we must begin by first nurturing a new leadership mindset for the future and the leadership competencies that go along with it.

Luckily, we already have some outstanding thinkers on the subject of our economic prosperity and the new strategic thinking it will require. This includes Roger Martin from the University of Toronto (U of T) and Henry Mintzberg of McGill University. Martin has been the Dean of the Rotman School of Management at U of T since 1998 while Mintzberg has been Professor of Management Studies at the Desautels Faculty of Management, part of McGill University, since 1968.

Sadly, there are still too few spokespeople in the leadership field in Canada, and their voices are muted in the boardrooms of business because the voices we do hear tend to come from the halls of academia. We need to fill that void with a robust national dialogue on the subject of what constitutes global business leadership for the future, and then we must begin to develop the type of leaders dictated by the context in which we live. We need Canada's brand to be known, admired and respected around the world, not just for our products and services, but also for our leadership capabilities and the Canadian way of doing business.

Transformational leadership is different than the day-to-day administrative or transactional leadership we have been accustomed to. Transformational leadership is the very special type of leadership required at those moments when you reach a key intersection or a strategic inflection point. It is not the old-style, reactive leadership that Dr. Jonas Ridderstråle and Dr. Kjell Anders Nordström of the Stockholm School of Economics warn us about in their books *Funky Business* and *Karaoke Capitalism*, and which Ridderstråle then addresses, in even more detail, in his book *Re-energizing the Corporation*. It is not the sad, watered-down herd mentality or imitation leadership that is a second-rate copy of the original.

Different types of leaders are required at different times. Transactional leadership is for a "business as usual" time and place. Transitional leadership is suited for the purposeful pause between periods of change, when we just need to catch our breath and reorient. Transformational leadership, on the other hand, is for those unique "business as unusual" circumstances, like right now.

8

The Canadian Mosaic, Version 2.0

Canada is a tough, rugged, resilient country that always seems to do especially well when the chips are down, whether on the battlefields of Europe or ice rinks around the world. We have a history of attracting hard-working pioneers who were willing to venture out into undiscovered territory, make do with what they had at their disposal and not whine about hardships. We are also a country populated by a diverse collection of immigrants who saw new and better opportunity in Canada and risked venturing out on their own to make a home in a new land that offered more for them and their families than what they left behind. We are a country who has come together from elsewhere over time or in recent years, and we understand we will be stronger because of our diversity if we can only find a way to release our collective potential.

It was author John Murray Gibbon who first wrote about the unique Canadian approach to immigrants, which he suggested differs significantly from the American melting pot, in his 1938 book *Canadian Mosaic: The Making of a Northern Nation*. However, not even Gibbon could have imagined that Canada would become a nation where the Chinese languages and Punjabi have become almost as prevalent as French or English and where our modern-day hockey heroes come from other countries and carry unusual names on the backs of their jerseys, such as Ovechkin, Malkin and Bryzgalov, rather than the more familiar names of Lafleur, Orr and Hull.

Our diversity places added responsibilities and demands on us in terms of ensuring we can accommodate where we need to and remain aligned and consistent where we must. We need to be able to read the shifting environment, understand the future implications and adjust in the business world, as we would in music. There is a difference between the right time for the precise form, elaborate content and soothing cadence of the classical masters, such as Beethoven, and the time for the more passionate, chaotic and invigorating jazz of an Oscar Peterson or Jean Derome. Our diversity, the Canadian mosaic, makes this a challenge at times, but it suggests a sense of chaos is inevitable because of who we are and how we have come together.

These times are different, and we need to understand in what way. These times demand a certain melody to be played in order for the leader to be in sync. As much as we might prefer it, we don't live in the calm, orderly, dignified and refined times of the grand salons and elaborate music halls. Instead, it is our fate to live in the crowded, overheated and frenetic jazz bars of the global marketplace. These are fluid and chaotic times. There is no script or score to help guide us, only the same skills and attributes employed by the great jazz musicians—imagination and improvisation.

9

Spirits of Our Past

In the rugged, dangerous and unexplored terrain of early Canada, in the years of Cabot and Cartier, Champlain and Jolliet, Hudson and Frobisher, there were no answers to the uncertainties they faced, no matter how much they might have had wanted them. There were no safe, certain paths that had been conveniently carved across the frontier. There were no convenient signposts that had been erected along the way. There were only questions to be asked and choices to be made at every stage of the journey. Decisions had to be made in the face of uncertainty and in pursuit of an undefined opportunity, which they hoped would lay just over the horizon.

So it is today, and so it will be for the foreseeable future!

While we have undeniably prospered as a nation under the management model that has been in force since 1945, during a much more rational and certain time, it has been easier for us to willingly follow a course chosen by others. However nostalgic we might want to be, though, it is now time to pivot and embark on a new course and a new journey of discovery. At the end of the day, we simply have to find a better, smarter way to identify and seize emerging opportunities, and then execute them in a manner that is more profitable, but also better balanced, more sustainable and unwaveringly ethical. All of that comes down to the way in which leaders evaluate the landscape, make sense of the environment, proactively shape the opportunities they find and then decide which to pursue.

In the current context, the future is optimized when core organizational strategies are framed by a mindset of exploration and discovery, rather than one of exploitation and defence. A strategy based on the old model of exploiting a particular product, market segment, customer group or type of technology is fatally flawed in the world we now live in. Strategies based on the old model have a half-life that is shrinking and are a sure path to competitive disadvantage when events unfold in the unpredictable, non-linear and even irrational fashion in which they almost assuredly will.

On the other hand, a strategic mindset fuelled by curiosity, exploration and discovery will produce a higher rate of opportunity creation than would ever be possible through the old methods. It is the more nimble, fleet of foot approach that is better suited to the times in which we live and the competitive marketplaces in which we do business. The choice has effectively been made for us by the context in which we have been asked to operate.

In the face of the new world order and the emergence of new players on the world stage who view things differently, we are at a point where Canada needs to rebuild its national business franchise and global brand. The old game will not allow us to be successful going forward. The truth is, Canada has been relatively successful up to this point not because of our intellect or our innovative capacity, but because we had things that would have been the envy of any developing nation.

We had abundant natural resources at a time when they were relatively scarce elsewhere in the world. We had productive farms at a time when China, the Ukraine, Mexico and Argentina had not yet learned how to maximize their own agricultural machine to feed their own people, let alone export. We had ample oil and natural gas before the Middle East and the North Sea had been tapped for their own energy riches, and well before the United States woke up to the idea of domestic energy independence. We were benefiting from our mineral wealth before countries like Chile, Russia and South Africa realized they too could benefit by extracting their own natural resources to fuel the expanding and increasingly global industrial economy.

Unfortunately, we were so busy enjoying the benefits and lifestyle that our natural endowments provided that we failed to notice the fundamental shift in the ground beneath our lakes, farms, mines and forests. We should have known better, but while we sat comfortably on our bounty, and in a position of relative advantage, our lead over others began to shrink. We have seen other non-traditional national franchises come to play and, they somehow seem fitter, faster and better trained than we are.

Leadership has always been wrapped in the uncertainty that comes from exploring new domains, whether they be geographic, technological or social. The greater the uncertainty, the more we need leaders who are not paralyzed by potential risks but rather invigorated by hidden possibilities. The biggest risk we face as a nation is in allowing ourselves to be too cautious in an environment that demands courage. The benefits we reap will be directly proportional to the risks we take, and the risks are small in relation to our potential.

STRAIGHT TALK NEXT STEPS

Organizational Effectiveness Scorecard

Leadership has always been a challenge, and today our leaders must not only understand and master each of the 10 individual elements of organizational effectiveness listed below, but they must also maintain the delicate balance between five broad categories. It is a demanding role and, in return, we should demand excellence from our leaders in all of the elements that define success in the modern world.

These include:

Operational Effectiveness

- Crisp strategy and clear objectives
- Sound organizational structure and solid alignment

Relationship Effectiveness

- Genuine collaboration and honest communication
- Unqualified trust and total respect

Transformational Effectiveness

- Unbiased critical thinking and decision making
- Productive change management and daring innovation

Learning Effectiveness

- Seamless knowledge transfer and continuous growth
- Thoughtful talent management and development orientation

Performance Effectiveness

- Sharp focus and ruthless execution
- Total accountability and full commitment

PART II

Meeting the Future Today

The business leaders of today and the future need to reset their thinking, adjust their perspectives and bolster their leadership toolkits. The challenges faced by businessmen and women are different today than in the past, and they will be different again in the future as the waves of change continue to pound the shores of business as we know it. As a result, the leadership skills, capabilities and competencies of the future will be markedly different, and Canada can no longer delay establishing the frameworks necessary for our long-term success.

In Part II, we review the four key challenges facing all business leaders and describe the eight leadership competencies required to proactively improve our chances of success and our relevance in a rapidly changing world. The process of transformational change begins with developing a new leadership mindset that liberates us from the vicious spiral of reactionary conservatism we have allowed ourselves to be caught up in. We need to place our national stake in the ground and shift to a more offensively minded business game better suited to the conditions we face, the assets we have at our disposal and the opportunity that Canadians can seize if we have business leaders prepared to lift their own game.

10

Lead, Follow or Get Out of the Way

Before defining the transformational leader of the future in terms of the eight specific leadership competencies required to approach the four most critical leadership challenges we face, we need to address two key, tightly interwoven factors that contribute equally to the success of the transformational leader—experience repertoire and mindset.

A leader's "experience repertoire" consists of the number and variety of unique experiences collected by the individual over the course of his or her life. This is not the deep technical knowledge, tenured experience or well-honed professional skill sets developed in a very specific and narrow area, but rather the broad portfolio of diverse experiences at all levels, both professional and otherwise, that serve to provide the rich, unique perspectives that allow the leader to make the connections and linkages not available to others.

The second factor that underpins transformational leadership acumen is "mindset," by which I mean the particular way these leaders look at the world—the lens through which they see things and come to understand them. It is the difference between an open mindset and a closed one; for example, the difference between a mindset that reacts to risk with fear and one that perceives opportunity. The difference between a mindset predisposed to exploiting the current or exploring the future. The difference between a mindset with a default set to defend or to discover.

We are living in some of the most exciting, opportunity-rich times ever. Traditional barriers to entry in most industries have fallen. Information is not only more plentiful and more readily available, but you can access it at a fraction of the historical cost. Knowledge is more freely exchanged today than ever before on a 24/7/365 real-time basis; it is essentially unregulated and, more importantly, available equally to the big and the small, the rich and the poor.

This all combines to change the fundamental competitive landscape. In this regard, authors Jason Jennings and Laurence Haughton had it right when they observed how the environment has changed and used it as the title for their book: *It's Not the Big That Eat the Small . . . It's the Fast That Eat the Slow!*

FOUR LEADERSHIP CHALLENGES, EIGHT LEADERSHIP COMPETENCIES

Canadian business leaders can and must play a much bigger and more active role in defining, shaping and building the global marketplace of the future. It is the future we will all live in, whether we help shape it or not, and it is obviously in our best interest for Canadian hands to be active in the wet cement of the new foundation that is currently being laid.

In order to do so, we need to improve our ability to see, act and react with more speed, courage and foresight than we have in the past. We have to get out of the shadows and become the more reasoned alternative, proposing new ideas and setting new standards.

This will require us to master the eight specific leadership competencies required to meet the four broad transformational leadership challenges we face:

1. Sense Making and Sense Shaping
2. Clarity and Credibility
3. Understanding and Perspective
4. Creating Winning Conditions

11

Challenge #1: Sense Making and Sense Shaping

Making sense of the world in which we live, decoding it and then shaping it in ways an organization and its people can better understand and willingly accept is the first challenge facing the transformational leader.

This challenge is about helping people connect the dots. It is about allowing people, at all levels, to get past the noise, chaos and distraction in order to arrive at a simpler, cleaner and less cluttered understanding of the situation.

It's about opportunity identification, opportunity management and opportunity maximization. It's about taking advantage of the opportunities that present themselves in the midst of discord.

The two specific leadership competencies this requires are *contextual intelligence* and *strategic intelligence*.

CONTEXTUAL INTELLIGENCE (CQ)

This is the ability to sense subtle shifts in the environment, to become aware of those changes before anyone else and to predict their likely implications going forward. It is the ability to put things into crystal clear perspective and then accurately frame the picture so others can understand it. Naturally, there is then the need to communicate the picture in a way that others can grasp and comfortably relate to. The crafting of the message is more art than science, and we know that an appeal to emotion is critical to having people make adjustments to their previously held mental models.

This, in turn, requires the leader to have an intuitive sense of the changing environment and what it portends and confidence in the new direction it requires the organization to go. CQ is like a highly sensitive radar system, constantly scanning the environment, looking for signals to pick up. CQ is what the great leaders of the past have always seized upon to drive their businesses forward. It is the ability to connect disparate elements and combine them into a vivid picture of a future state.

It is what propelled Moses Znaimer and John Martin to launch MuchMusic and turn it into one of the most recognizable youth-oriented music and video broadcast brands today, spanning multiple different platforms.

It is what led Arkadi Kuhlmann of ING Direct to understand there was room in the financial services market for Internet banking in Canada, without the need for costly bricks and mortar.

STRATEGIC INTELLIGENCE (SQ)

Strategic intelligence encompasses a trio of capabilities:

1. Deep insight into the issues
2. Clear foresight as to how things will play out
3. An acutely sensitive peripheral vision

Peripheral vision is perhaps the single most important of the three in terms of usefulness in the current and future marketplaces. It is essentially what will help a leader avoid the risk of being sideswiped by a random event or being bypassed in the fast lane.

This is the ability to manage what George Day and Paul Schoemaker have called the "vigilance gap." Ted Rogers, the founder of Rogers Communications, demonstrated it when he sensed that the vacuum tube radio technology of the past would give way to the wireless handheld devices of the future, connecting people in real time, in new ways.

Michael MacMillan did too, when he built one of the world's premium film entertainment organizations. He eventually merged it with a similar organization founded by Robert Lantos, creating Alliance

Atlantis Communications at a time when others thought film production and going to theatres was a dinosaur social proposition.

Together, contextual intelligence and strategic intelligence effectively turn away from the practices of the past. They discard the slow, safe, linear, incremental strategic planning process that many companies still practise. They replace it with a new, modern emphasis on the much more important, upfront and intellectually demanding strategic thinking and cognitive processing capabilities of its leaders.

12

Challenge #2: Clarity and Credibility

The second challenge of the modern transformational leader is ensuring that the organizational purpose, objective and intent are clear and then underpinning that clarity with an unblemished level of personal credibility, which serves to bolster followership. Clarity and credibility together are the non-negotiable baseline essentials necessary for a leader to secure "permission" to lead from those who follow.

Dr. Steven F. Hayward put it very well in his book *Churchill on Leadership* when he described the essential aspects of Churchill's character as a leader. He listed four attributes:

- candour, courage and plain speaking
- decisiveness
- historical imagination
- balancing detail with the big picture

It is this combination of attributes that determines whether a leader's message resonates and whether his or her judgment is trusted. Some people like to think of it as a measure of the leader's personal brand equity, personal stock price or the amount of goodwill they have been able to build and upon which they can then draw in order to make tough decisions. However you choose to define it, it is the foundation required to galvanize others to commit to transformation and change.

The two leadership competencies this requires are *emotional intelligence* and *decision-making intelligence*.

EMOTIONAL INTELLIGENCE (EQ)

This is the ability to know yourself, manage yourself and build effective relationships with others. It has been written about extensively in recent years, yet, surprisingly, it is still not well understood by everyone in business, let alone perfected and practised by leaders at all levels. In its simplest sense, EQ requires leaders to have a solid understanding of their own emotional construct and to have the ability to manage and regulate their emotions. In addition, EQ requires the ability to understand the emotional tone and motivations of others.

EQ allows leaders to better manage relationships within an organization's social environment. The better the leader does these things, the more resonant the leader becomes and the more willing the followers are to trust that person, especially on a journey to a new and better, but still unknown, place.

It is what Guy Laliberté of Cirque du Soleil understood when he realized you could build a viable commercial business proposition by touching the emotions of people, because people of all ages can relate to the joyful emotions of a circus when it is combined with a new, modern twist.

It is how Ron Joyce came to see the social and emotional connection with people that could be fostered over a simple cup of good coffee at Tim Hortons, well before Howard Schultz and Starbucks followed suit and took it to another level at the premium end of the market.

DECISION-MAKING INTELLIGENCE (DMQ)

This is the ability to solve problems, resolve issues and come to conclusions that satisfy the various stakeholders and leave them feeling fully and clearly committed to the decision. It is about personal credibility and trusted judgment. In order to be credible, leaders must combine their EQ with a proven track record of superior decision making under a wide variety of circumstances and across a wide portfolio of business matters. The leader must have the ability to understand and master the complex elements involved in the decision-making process, including the rational and interpersonal components, as well as the divergent and convergent phases.

These abilities embody the essence of decision making within what is known as the field of behavioural economics. Our current understanding of this science comes from a growing pool of notable experts, such as Daniel Kahneman and Daniel Ariely, who have helped us better understand the mechanics of decision making and the phases we go through as we make business decisions.

It is what Peter Munk of Barrick Gold understood when he decided he could build a global mining powerhouse and an internationally recognized brand on the back of a modest, Canadian-based natural resources foundation.

It was the strength of his decision-making conviction that allowed Robert Deluce to conceive of Porter Airlines after his several previous attempts had failed and when others continued to believe the airline industry was nothing but a deep, dark hole of misery and financial loss.

Together, the powerful combination of EQ and DMQ represent the fundamental building blocks upon which leaders develop their legitimacy. In other words, as Barbara Kellerman points out in her book *Followership*, leaders will not be able to lead effectively unless their followers have determined them to be worthy. Legitimacy, defined in this way, is something granted to the leader by his or her followers. As such, it could be argued it actually puts the followers in control. If legitimacy is not achieved, two things can happen:

- The followers will not be fully committed or fully invested, and the organization will seriously underperform as a result.
- The followers will ultimately undermine the leader, using a variety of different methods ranging from outright sabotage to careless neglect to lack of carry through.

Either way, the inevitable result will range across a broad continuum of organizational failure, from mildly suboptimal to totally dysfunctional. In the process, the social architecture of the organization will deteriorate to the point where the leader can push all the buttons he or she wants, but the organization will just not respond as it should. At that point, it's game over for the leader!

13

Challenge #3: Understanding and Perspective

The third challenge for the transformational leader is ensuring a deep and broad organization-wide understanding of the mission, the objectives and the means. This thinking has to be wrapped in a rich and complete narrative that people at all levels can not only understand but also relate to. This means the leader's own perspective and way of looking at things must be sharply defined and skillfully packaged into a storyboard that not only makes sense and connects the dots for others to understand but also fills in the gaps in comprehension that can so often block change, even long-desired change. Storytelling is an essential part of leadership and communication, and it does not always get the consideration it should when there is a need to alter people's perspectives. The ability to weave a good story is often what allows people to break from the past and take the risk of venturing into the unknown.

The leader must have the ability to help the organization "think in the future tense" and, therefore, more comfortably compete in the realm of the unknown. This ability, the definition of which was coined by cultural anthropologist Jennifer James, is very likely to be in increasingly high demand in the uncertain future we face.

Leaders who do not have the ability to properly and accurately orient themselves and their organizations in time and space will very likely find themselves sucked into a "black hole." Leaders must bring a sense of fresh perspective to the table, not about the past, which we already know, but about the future we do not yet understand. In his book *Churchill on Leadership*, Steven Hayward quotes Churchill: "In a quarrel between the past and the present, we shall find we have lost the future" (more on this later). The two competencies this challenge requires are *innovative intelligence* and *ambiguity intelligence*.

INNOVATIVE INTELLIGENCE (INQ)

This is the ability to inspire, imagine and invent. It combines a number of different concepts and principles flowing from the theory and practices of what Roger Martin of the University of Toronto has called "Integrative Thinking," as well as the principles of "Design Thinking," as practised and promoted by Tim Brown, the CEO and President of IDEO, the world's most formidable design and innovation consultancy firm. In both cases, they have helped us come to better understand that

- innovation is not a magic trick that only some people are capable of mastering; and
- it does not flow only from people with a certain creative mindset, natural disposition or artistic temperament.

Thanks to Martin, Brown and others, such as Harvard Professor Clayton Christensen, we now understand that innovation is a disciplined way of thinking about and solving problems. As a result, it is something we can instill in our organizations, if we choose to implement the support processes necessary and then foster the requisite mindset.

Innovative intelligence is what Arthur Erickson practised when he built his personal brand as an architect and urban planner into a globally recognized and sought-after source for original, creative thinking in the modern context.

It is what Canadian singers and musicians, from Anne Murray, Celine Dion and Shania Twain to The Guess Who, Neil Young, Diana Krall and even Justin Bieber, have understood and practised for a considerable period of time.

AMBIGUITY INTELLIGENCE (AQ)

This is the ability to live comfortably with uncertainty and not allow yourself to become physically frozen or mentally incapacitated with not knowing. There are very few things in life that are simply black or white. No matter how much easier it would be if our only choices were conveniently positioned at one end or the other of two stark, polar opposites, that is rarely the case. Unfortunately, grey is very likely to be the most popular colour of the future. As a result, leaders in the future are going to have to learn how to become comfortable living in a world of ambiguity and uncertainty.

If leaders are paralyzed by uncertainty and cannot operate comfortably within an environment filled with the thick fog of ambiguity, they are not going to be able to make the kind of decisions necessary to keep their organizations moving forward. Leaders must work harder than ever before on improving their coping skills and finding ways to maintain their equilibrium under a wide variety of circumstances and conditions.

AQ is the intelligence necessary to avoid rushing to premature judgments and knee-jerk decisions. It is the ability to stay calm and find other ways to orient yourself when in the midst of something new or different. To paraphrase the poet Rudyard Kipling, "It is about keeping your wits about you while all others are losing theirs and blaming it on you."

It is what George Cohon understood and was comfortable with when he brought the McDonald's brand into Canada and then subsequently used Canada as a launching pad for the company's eventual entry into the Soviet Union, well before the wall fell and others ventured into what we now call Russia.

It is what Allan Taylor of the Royal Bank understood when he displayed the foresight and confidence to build on the bank's well-honed international reputation at the very start of the strange, new euro-market phenomenon and took steps to strengthen its global presence in corporate and investment banking.

Together, INQ and AQ are essential for a leader to confidently navigate the future, where there will be fewer and fewer precedents from the past to rely upon, and where the half-life of any knowledge you have today is likely to get shorter and shorter.

In this environment, successful leaders will no longer be judged by how much they know about something, but rather how good they are at accessing what they need to know when they need to know it. As author and professor Mihaly Csikszentmihalyi described so well in his book *Flow*, success in the leadership world of tomorrow is no longer about accumulating stocks of information, it is about accessing the flow of knowledge.

14

Challenge #4: Creating Winning Conditions

The final challenge for the transformational leader is finding the right balance between the focus required to meet the pressing demands of the day and the focus necessary to address the emerging challenges and opportunities of the distant future. It is about creating the right set of winning conditions necessary to achieve excellence in both worlds.

This is about setting and nurturing an organizational environment within which people are free and able to do their very best work. It is about building effective teams, developing superior talent and building a culture of total engagement. It is about creating a positive "investment" climate so people choose to invest more of themselves in the success of the organization. The logic is the same for a city, a province or a country in terms of what they need to do to create an attractive environment to encourage financial investment. It is obvious that if the physical infrastructure is not world class, if the labour pool is weak and if the tax environment is not supportive, businesses will simply not invest in that location, they will move on to find a more favourable place.

It is the same thing within an organization. If the management structure is cumbersome or confusing, the quality of employees and teammates is low and the barriers to performance excellence and personal growth are too high, then employees will not choose to make the discretionary personal investment that is necessary. A poorly run and weakly led organization taxes its people on many different levels. It is the leader who is responsible for the quality of the investment climate, and for creating the right winning conditions.

The two leadership competencies this requires are *talent intelligence* and *collaborative intelligence*.

TALENT INTELLIGENCE (TQ)

This is the ability to spot, develop and release the talent that resides within each person, according to their own desires and capabilities. Talent management is very often an area in which most organizations like to pretend, or believe, they are doing a better job than they really are. As a result, it is a blind spot that can be especially fatal in an environment where the "War for Talent," as first described by McKinsey & Company in 1997, is getting more and more heated.

Most often, the underlying problem is that organizations place too much emphasis on managing the performance of average employees and too little on managing the potential of the supremely talented people. In the majority of cases, organizations do an adequate enough job of performance management, believing that if they can master that part of the process, they will be successful at talent management. In reality, the focus should not be on the performance equation, but rather on the other part, which is harnessing untapped human potential. Unfortunately, very few organizations apply the necessary focus, discipline or rigour to this part of the overall talent-management process.

As a result, we all too often march forward in blissful ignorance of the waste created by our neglect, and we are oblivious to the pollution we create within the organizational environment. While we religiously monitor a wide variety of performance and productivity ratios, such as ROA, ROI, ROC and ROE, we have not yet developed a sophisticated awareness of the need to focus on the modern talent ratio of ROP (return on potential), whether it be personal, organizational or national.

TQ is what John Beck of the international construction giant Aecon understands in an industry where top talent can command a premium and where treating your talent well can make a major difference in how well you can serve a very discerning global customer base.

It is what Marc-André Blanchard of the law firm McCarthy Tétrault LLP understands as he continues to transform his law services partnership in new ways by focusing on how to create a strategy and a culture where the top talent in the industry can find rewarding work in a demanding profession known for chewing through talent and burning out top performers.

COLLABORATIVE INTELLIGENCE (COQ)

This is the ability to connect with others and work comfortably within formal and informal networks and groups of people. In a world of increasing complexity, brilliant diversity and confusing organizational structures, learning how to master the skill of genuine collaboration, in the organizational context, is one of the keys to effectiveness, efficiency and productivity.

Somehow we need to move beyond the simple-minded belief that some people still have: that teamwork is somehow a second-class soft skill that is more a luxury than a necessity in today's business world. We need to update and modernize our thinking in this regard so that everyone understands that collaboration is a business essential and a true competitive differentiator. We have a long way to go when you consider how few organizations have mastered this competency from top to bottom.

Collaboration is about tapping into the diversity of thought necessary to remain nimble and relevant in a changing world. However, as Morten Hansen says in his book *Collaboration*, it is important for "leaders who pursue disciplined collaboration to never lose sight of this dictum: collaboration is a means to an end, and that end is great performance. This means that often it may be better not to collaborate, because there is simply no compelling reason to do so. To be disciplined about collaboration is to know when not to collaborate."

There is a huge competitive advantage to be found in moving to genuine collaboration, defined as a sincere blending of strongly held opinions without the dilution that often comes from a lack of willingness to advocate for a point of view and then surrender it for the sake of peace and harmony. This new, richer and higher definition of collaboration requires us to re-evaluate our vocabulary and sharpen our understanding of the differences between compromise, consensus, co-operation and collaboration. While often joined in the same conversation and considered interchangeable, they are simply not the same thing, and the highest level of proficiency only occurs in the collaborative space, where high levels of co-operativeness are met by equally high levels of assertiveness.

When we begin to weave increasingly unconventional networks of diverse people together, we are bound to generate fierce dialogue, occasional friction and constructive tension. We need to see these as necessary performance enablers, not nasty by-products to be avoided at all costs. They are the fuel required for generating breakthrough solutions. We need to master collaboration and use it to steer the problem-solving and decision-making processes to a productive and optimal conclusion.

We will have to overcome generations of business training that produced a tendency for us to naturally default to either the lowest common denominator solution, achieved through consensus, or to the urban myth "win-win" solution, achieved through negotiations focused on arriving at a compromise. Neither of these two answers will do. We have to be stronger and more determined than we have been to master truly collaborative outcomes, rather than settling for second best. We need to unlearn some very bad habits that have crept into our accepted leadership practices, and we need to realize that the world has moved on, even though our thinking has not yet caught up.

Alain Bouchard of variety store mega chain Alimentation Couche-Tard Inc. (the owners of Mac's) demonstrated his COQ as he created a model across North America that depends on forming and maintaining deep collaborative relationships between owners, operators, suppliers and everyone who forms part of the value chain.

So too did Monique Leroux of the Desjardin Group, the largest association of credit unions in North America, who is building on the traditional collaborative community-based financial services model and taking it to new heights in a modern context against formidable competition from the big banks. Together, TQ and COQ are about unleashing the full potential of people, teams and the enterprise. They are about creating the conditions that allow every employee to do their very best work and maximizing the discretionary investment level of people for the benefit of driving organizational performance and allowing people to achieve their own level of potential.

The eight critical competencies for transformational leadership operate as a balanced suite of personal leadership capabilities. They are interdependent and are certainly not the bland, garden-variety leadership competencies we have become accustomed to. They are new, demanding and different, and they require a leader to master a much higher level of sophistication. They redefine the way we look at opportunity and people, and they represent a framework to guide organizations into the future.

LESSONS FROM CANADIAN BUSINESS

There are two rather stark Canadian examples of the failure to practise responsible leadership, and each of them contains some valuable lessons and important warnings for other Canadian business leaders. More than anything else, they highlight Canada's seeming inability to remain competitive outside of our traditional strength industries of natural resources and financial services.

Nortel Networks Corporation

Founded in Montreal in 1895, the company was originally known as Northern Electric and Manufacturing Company. It was a giant of Canadian industry and one of our major exporters and job creators for many years. During its heyday, it not only defined the very nature of the technology market in Canada, but it also represented one-third of the total valuation of companies on the Toronto Stock Exchange. At its peak, it employed 94,500 people worldwide.

In 1976, it announced its intention to take on the world and become a leader in the emerging digital communication space. Its fortunes blossomed throughout the following years, right up to the time it celebrated its 100th anniversary in 1995. Much of its success came from riding on the back of the global tech boom. Nortel was a Canadian darling, and it seemed it could do no wrong.

The company grew in almost a straight-line progression over many years under John Roth, with its shares hitting a peak of $124 in 2000. The problem was that the company was in trouble, but few on the outside knew it. Beginning in early 2000, the company's market capitalization began to fall, shrinking from almost $400 billion to less than $5 billion in two years. The stock price naturally plunged, along with profits, to a low of $0.47. Roth's controversial departure in 2004, with a settlement package amounting to $139 million, led to Chief Financial Officer Frank Dunn being chosen as his replacement. Things got worse very quickly over the next two and a half years, ending with Dunn and two of his finance department deputies being fired in 2004 for alleged financial statement irregularities. The company turned, on an interim basis, to retired U.S. Navy Admiral Bill Owens to help it project a sense of propriety, but his term lasted only 18 months. It was clear that leadership in the American Navy was not the same as leadership in a Canadian high-tech company gone bad.

The directors, a veritable who's who of the Canadian business elite, had been expected, as any board would have been, to act as the responsible check and balance on a weak management team. Around the boardroom table, there were many notables, including John Cleghorn the former Chairman and CEO of the Royal Bank of Canada; Lynton "Red" Wilson, former Chairman of BCE; Frank Charles Carlucci III, who served as the United States Secretary of Defense from 1987 to 1989 in the Reagan administration; and James Johnston "Jim" Blanchard, who had served in the United States House of Representatives, had been Governor of Michigan and was then United States Ambassador to Canada. However, they were either asleep at the switch, blind to the facts or simply oblivious to the signs and signals.

The new CFO, appointed in 2005 after Dunn left, was Peter Currie, previously the Chief Financial Officer of Royal Bank under Cleghorn. He eventually left of his own volition in 2007, after some investors suggested he be fired. Shortly after his departure, the Securities and Exchange Commission in the United States filed civil fraud charges against Nortel, alleging accounting fraud from 2000 to 2003.

In mid-2005, as the company continued to slide into desperation, the board sought a new saviour in Mike S. Zafirovski, an American who had served as President and CEO of GE Lighting and then as Motorola's President and COO. Unfortunately, or inevitably, despite all his leadership and business training at the famous General Electric "executive school" created by Jack Welch, he could not save the day for a company that had lost any ability to steer a safe course in the rapidly changing technology waters.

(continued)

As Nortel rushed toward bankruptcy, Zafirovski ultimately resigned and subsequently took on a senior advisory role with the U.S. financial advisory and investment firm Blackstone Group. At the end of the day, Nortel filed for bankruptcy in 2009 and was ultimately liquidated, leaving 60,000 employees plus pensioners and other creditors in the lurch.

While the final chapter is not yet written, Nortel was brought to its knees by many of the same flaws in character, ethics and greed we have now recognized were also at the heart of the economic crisis of the past four years. Nortel's leadership, at all levels, including the board of directors, was either unable or unwilling to see and acknowledge their flawed thinking and poor judgment, and their demise was, therefore, inevitable.

Its demise can be traced back to shortcomings in several of the eight leadership competencies we referred to previously, but chief amongst these was a track record of poor decision-making intelligence at all levels over a period of many, many years, including decisions about who the right executive leaders should be. Each bad decision led the company down an even darker path, where every attempt to correct a prior bad decision was compounded by yet another, making things worse and worse as time went by.

T. Eaton Company

To generations of Canadians, well before the arrival of the new economy and the technology-infused time of Nortel, Eaton's was the model for what we believed a successful company should be. It had been a very successful department store chain right from its humble beginnings in 1869, two years after Confederation. However, by the time it went bankrupt in 1999, its glorious past was not enough to prevent it from succumbing to the pressures of the future and demands of the new world in retailing. This included a revolutionary series of customer-focused changes, brought to us courtesy of the brute retailing muscle of American giants like Walmart and Costco, that excelled at logistics as well as the pure retail experience.

Eaton's failed not because Canadians wanted American solutions. Eaton's failed because its management was not able to reinvent its business model and respond to the global trends, which were there for all to see. Canadians, if anything, are pragmatists, looking for the same good deal as anyone else, no matter what flag it is wrapped in. As Eaton's failed to keep pace with its foreign competitors, its customers voted with their feet, and it lost its historical consumer base.

Like so many other companies that fail, there was more than one cause of Eaton's failure, but its lack of both contextual and strategic intelligence is what ultimately resulted in it missing or ignoring virtually every signal that was being sent about how mass retail in Canada was changing forever. Either its leaders did not hear the footsteps of consumers leaving their stores to shop elsewhere or they could not come to grips with how new purchasing choices and experiences were driving customers to other, more relevant stores both large and small.

These two companies, and countless other large and small enterprises, from St. John's to Victoria, have exited the marketplace because they failed to manage themselves in the way Canadians deserve and expect. These two organizations are particularly guilty of the business crimes of gross neglect and severe myopia. They are amongst the worst examples of how an organization should be managed and led. The many faithful former employees of Eaton's and Nortel would have every right to feel cheated and disgraced by the human and financial losses incurred due to poor leadership and the inability of these organizations to transform in a smart and timely manner.

15

Mistaken Beliefs and Naïveté

In far too many organizations, the word collaborate means slow down, play nice and consult with as many people as you can. When that is the definition of collaboration, it is almost a given that neither the leader nor the people below actually understand what it looks like, let alone what it means inside the social reality of the modern organization. Collaboration, by definition, is an act of exploration. Collaboration is the pursuit of new, better and different answers. When you genuinely understand the collaborative process, you realize it is all about achieving the benefits of "dynamic tension." It is the belief in, and commitment to, the process of bringing diverse opinions and experiences together and allowing them to violently collide in an open marketplace for ideas, where only the best ideas survive.

This is the exact opposite of what most organizations do. Instead, they involve mostly like-minded people, with narrow points of view and very limited ranges of experience, to come together in a controlled environment where the final answer is typically just a shade above the lowest common denominator. This cannot possibly create better value, and it will not and cannot produce a competitively advantageous outcome from which significant new economic value can be created. It suggests that incremental mediocrity is the answer, when what the market wants and really values is novelty.

The art of business leadership is thousands of years old, but in a frustrating and paradoxical way, we have still not discovered how to master it reliably on a mass scale. As a result, a huge loss of value occurs each and every day due to poor leadership. While many have tried to improve the ultimate performance of their organizations through process-efficiency-biased solutions, like the well-known Six Sigma methodology popularized by Jack Welch at GE, not to mention endless reorganizations and countless restructurings, we have not devoted the same time, attention and dollars to the most insidious, irrational problem of all, the loss of value due to the organizational dysfunction that results from poor leadership.

Let's stop kidding ourselves. Truth be told, we have failed to develop the necessary level of sophistication in our understanding of the human condition as it plays out in the modern organization. As a result, we remain locked in a set of time-warped paradigms that no longer apply. Conflict, discord and tension are not the bad things we think they are. They are actually the essential elements of creativity and value creation we need.

The real failure is our unwillingness to master the leadership competencies necessary to turn the heat of debate and the energy of disagreement into genuine, distinctive and differentiated value. It seems as though we would rather avoid the hard work, bury our heads in the sand and call conflict, tension and disagreement the enemy than do what we need to do to maximize the benefits of diversity of thought, experience and ideas.

16

Raising the Flag

There is often a huge disconnect between what leaders say they want to accomplish and the processes, mindsets and cultures they create in order to help achieve it. Whether born or made, there is no question we need leaders who can create and harness the energy and potential of their organizations by mastering the skills and developing the competencies necessary to be transformational. In the process, these transformational leaders can not only improve the domestic market, but can help create a Canadian voice at the global business table, leveraging our brand and making sure the Maple Leaf matters to the world.

Transformational leaders are needed to help put Canada in the position of greatest advantage and allow us to make a difference, both at home and abroad, in a unique Canadian way. We are not talking about the kind of leadership competencies engraved on plaques or written on colourful signs and hung at various points around the office. We are talking about the leadership competencies that will help shape the future, drive progress and create sustainable value. They include:

- a belief in vigorous dialogue and healthy debate amongst diverse groups of individuals
- a belief in allowing opposing ideas to compete in the open, without fear of judgment or recrimination
- a belief in always striving to seek the optimal solution or outcome, not just the easy answer
- a belief in personal accountability and shared responsibility, not the puffing up of abundant egos

At the end of the day, the leader who truly understands performance, potential, opportunity and wealth creation also understands he or she is responsible for shaping the culture and creating the conditions that allow the very best people to do their very best. It is the credibility, character and commitment of the leader that form the basis for transformational change.

STRAIGHT TALK NEXT STEPS

Stepping Up to Transformational Leadership

The reasonable question for anyone to ask is, "How can we possibly embrace such a radical approach to leadership and organizational effectiveness, without destroying the very thing we are trying to improve?"

Here are some suggested steps that can help you begin the journey.

Step 1: See Beyond Your Own World

We are all victims of our own experiences, many of which are too narrow, too bland and too constraining. The secret is to embrace the experience repertoire that others bring to us, and to use it to help broaden the tapestry of possibilities. As a result, we need to be willing to push out the boundaries of our imagination and play more comfortably with the ambiguity around the fringe. Today, if you are not hyper alert, you are probably in trouble, but blissfully ignorant of that fact. When you wake up, you might be shocked to see the trouble you are in. A better-tuned radar system will push you to attention and open your eyes.

Step 2: Have Crucial Conversations

The art of good conversation, thoughtful mature dialogue and honourable spirited debate has been lost. We are either too distracted at one end of the spectrum or too concerned with winning at the other. In either case, we seem to have lost the

(continued)

---

ability to raise the calibre of the conversation to meet the challenge of the moment.

Leaders need to engage their organizations in a rejuvenation of the much higher level of dialogue needed to shift from a dead-end path to another path with more promise and opportunity. This means holding people accountable for having a well-reasoned and well-informed point of view, and demanding they bring it to the table. There can be no room for tepid opinions and loose logic. A leader has to set the tone by demonstrating a willingness to converse in meaningful ways, not just in corporate jargon and political speak.

Step 3: Bridge the Solitudes

Making peace with the future means building bridges from the past. These bridges are of new understanding and mutual benefits that can only be built on common ground and shared interest. If we enter the transformation debate with a commitment to building these bridges, chances are we will find opportunity.

Divisions and differences of opinions are a healthy by-product of any good debate. In fact, they are the very source of energy we need to break free from complacency, but the outcome needs to bring the sides together in resolution. Wounds that are left unattended will undermine the foundation at both the personal and the organizational level.

Final Thoughts

Leaders need to play a visible, activist role as facilitators and mediators of spirited dialogue within their organizations. They need to show the organization it is all right to disagree and to have strong opinions (albeit loosely held), and they also need to ensure that the expectation will be resolution rather than permanent division amongst people, their ideas and the collective outcome of the dialogue.

Passive-aggressive behaviour that effectively forces the tension underground cannot be tolerated in the high-performance organization of the future. Leaders cannot afford to be conflict avoiders, and they cannot allow conflict-avoiding behaviour to exist in their organizations unless they wish to hasten their own demise. Leaders must take responsibility for managing the health of the social architecture of their organizations, not just the structural, process and financial components of the operational architecture.

PART III

Preparing for Transformational Leadership

The first thing transformational leaders must do is develop an accurate understanding of the context or environment in which they will be asked to lead in the future. In the process, they must define with precision what the specific leadership demands and challenges will be.

In Part III, I will paint a picture of the evolving future and suggest how leaders must do a much better job of strategic soothsaying based on a fundamental shift in outlook and perspective. Like so many other developed countries, we have allowed the self-proclaimed wisdom and superior knowledge of money managers, stock market traders and speculators to shift our thinking into such small increments of time that we end up dizzy, frightened and insecure about the long-term future. As a result, we find ourselves having defaulted to short-term thinking and prone to reacting impulsively to daily signs and signals rather than steering a confident and steady course to the future that lies just over the horizon. This pattern must be broken or Canada and its corporations will never fully leverage our national brand or realize our full potential.

17

Rebuilding the Franchise

Leading a group of people, a team, a department, a business unit or an organization is a privilege that comes with certain very serious obligations. While there is no single "right" style or textbook approach, because circumstances and situations vary too greatly, there is a common obligation to lead from a set of core principles that keep people pointed in the same direction and focused on the same objectives. As a result, ensuring and maintaining alignment at all levels is key, and it is also one of the most difficult challenges facing any leader, especially in times of turmoil and transformation.

People easily become lost and confused when their focus is diverted from the path immediately in front of them, and they can often miss the signs telling them to turn left or right. One of the most important and fundamental choices of modern leaders is to decide whether they will lead by map or by compass.

Command-and-control-style management is about maps. It is about strict adherence to a chosen course, with no deviations allowed. It assumes someone at the top already knows the best path. It is about discipline, control and compliance. The problem is it creates a dependency mentality because management is about having the answers.

Transformational leadership is about a compass. It is about a process of discovery, which assumes we will learn as we go and get stronger as we gain experiences, collect insights and make decisions along the way. It assumes there is more than one right path, and no one person is smart enough to know which one is best. It is about personal freedom and collective accountability. It serves to create an independence mentality because leadership is about asking the right questions.

This fundamental difference in philosophy and approach takes on epic importance in times of chaos, instability and change. An organization trained to religiously follow detailed maps, which have been provided to them by emotionally detached, narrowly focused and perhaps even small-minded managers, will simply not be equipped to survive in the wild. An organization wired to follow maps other people have drawn will not be able to improvise, change course or confidently embark on a journey of discovery when conditions change and they need to respond accordingly.

When we allow an organization and its people to become dependent upon instructions, policies, procedures and processes to guide their activities, they can only respond in the way they have been trained to, by adhering to choices made by someone else. Transformational leadership, on the other hand, requires not only self-confidence, determination and grit, but also that choices be made by people other than the leader. It is the granting of choice that allows people to assume personal accountability, carve a unique path, fulfill their true potential and pursue opportunities.

18

Winning Is an Attitude

Canadians have long defined ourselves more by our national game than our business acumen. Hockey is a material part of our national psyche, our pride, our passion and our identity. We know how to play the game very well, and we can produce generation after generation of talented players. However, the sad truth is we don't know how to build serially successful franchises that, even as the game changes, are able to lift the Stanley Cup.

We still pack the arenas from coast to coast and religiously glue ourselves to the TV every Saturday night, but we don't demand better leadership and a more competitive product when our favourite team fails to win, let alone make it to the playoffs. We somehow seem permanently resigned to settling for the disappointing results produced year after year by the perennially hapless Maple Leafs and the ever-frustrating and underperforming Flames and Oilers or the teasing results of the Senators, Habs and Canucks, who sometimes get close but never do so on a sustainable basis. In the meantime, the Kings, the Bruins, the Ducks and even the Hurricanes bask in victories still largely built on the back of our talent, but managed by individuals and organizations that have the hunger, determination and strategies that have proven to be successful. We need to wake up from our slumbering complacency and start becoming far more indignant about our serial mediocrity.

It's been the same sad story on our business front, and it's time to rebuild the foundation upon which our national business franchise has been standing. It's time to challenge the fundamental premise from which we operate. It's time to build organizations, leaders and teams that will allow us to wear our national business jersey with legitimate pride. It's time to enjoy the exhilarating taste of victory, not just feel the sour sweat of a game played hard but lost.

It has been said that strategic business leadership is art, and operational business management is science. Leaders paint, managers prove. Unfortunately, in most Canadian organizations, the science part of the leadership equation seems to have overtaken the entire process. The delicate and necessary balance between the two parts of the process has been destroyed by extreme overcompensation and an unfortunate default to the rigid science of risk-averse planning. To put a not-so-subtle point on it, you simply cannot plan for what you do not know, and what you do not know is a heck of a lot more than what you do!

In simple terms, you can't improve the desired outcome by working harder and harder at putting things into more logically organized, but ever tighter, smaller and more confining boxes. Nor can you improve the outcome by then validating those choices by endless amounts of clinical over-analysis that could never prove the facts in the first place. In other words, you can try to systematize and refine the analytical process in an effort to reduce the risk, if you like. However, don't be surprised when you are caught flat-footed by events that unfold in unpredictable, illogical ways and at times that are seriously inconvenient for you.

It seems that leaders of too many organizations have tried to control their destiny and their market space by applying extra layers of logic and additional doses of linear thinking to what is essentially an unpredictable and chaotic world. Hockey is not baseball or football, where the game unfolds at a slower, more predictable pace. It's not a game where set plays are designed ahead of time by the coaching staff who simply ask the players to execute the play. Hockey is more like the world of business. It is a violent game that happens at high speed, with naturally occurring ebbs and flows that cannot be predicted and where the trick, to paraphrase Wayne Gretzky, is for players to stay in motion and anticipate where the puck will go next, not where it is at the moment.

19

Playing the Canadian Game

There is a shift occurring in the business world, and it is long overdue. If Canadian business leaders can adjust and begin to play the international business game more like the fast-paced game that Canadian hockey players play, rather than the less intense, more casual and frankly boring approach of American baseball players or British cricket players, then we have a good chance of ensuring we will win way more than we lose. The choice is ours, but today's game calls for our grit and determination to be matched by our creativity and passion.

On the premise that business leaders can never know enough or be fast enough, even in our technologically supercharged information society, to stay ahead of the curve, the traditional strategic planning process used by most business leaders may have run its course. If this is true, we need to shift toward an approach more suited to the conditions we face and more appropriate to the circumstances surrounding us. Breakthrough, game-changing strategy is derived from superior thinking, not from more and better planning. The thinking part is the valuable raw material and it has to come first, not second, if we want to produce a finished product that has relevance in a value-hungry global economy.

Organizations have been short-changing their future for quite a while now, faking it, creating the illusion of being in control of a situation where complete control is just not possible. The more responsible and sensible thing to do would be to put the majority of effort, both physical and cerebral, into improving the strategic-thinking process, not trying to lock down the perfect strategic plan. The strategic plan, at the end of the day, will only be as good as the thinking that goes into it anyway, so why not put the emphasis where it will have the greatest impact?

There are at least three fallacies embedded in the flawed traditional doctrine of strategic planning, as we have come to know it:

Fallacy of Prediction—believing we can, in fact, predict future events with great and reliable accuracy

Fallacy of Formalization—believing we can come to better outcomes by better organizing and justifying our logic

Fallacy of Detachment—believing we can be totally objective in our judgments and detached from bias

Leaders are human, so they are prone to the same flaws in judgment and other forms of misguided behaviour as the rest of us. The difference is, they are in a position to tap into the collective wisdom of their organizations and take advantage of the series of checks and balances that should mitigate the worst of their mistakes. It is when the culture of an organization breaks down that this safety check fails to enable itself, and the consequences are typically not very good for anyone, especially those further down in the organizational food chain.

20

Benefits of Healthy Paranoia

It was almost 20 years ago that Andy Grove, the former CEO and Chairman of Intel, wrote the controversial but popular book *Only the Paranoid Survive*. His thesis was pretty simple and to the point. He believed that leaders require a certain disposition to succeed, and they should remain in a state of mild to medium paranoia about the future. He believed that both threat and opportunity occur in periods of dise-quilibrium, or discontinuity. He coined the phrase "strategic inflection points" to describe these particular moments. Grove went on to explain how successful leaders seem to have a certain uncanny sense of timing and a knack for knowing just the right moment to shift position, even if the shift needs to happen at the height of maximum effectiveness, rather than the valley of total despair.

Grove was talking about the organizational ability and capacity to abandon, the willingness and courage needed by the leader to give up one position and adopt another, to know exactly when to move on, when to leave things behind and when to take a bold step forward. Grove understood the advantage created for an enterprise when its leader has the confidence to shift to a new frontier right at the apex of success, rather than ride the downward curve of diminishing influence, profitability and relevance. In more recent times, Steve Jobs adopted this same approach at Apple, and took it to new and even braver heights. In so doing, he became the poster boy for serial exploration, not to mention financial success, value creation and brand excellence.

In both cases, these transformational leaders understood the nature, power and benefits of a mindset of exploration, and the limits of a culture of exploitation. They knew that planning for an unpredictable future could only be the second-best approach to building a resilient organization, capable of constantly improving its ability to sense the future by doing a better job of thinking about the future. The leadership stories that follow are replete with courage, bold moves and grit—necessary to create the future, not subsist in a status quo and fail because of it.

LESSONS FROM CANADIAN BUSINESS

We can point with pride to some instructive examples of Canadian leaders with the ability to take advantage of these strategic inflection points. They include William Edmund "Ed" Clark and his highly successful stewardship, as President and CEO, of Toronto-Dominion Bank Group since 2002, and Phillip Crawley and his bold re-imagination of *The Globe and Mail*, of which he has been Publisher and CEO since 1998.

Dorothy Leonard and Walter Swap, in their excellent book *Deep Smarts*, do a very good job of helping to define and crystallize the thinking that Grove, Jobs, Clark and Crawley practise, which revolves around how you need to constantly redefine and out-think your competition in order to remain one move ahead of them at all times. They provide some answers to the question of why some leaders and organizations outperform others in making choices about their strategic direction.

Folded into the stories of these two brilliantly successful Canadian organizations and their leaders are lessons on how to maximize opportunity in the new economic reality. They reinforce the findings of Leonard and Swap and support the premise that suggests a leader's strategic-thinking ability is developed and enhanced by the wealth of their "experience repertoire."

In other words, they are suggesting that the number, breadth and variety of unique experiences (and not just work experiences) a leader has accumulated over time are directly linked to the quality of the insight and thinking they are able to bring to the table. If the quantity, quality and variety of the experiences are high, the leader is better equipped to view situations with heightened perspective, greater awareness and a much better set of future-oriented strategic lenses.

Toronto-Dominion Bank Group

Ed Clark is not your typical banker. He did not begin his career as a teller like so many other bankers of his generation. In fact, he is an economist by training and persuasion, and he earned his Master's and Doctorate in Economics at Harvard. He was also a senior mandarin within the Canadian federal government. In 2010, he was named Canada's Outstanding CEO of the Year, an award given out by Caldwell Partners.

Despite his non-traditional banker's background, Clark has built a formidable financial services powerhouse on both sides of the 49th parallel. He has done so on the basis of promoting a unique culture and collaborative philosophy that he coined "The Federated Model," an apt description for the Canadian way of doing things.

TD Bank has pursued a transformational agenda, both internally and in the markets it serves. The first bank to adopt weekend banking hours, it differentiated itself with its customers by breaking from the rigid grips of old-style thinking and doing something that was small, but met the test of common sense. Even though TD was considered to be within the second tier of Canadian banks not that long ago, after Royal, CIBC and Bank of Montreal, it has steadily climbed the league tables. Today, it finds itself in second place by virtue of market capitalization, and it made the move with an astute combination of growth from the core and adding on important, synergistic acquisitions.

Its acquisition of Banknorth Group in 2004 was an important step in building a Pan-American retail banking powerhouse that could be equally recognized on both sides of the border. The Royal Bank, on the other hand, badly fumbled its entree into the United States, with several ill-considered acquisitions, including that of Centura Bank. They came to the game very late, after both Bank of Montreal and TD had established a presence, and eventually ended up selling their U.S. holdings in 2011 to PNC Financial for $3.6 billion, a huge $1.6 billion loss.

(continued)

On the wealth management and brokerage side of things, TD initially acquired interests in Ameritrade and Waterhouse Securities in the 1990s, and since then has steered these investments and interests to great success under the TD Waterhouse and TD Ameritrade brand names. It also expanded its consumer presence through the acquisition of Chrysler Financial Services in 2011 and Target's retail credit card portfolio even more recently.

While his leadership is rooted in the very best qualities of Canadian common sense and pragmatism, Ed Clark has succeeded because he has not been afraid to rethink the business model and reshape it along the way. His leadership is widely recognized, as demonstrated by the fact that *Barron's* magazine included him in their 2012 list of the Top 30 CEOs in the world; a list that includes 18 CEOs from the United States, seven from Europe, three from Asia and one from Australia, and puts him alongside Warren Buffett and Howard Schultz of Starbucks.

To top things off, Interbrand named TD the most valuable brand in Canada in its 2012 report.

The Globe and Mail

Phillip Crawley came to *The Globe and Mail* at a time when "Canada's National Newspaper" was being threatened by some new and aggressive competition. He arrived with a mandate from the owners to "defeat the upstart *National Post.*" Crawley was well equipped to do so, having been shaped by experiences gained in the tough media markets of the UK, Hong Kong and New Zealand.

Crawley has had to fight off not just the traditional newspaper competition, but also navigate through the unprecedented changes in new forms of digital media. He has been able to transform *The Globe*, not an easy task in an industry that is about as set in its ways as any in the world of business.

Traditional newspapers, *The Globe* included, are often thought of as being rigid, arrogant and stubborn, exactly the kind of environment in which change comes very slowly, if at all. The fact of the matter is that a news organization actually needs to be extremely creative in order to survive. Their core business of synthesizing, packaging and disseminating the daily news requires them to, in Crawley's words, "create a new product, from scratch, every day," and that represents the type of time-pressured, relentless creative pursuit that would terrify most leaders in other industries.

The key to the transformation of *The Globe and Mail* from a traditional, ink-stained newspaper to a modern media powerhouse is, in large measure, due to the process Crawley launched in 2003, which is referred to internally as the "Reimagination Project." This marked an entirely new approach to collaboration, wherein a dozen or more cross-functional project teams were launched to reimagine every single part of the paper using a zero-based, clean-sheet thinking approach. The teams began by taking an outside-in approach, which included scanning every part of the world for new ideas and novel concepts. They had a mandate from Crawley to be bold, and they were!

At the same time as the traditional core business was being rebuilt, the digital side of the news business was growing by leaps and bounds, as more people felt inclined to read the "paper" on their computer or mobile device. This created a parallel universe in which news had to be presented in new ways and in a constantly updated, real-time stream over the full 24-hour news cycle. The challenge was huge, and there were only a few other news organizations in the world that were prepared to embark on the same transformational journey. The second phase of the redesign process was launched in 2010 with an even bolder new design, additional eye-popping graphics, much more vivid colour and a new glossy format to appeal to both readers and advertisers alike. In order to achieve this lofty goal, Crawley needed to invest large amounts of money in new print technology and reposition content, with a shift to articles

(continued)

aimed at creating more of a national debate and, in the process, move the presentation of the news from dry information sharing to sharply argued insight.

His success can be measured by the continuing high regard in which *The Globe* is held by both readers and advertisers alike, and by the fact that under his tenure, *The Globe* and its staff have won over 50 National Newspaper Awards.

21

Thinking about Tomorrow

In a world of increasing complexity and chaos, set against an environment of rapidly changing social norms and the ever-faster availability of information, the advantage will go to the leader whose organization has the best strategic-thinking radar and the best customer-focused market sensitivity. These attributes can only be developed and enhanced when the leader understands the importance of assembling a team with a varied set of rich and diverse experiences.

The words of the song made famous by the popular 1970s band Fleetwood Mac, and used very creatively by Bill Clinton as a presidential campaign mantra, "Don't Stop Thinking about Tomorrow," could very well become the theme song for any leader who wants to guide his or her organization into the future.

In simple terms, the rise of the wise and experienced generalist may be about to overtake our previous faith in the superior aptitudes of the deep, but narrow, über specialist. The pendulum is swinging because in a slower-moving, less confusing and more predictable world, things just didn't change too much, too often or too dramatically. The problem now is that world does not exist anymore! As a result, the mindsets, attitudes, beliefs, processes and leadership competencies that might have very well been good enough even 10 years ago, are just not likely to be appropriate today, or in the near future.

If not, it begs the question—then what?

The answer is clear, and transformational leadership is the essential means to unlocking an organization's sustainable business performance and opportunity-seizing potential. It is a robust experience repertoire that enhances the ability to think fast forward and sharpens contextual awareness to a fine point. This requires a certain set of smarts that act as the intellectual and spiritual catalyst for transformation.

22

Clear Vision and Sensitive Radar

The argument has already been made that what sets the accomplished transformational leaders apart from the rest of us is their ability to gauge the subtle shifts in context and meaning that are the precursors to driving significant change, which allows them to seize emerging opportunities. The leader's ability to accurately assess the context and connect the dots, his or her sense-making or contextual intelligence, is a major part of this competence. It helps the leader create the vivid image of the future that is necessary to galvanize change, overcome inertia and shift an organization onto a new path.

Royal Dutch Shell has, for many years, practised a version of this imaging approach, and it has come to see scenario planning as a valuable means to help guide better strategic decision making.

A futurist and co-founder of the Hudson Institute, Herman Kahn is most often credited with introducing scenario planning through his work with the U.S. military in the 1950s and then at the well-known think tank the RAND Corporation. Since then, it has morphed from its original use as a military intelligence tool and has been shaped into a business application by organizations such as Royal Dutch Shell.

Scenario planning essentially divides knowledge into two categories—the things we believe we know about something and the things we consider uncertain or unknowable. It then blends the known and the unknown into a limited number of consistent views that offer a wide range of possibilities about the future.

Since the 1970s, Shell has taught its leaders how to envisage multiple futures, rather than lock in on just one. It requires its executives to think deeply about each alternative and, in the process, prepare for several different eventualities. As it turns out, the good folks at Shell were way ahead of their time and have been using exploration and design thinking techniques for many years based on the work of prescient thought leaders like Manfred Kets de Vries.

Scenario planning, as a transformational leadership tool, is founded on a belief that there simply is no such thing as absolute certainty and, therefore, no possible way of predicting specific outcomes in the future. However, by adopting the rigour and discipline to pursue multiple possibilities at the same time, and holding multiple futures in your mind simultaneously, you achieve perspectives or clues that would otherwise be missed. The net results are a level of preparedness that is significantly higher and a view of the universe that is much broader. In the process, you are putting yourself in a better position to identify what others have called the "faint signals from the periphery." It is these signals emitting from the future that are so necessary and so useful in orchestrating a timely, rational and appropriate response to emerging events.

Along the same lines, the concept of "Futurescapes" was developed in the early days of three-dimensional CAD technology to describe the methodology of constructing a visual image of a possible future state. In essence, it is a forward-focused mental model that connects a series of apparently random elements into a coherent, integrated picture. Consequently, it provides a means to visualize and understand the various important parts of the puzzle and, more importantly, to gain a better understanding of the relationships and interdependencies between the various elements.

Futurescapes appeal to the part of our cognitive capacity that relates much better to pictures than words, let alone dull spreadsheets, complex Gantt charts and detailed tables of dry data. Futurescapes have the added advantage of serving as a tangible, visual representation of what otherwise might be an intangible story about a vague and ill-defined tomorrow.

In the field of strategy design, Tim Brown of IDEO, the California-based design company, would say a Futurescape is to the business executive what a prototype is to the designer. It is a way of visualizing various possibilities so you are better able to understand the shifting components. In that way, it is perfectly designed for the strategic-thinking and scenario-planning model. It is based on a core premise that flexibility, adaptability and responsiveness are more important to building the business value proposition than binders of densely filled projections, crafted within limited, fixed boundaries and cemented into place with an obsessive doctrine of following the plan as originally crafted.

STRAIGHT TALK NEXT STEPS: CRITICAL COMPETENCY

Contextual Intelligence (CQ)

Canada needs to develop transformational leaders in every sector of the old and the new economies. We need to aggressively and proactively seize the opportunity embedded in the new hyper competitive global economy. In the process, we must shift the very way in which leaders and their organizations go about the process of creating their business strategies.

The irrevocable driving force behind this move is the quantum change in the global business environment, which requires us to develop new tools, techniques, practices and mindsets that are better suited to the world we live in—rather than the one of the past.

The new conditions and the changing marketplace of the future suggest leaders would be well advised to begin charting a new course, one more in keeping with the contextual realities we currently face. Leaders can begin this shift by taking a few simple steps to help jump-start the transformation process.

Step 1: Change the Mindset, Change the Conversation

It all begins with changing the mindsets and mental models we use to shape our view of the world. The process requires the leader to assume responsibility for articulating a disruptive call to action based on the puncturing of tired beliefs and old fallacies. The transformational leader needs to present a vivid, compelling alternative view of the future.

There has to be a clear, believable appeal from the senior leadership team that makes it obvious the organization must and will embark on a new course of exploration. The leaders need a manifesto for change that begins to reshape the narrative and that they can use to engage the organization in a vibrant dialogue about the new future.

This process of dialogue is an essential part of building the shared understanding upon which specific ideas, insights and initiatives for change are then built. Transformation is a story that must be written chapter by chapter and, to quote Peter Denning and Robert Dunham, authors of *The Innovator's Way*, this is because "there is nothing like a compelling story to capture our hearts and imagination."

Step 2: Assemble the Thinking Team

The senior leadership team must have the courage to pull together the very best thinkers in the organization, regardless of level or tenure. The criteria for membership in this strategic-thinking council is the quality of the insight they bring and their ability to fluently engage in powerful debate. In most cases, this likely means a small, dedicated group of highly motivated thinkers who may very well be short on functional expertise, but long on pioneering character and passion.

The thinking team then needs to embark on a serious and totally objective look at the macro trends impacting the current business model, beginning with an outside-in view and a customer-based perspective, and then work backward. The objective of the team is to search out and listen to the faint signals from the periphery that denote the clues to necessary changes.

They must begin the search for a new strategic context by identifying the megatrends and seismic shifts that are providing the clues that will, in turn, impact the market, the social environment and the way things are being done, however uncomfortable those shifts might be to acknowledge.

Step 3: Build a Futurescape

Designers know the best step to take after their initial search for external insights is to shape those insights into an initial
(continued)

prototype to test their emerging theories and beliefs. The best tool for assisting in the design of business strategy is the creation of a Futurescape, in essence a visual prototype of the environment and the organization's response to it. This helps those in the organization understand the new reality by identifying the dots and connecting them into a visual representation that assists in ensuring relationships and dependencies are clear to everyone.

The key is to focus on the whole picture and the connections, not the individual parts. This requires a different set of behaviours that includes, amongst other things, not rushing to early judgments. Instead, there must be an ability to ask brilliant questions and a willingness to allow answers to emerge that, in time, will reveal the secrets of the evolving Futurescape.

Final Thoughts

The world of tomorrow will be an exciting place where the speed of change will pick up momentum at every turn, like a snowball rolling down the mountainside. As a result, the transformational leaders who are smart enough to play the new game will also need to understand that once they begin, they can never stop. The commitment to transformation will require wave after wave of continuous change, to the point where it will appear that there is no stability whatsoever.

The new game is one of perpetual transformation, where stability, comfort and complacency are the avowed enemies, and where the leader must instill a capacity and comfort with the unrelenting pursuit of the new tomorrow. In this world, there is no time to stop and smell the roses, only the promise of more work to come. It is clear that not everyone will be suited to this pace and these conditions, so it is imperative that leaders surround themselves and fill their organizations with people wired to excel in this set of circumstances.

PART IV

The Basis of a
High-Performance Culture

Littered across our business landscape in every sector, region and industry, we find underperforming organizations led by underperforming leaders with underperforming workforces. Yet, despite the fact that we generally know this to be true, we still fail to take the bold action necessary to develop the essential healthy DNA of what we know the high-performance organization to be.

In Part IV, we help business leaders come to terms with what they must do to transform the genetic makeup of their organizations. The process begins by making the deliberate choices necessary to build sustainable high performance in our organizations and, in so doing, avoid continuing our decline into the mind-numbing embrace of even greater national complacency. We make the case for improving the ability of our business leaders to guide their organizations in the midst of permanent ambiguity. We must avoid the misplaced belief that everything in business must be locked down with certainty, proven with fact and supported by rigorous processes that lock our organizations and their people into a deep freeze, where brilliant people and high performance is undermined in homage to avoiding risk and limiting flexibility.

23

Teamwork vs. Team Performance

Canada has always been able to produce reliably high-performing hockey players capable of competing on the international stage. We have done so generation after generation, despite changes to the way the game is played and the emergence of new hockey superpowers, ranging from Russia to the Nordic countries. Our best players typically come from small, salt of the earth, blue-collar towns such as Flin Flon, Manitoba, Floral, Saskatchewan, Cole Harbour, Nova Scotia and Chicoutimi, Quebec; places not exactly high on anyone's list of world-class cities. Despite this, we produce world-class hockey players who can skate, shoot, score and fight with the best of them.

Unfortunately, the same level of sustainable, high-performance excellence remains the elusive goal of far too many Canadian business leaders and their organizations. Our track record of reliable success on the world business stage is spotty at best, save for a very few examples, several of which will be highlighted throughout this book. The more common story, from coast to coast, involves organizations that are currently paying a huge price for the failure of their leaders to pay proper attention to high-performance organizational effectiveness. We can all see the visible pain and dislocation being suffered by those who failed to build a solid foundation in good times, something on which they could depend when the going got tough.

Simply put, while it's easy to ignore imperfections in culture and organizational effectiveness when times are good, those small cracks can become giant chasms if they are not addressed. A destructive chain reaction is then set in motion, one that ultimately impacts both individual and organizational performance when the game changes, the pressure rises and high performance really matters.

The minute you bring any group of people together, let alone the hard-charging, high-achieving, super-innovative types we all want in our organizations, you are bound to ignite tensions. The human dynamic provides for an endless number of psychological variables that even the very best leader can find challenging. High-performance organizational effectiveness can inevitably end up twisted and distorted by underlying tensions that impact performance, harmony and survival.

First, there are the cognitive tensions, which arise from inequities in the distribution of mental firepower and the resulting inability to reach shared, common understanding because of basic differences in the way people process information.

Second, there are the emotional tensions, embedded deeply in the character, motives, intentions and fears of the various members of the team. The emotional and behavioural foundation of an organization is what shapes the culture and is reflected in the habits, preferences, methods, approaches and styles of the people. Culture is a powerful force that can act for the good, but equally for the bad.

Almost anyone who has ever been part of a team has been exposed to the team performance theory embodied in the "Forming, Storming, Norming and Performing" model, introduced by Professor Bruce Tuckman in 1965. Unfortunately, that model is far too primitive to be of much use in today's more challenging environment where the complexity is greater, the social fabric more diverse and the heat from the fire more intense.

Author and academic John Kotter has significantly advanced our thinking around team effectiveness, and he has taken it to a new level when he talks about the fundamental difference between teamwork and team performance. He suggests we often settle for the former when we really want the latter.

Kotter argues that, all models and theories aside, for leadership teams to perform effectively in the organizational context, they need to do some "real" work together as a team. In other words, they can only learn to perform and trust each other when they are faced with genuine work to do. Performance and trust are outcomes, not inputs, and they are only achieved through actual work.

However, Kotter points out that the work we give most senior teams is rarely taxing enough, at either the cognitive or emotional level, to embed real team performance effectiveness. It very seldom requires them to punch through the wall and reach the breakthrough on the other side, where permanent high performance becomes an everyday reality rather than an occasional occurrence.

Instead, most teams stumble along, avoiding the really tough work required for them to get in shape. Senior leadership teams confuse the mild pain of the annual executive retreat or the quarterly operations review with the hard work and time they need to devote to practising together in order to get better together.

24

Mistakes of Leadership

At the macro level, sustainable performance excellence depends on the willingness of the team to measure its effectiveness in a rigorous manner on a regular basis and with a focus on getting better, not just getting there. In other words, leaders need to understand and accept that there are a set of well-known hurdles to cross and a continuing series of ever-escalating levels of proficiency to master on the road to high-performance team effectiveness. Over and over again, teams make the mistake of setting the bar too low, declaring victory too soon and not pushing hard enough to get through what author Seth Godin calls the "Dip." This is a concept he explains in his book of the same name, which suggests that leaders need to take stock up front and be both willing and committed to paying the price of hard work and effort it takes to get through the tough times as a prerequisite to earning the right to success.

There are some common symptoms and visible signs that indicate high-performance struggles within a team, including:

- a leader who fails to become maestro of the various personalities, resulting in teams who operate in silos or who move in small packs for protection
- a leader who uses a hub-and-spoke style of dealing with individual team members, resulting in teams who fail to fully define the common ground on which to then coalesce
- a leader who avoids confrontation and fails to hold members of the team to task for bad behaviour, poor performance or lack of original thought

At the end of the day, the first thing to visibly deteriorate in an executive leadership team is accountability, both individual and collective. It often begins with a loss of trust and respect, but those are often well hidden or even invisible. When lack of accountability rears its ugly head, it typically triggers a decline in credibility, which almost inevitably leads to a relatively quick slide into turmoil, dysfunction and ineffectiveness.

High-performance teams never shirk accountability; they tackle it to the ground and demand it of themselves and each other. They master conflict and are not paralyzed by tensions or dissension. They know how to overcome, bounce back and learn from setbacks. They commit to nothing less than achieving total mastery.

25

Middle Management Malaise

One easy litmus test with which to gauge high-performance leadership effectiveness is to ask a typical group of mid-level managers or front-line supervisors to summarize their organization's strategy. You will inevitably find a frustratingly wide range of misunderstandings, misinterpretations and blank stares, despite what the senior leadership team will tell you have been their Herculean efforts to communicate the strategy. Senior leaders often simply fail to appreciate the fact that this breakdown occurs not because of problems with the quality or quantity of the communication, but rather due to a failure on their part to provide meaning or relevance to those middle managers.

There is no more predictable cause of organizational ineffectiveness and underperformance than a lack of personal connection and commitment to the strategy, at all levels, but especially amongst mid-level managers. The middle management constituency within most organizations is typically the most underappreciated and misunderstood. Few senior leaders understand that this cohort is the real engine of high performance, and it represents the most important group of people in any organization. They are the influencers, the interpreters and the translators. They are what Art Kleincr, the Editor of *Strategy and Business* magazine, refers to as the "core group"—the people who really matter.

Despite the critical nature of their role as connectors, middle managers continue to receive far too little attention and are often amongst the most disconnected and disempowered employees in any organization. The middle managers we are talking about are the store managers in a retail chain, the supervisors on a factory floor, the managers and directors in a large multinational organization. You can tell you have a challenge with this community when you walk the halls, tour the floor or visit the cubicles and notice lack of eye contact and a low level of vitality. Middle managers who are heads down and hiding from those above and below are not likely to be driving high performance.

Organizations and their senior leaders need to change the way they view, manage and communicate with this vital constituency, and that begins with understanding the performance benefits that can be gained from releasing this bottled-up reservoir of underutilized capability and engaging it in the transformation process.

26

Coaching to the Bell Curve

Most half-decent hockey coaches across the land, at any level, intuitively understand one simple fact about the makeup of their teams. They understand that every team, both their own and the other guy's, is made up of A, B and C players. The A players on one team are generally just as good, and as capable, as the A players on the other. Similarly, the C players on both teams are the same type of grinders, role players and limited-capability individuals. The real and important difference lies in the middle, with the nature, motivation and potential of the B players.

The ultimate objective of the head coach of a hockey team, or the CEO of a business, is to find a way to get their B players to outplay and outperform the other team's B players. If you can get even a marginally superior level of performance out of the B community, chances are you will win. In the organizational context, the middle management ranks are supposed to be the farm team for eventual promotion to senior management. Generally, those ranks are filled with an abundant number of B players, and so it makes sense to focus on them disproportionately, for many different reasons.

Unfortunately, this is simply not the case in most organizations. They have no real sense of where the hidden talent resides, and they don't do a very good job of identifying those individuals with the most upside potential. They tend to view middle management as a homogeneous band of people, more like a commodity, a mass group of interchangeable and replaceable parts, especially in a tough job market.

The neglected and underappreciated middle management ranks need to depend on the effective and timely cascade of information, insight and instruction from the level above. Unfortunately, when they do come, those messages tend to come late and they certainly come filtered. As a result, middle managers begin in a disadvantaged position from an understanding point of view, and they are often forced to submerge their own frustrations and confusion in favour of quiet compliance.

Another way you can think about the importance of middle managers is to see them as the equivalent of the swing voters in an election. They are very likely the ones most inclined to change their allegiance from one election to another, rather than follow the intellectually lazy practice of voting for the same party they have always supported, regardless of leader or platform. In this regard, the middle managers in any organization actually control the balance of power. They effectively decide what matters and what does not, what gets done and what does not, what people believe and what they do not. The middle managers in any organization are the source of the best cultural intelligence you can find, and they are ultimately the secret ingredient to achieving superior performance.

27

Culture of Grit and Determination

Truly resonant, transformational leaders take their job as communicators very seriously. They work extraordinarily hard to ensure not only a clear and unwavering understanding of organizational intent that everyone can align with, but they also ensure that it is accompanied by the discipline, willingness and fortitude to get things done. They ensure that the chosen playing field is sharply defined, and they have the fierce resolve to establish priorities, make decisions, drive effort and anchor accountability.

Leadership teams fail or, perhaps even worse, just limp along wistfully, because they do not make dependably smart choices, at all levels up and down the organizational hierarchy, about two things in particular—what they do, and what they do not do!

Over and over again, organizations fail to use the strategic filter as a means to rigorously prioritize their actions. They are not disciplined enough in maintaining their focus and, as a result, have difficulty conserving their energy. They mix short-term tactical and operational issues with long-term strategic priorities at critical moments, and then wonder why things stall or people become overwhelmed and confused.

You will have performance gaps when there is anything short of absolute clarity about the organizational goals and objectives and the strategy chosen to achieve them, and anything less than total zeal to focus only on what really matters. Over time, organizational ineffectiveness will seep into those gaps and, more often than not, it will be with rather dire negative consequences.

28

Battling Stagnation

Very often the end game might not be as clear, the trophy as symbolic or the timeline as finite as it is with winning the Stanley Cup. However, having a clearly articulated and motivating goal is just as important in business as it is in hockey, because it can galvanize attention and focus effort. The sad fact of the matter is, while a clear vision and audacious goals are touted as the most important parts of a winning strategy, the equally important role of culture is constantly ignored, or at least deeply discounted. Too many leaders do not see culture as a source for driving performance effectiveness in the modern organization.

How wrong that belief is, and how dangerous it can prove to be when the chips are down. A sound, healthy, progressive organizational culture is like a rainy day fund. You may not need to draw down against it in good times, but when the going gets tough, it's a great alternative to crossing your fingers and hoping things will hold together. In tough times, you need the cultural glue to help hold things together when everything else is going wrong.

Culture is the foundation upon which a sustainable high-performance organization is built. Culture is what attracts and retains great talent. Culture is what ensures that people do the right thing, even when nobody is watching. Culture is the sum total of all the habits and rituals acquired by the organization and its people over time. It includes the social capital, both good and bad, that the organization has built and that it can use to stimulate even higher levels of performance in difficult circumstances.

The choices we can make with respect to how we wish to manage and improve culture are pretty simple:

- we can choose to ignore it and hope for the best;
- we can choose to embrace it timidly and promote it half-heartedly; or

- we can embrace it fully, embed it at all levels and make it the centre of what we believe.

A healthy culture, no matter how big or small the organization, represents the values, beliefs, aspirations and behaviours the organization stands for and the people within the organization choose to live by. It is the internal equivalent of the external "brand proposition," and it is equally important. It is the promise you make to your employees and your willingness to keep it. The "brand" either resonates within the organization or it causes dissonance, and the leader must assume equal responsibility in each case.

The failure to understand the costs and consequences of a poor cultural brand can cut multiple percentage points off your bottom line and make everything you do harder, slower and more expensive. John Kotter and James Heskett have shown this to be the case in their seminal book, *Corporate Culture and Performance*.

29

The Team Is Not the Sum of Its Parts

It is not hard to detect when a team, or an organization, goes sideways. There are usually plenty of warning signals and symptoms. The only real surprise is how easy it seems for some leaders to ignore them. Symptoms include:

- cliques, subgroups or coalitions of mixed loyalty begin to form and work at cross-purposes
- side deals negotiated outside of the full team
- directives from the top go unanswered or are regularly second-guessed
- lack of candour causes the really important and meaningful conversations to go underground
- lack of self-regulating, self-aligning team discipline results in missed deadlines
- conflicting priorities become common and, sometimes, outright sabotage can occur

To make matters worse, all too often the leader fails to see or sense any of the symptoms.

The real problem with most ineffective leadership teams and underperforming organizations is that they are not so preposterously bad as to call for drastic remedial action, they are just weak, mediocre or partially inept. As a result, it is often easier to avoid the final push to excellence, rather than expend the dedicated effort and emotional investment it would require. Accordingly, we get trapped, or perhaps seduced, into accepting second best. In so doing, we lower our standards and expectations, and end up dying a slow death by a million cuts.

While you cannot fit all the complexity of team and organizational behaviour into a tidy formula or a convenient checklist, you can learn to examine the various elements in a more holistic manner. As John Kotter suggests, the real test of high-performance team effectiveness is how the team performs when it has to perform together, not how it performs as the sum of the individual contributions. He is right when he says the emphasis should be on knowing how and when to balance the collective and individual components of team effectiveness, not on accentuating one over the other. It's the combination of offence, defence, goaltending and special teams that produces winners, not just a blue line occupied by tough-guy enforcers, or a forward line full of prima donnas who won't backcheck.

Business leaders are often guilty of overdosing on fads, theories, models and frameworks. On the other hand, they are equally guilty of falling well short when it comes to developing meaningful metrics for culture and team effectiveness. Courageous, resolved transformational leaders must show a willingness and determination to use the power of good metrics to chart and maintain a course. The very same CEOs who watch, and even obsess over, every movement in the share price or in competitive market share conveniently choose to ignore a similarly rigorous and objective approach to tracking and measuring team, organizational and cultural effectiveness.

Building, maintaining and leveraging a high-performance culture is a difficult thing, just like winning the Stanley Cup. It requires you to not only have the necessary talent and skills to perform, but also the right culture and conditions to make winning a credible possibility. Talent and skill will not, on their own, guarantee victory, but when they are mixed with the right culture and conditions, they produce the intangible difference when it really matters.

30

Facing Reality in the Mirror

Despite all the frameworks, theories and elaborate models available to help guide and educate leaders about high-performance team effectiveness, leaders still seem to fall into one of two basic camps:

- those who believe they already have a highly effective senior team but who, in reality, do not
- those who know they have an ineffective senior team, but are afraid to do the hard work necessary to fix it

The former just don't seem to be aware enough, or perhaps just don't care to see the facts staring them in the face. They just carry on, not fully appreciating the cost of their own ignorance. Strangely, the latter group somehow find it easier to replace individual members of the team, in a wild game of Russian roulette, rather than fix the cracks in the fundamental foundation.

Admittedly, it is hard work cobbling together a diverse group of talented individuals and getting them all pointed in one direction. The number of unpredictable variables in the team performance equation is quite staggering, and random acts of emotional bias and negative influence can easily overwhelm even the most rational of leaders.

The key is to

- take honest stock of where you currently stand;
- determine exactly where you need to be, and by when;
- build the case for making the long-term effort it will require; and then
- have the tenacity, patience and resolve to carry it out.

Few things in life are more frustrating for a transformational business leader than a half-hearted effort. As a result, leaders have to hold themselves accountable for making the full effort necessary to ensure the team is fundamentally aligned, and not just superficially compliant. There is nothing sadder or more frustrating than a timid leader, with a lack of genuine commitment and a dearth of personal resolve to do what is needed to help his or her organization and its people achieve high-performance excellence.

31

Stocking the Credibility Bank

It is far too common to hear members of a senior leadership or middle management team imply, or even whisper, about the existence of a certain lack of trust within the organization, or amongst one another. Even worse, they might actually state it out loud. However, more often than not, it is anything but the dirty little secret they would prefer to think it is, hidden safely out of view. In fact, the lack of trust within a team can usually be easily spotted at 100 feet, through the porous walls of organizational delusion.

When trust is broken and incivility or passive-aggressive behaviour signal their ominous arrival, it is usually very quickly known throughout the organization. Very seldom is it a well-kept secret, and the result is a decline in the leadership team's credibility. The corresponding depreciation in the level of the leader's legitimacy results in a series of cascading accountability problems, political jockeying and performance failures.

Credibility is the currency we use to measure individual, organizational and leadership team effectiveness. Credibility is like a stock price. It rises and falls over time according to what the market (in this case, the people in the organization) determines it to be.

Determining leadership credibility is not the result of measuring employee engagement or employee satisfaction. It is much deeper, much more complex and far more important. It is the implicit value attributed to the level of confidence the organization has in the leadership team's ability. Specifically, it is the ability to navigate a chosen course to a safe and desirable destination, and the corresponding willingness of the members of the organization to fully invest themselves in making that journey.

Credibility is not only poorly managed in most organizations, it is also poorly understood amongst the members of most senior leadership teams. This is despite the fact that credibility is essential to getting people to follow, to take intelligent risks, to innovate and to drive themselves forward aggressively, especially in turbulent conditions.

Credibility is the essential lubricant of high performance and, while it can be influenced by any number of things, the two most important drivers of the credibility currency are

- the quality of the decisions made by individual leaders and/or the senior team collectively; and
- the way in which relationships are built and nourished, at all levels, over time.

It's sad to say, but the privilege of worshipping at the altar of high performance does require some human sacrifice, just not the kind you may fear! It requires people to be willing to invest themselves fully in the pursuit of a worthy strategic objective and to make the personal commitment that can only come from a deep well of intrinsic motivation. You simply cannot have a high-performance team or organization without correspondingly high levels of discretionary commitment and investment at the personal level.

32

Discipline and Accountability

Discipline is a word that can get an unfair rap in some quarters. Naturally, there are countless forms of inappropriate or wrongheaded discipline. On the other hand, when it comes to senior team effectiveness, there is one elegantly simple discipline to insist on, and it can be summed up as the Say/Do ratio. In other words, the willingness to make a promise and the ability to keep that promise, no matter what it takes.

The business world typically loves its numbers, and most leaders have a preferred set of performance indicators that tell them how they are doing and help them stay on track. However, the set of numbers many choose to ignore is the one that would allow them to measure the cost of team and organizational ineffectiveness.

We can't afford to wait any longer for the accounting profession to come up with appropriate rules governing disclosure of this particular financial performance liability, or to figure out an appropriate way to include the cost in the footnotes of the Annual Report. Responsible leaders need to take steps of their own to begin to quantify and track this cost while moving to full disclosure and transparency. It's time to hold leaders accountable for the efficiency and effectiveness of their leadership, not just the results they produce.

High-performance, highly effective teams do many things differently than the vast majority of others, including the way in which they interact and communicate with each other. They have learned how to avoid the headlong rush to premature conclusions and knee-jerk reactions. Instead, they hold themselves accountable for ensuring the thinking and dialogue process is rich with original insight and fresh perspective.

The quality of the cultural environment within the organization really does matter, and senior leaders have the responsibility for shaping that environment. One good way to determine the health of the environment is to listen to the quality of the conversations, debates and dialogue taking place at all levels. Good leaders enable organizational dialogue and view it as a major component of ensuring they have a vibrant culture.

In most executive team meetings, the quality of the discussion is actually quite disappointing. People do not stay on topic, minds wander here and there and the important, hidden thoughts rarely emerge. High-performance teams, on the other hand, ensure the dialogue is infused with demanding intellectual commitment and courage.

Another way to judge a leader's commitment to fostering a healthy organizational culture is to note the commitment made with respect to fostering two-way dialogue and where the leader puts high-quality listening on the organizational list of priorities. The decision that a leader makes in this regard can have an important bearing on the type of environment created. There is no better time than right now to take a long, hard look at organizational culture and determine what can be done to ensure it is helping, not hurting, your chances for success.

33

Understanding Your Organizational DNA

The truth is that the DNA of a "healthy" culture cannot be reduced to a bland set of generic qualities. As with so many other things in organizational life, the context has to be taken into account, and it must help shape the necessary framework. It is more important to have the culture aligned with the context than to have it aligned to some supposedly ideal formula.

Organizations are living, breathing and dynamic communities. As such, they suffer from the same flaws, imperfections, obsessions and biases as the people who work in them and the leaders who guide them.

The possible dysfunctions of organizational life are many and the variations endless. However, there are a few basic "pathologies" that can help identify some of the more common diseases and discomforts. These include a list nicely packaged by Booz & Company Inc. and fully detailed at www.orgdna.com that includes:

The Passive-Aggressive Organization

This is an organization that seems congenial and conflict free, but that is only on the surface. Its leaders appear to come to agreement pretty easily and early. However, they then struggle to implement and carry through on the commitments they have agreed to. There is no stickiness to their decisions, and the real conversations always happen outside of the leadership circle and behind people's backs.

The Fits and Starts Organization

This organization is typically full of very smart, highly motivated and very talented people. However, they rarely pull in the same direction at the same time. High egos and siloed behaviour prevent them from having an aligned enterprise view on almost anything. The internal signs of distress are evident by low levels of trust and respect, while transparency is only a pipe dream.

The Overmanaged Organization

In this organization, multiple layers of overlapping management conspire to create a paralysis by analysis phenomenon that adds little value and slows the organizational metabolism down. These organizations are bureaucratic in nature, allowing policy, process and procedure to abound. Out of necessity, they tend to be highly political environments where side deals are often the norm.

The Outgrown Organization

This organization has grown in size and is now too large and complex to be effectively controlled by a small team. However, the team at the top is willing neither to concede control nor to democratize decision-making authority. As a result, mid-level executives and managers have no real authority, and all major decisions are channelled to the top. This creates a dependency culture, where the people below are sheltered from accountability since all decisions are made one level up in the organization.

The antithesis of these dysfunctional pathologies is what Booz Inc. and others have termed the "resilient organization." It is an organization flexible enough to turn on a dime and adapt quickly to shifts in the external market reality. At the same time, it is also disciplined enough to stay focused and remain aligned to a coherent long-term strategy, which guides critical decisions.

34

Modern Anthropology in the World of Business

In the real world, the world that exists outside the walls of big business, the super conglomerates and the large multinational corporations, we have long relied upon the work of anthropologists to help us understand culture. Whether in ancient Egypt, the rainforests of Africa or the mountain ranges of South America, the work of anthropologists is fundamental to helping us decipher and understand the rituals, customs and habits of a particular tribe. In the organizational context, the cultural anthropologist considers the attitudes, beliefs and behaviours of the people within an organization.

Whether we are in ancient Mesopotamia or modern-day Montreal, we know that certain cultures thrive for quite a long while; others thrive, but only for a short time; and still others fail to thrive, thus dying a quick and merciful death. The mindset, attitude, belief system and adaptability that the tribe chooses to adopt will ultimately make the difference. Choose well, you survive. Choose poorly, you die. Choose somewhere in between, and you suffer long-term pain, frustration and disappointment. In all cases, the culture that emerges is a choice rather than the result of a random set of events or the modern equivalent of a plague or famine.

The culture of an organization matters. It is the culture, the unspoken, the ephemeral and the unnoticed that actually shape the view the organization adopts and define the choices it puts before itself. Sitting just alongside the attitudes and beliefs of an organization is a companion set of attributes that round out the cultural blueprint. They include the core values, espoused by the tribe, and the behavioural competencies nurtured to drive performance, build talent and fuel innovation.

It is a pretty simple formula. So simple, in fact, that many seem to think they need to cloak it in complexity in order to justify their organization adopting of a set of basic principles. Organizations have a tendency to overcomplicate and overengineer almost everything they do, and it is usually to help them hide from the truth, rather than to sharpen their focus on the vital few things that really matter. The ruse is usually visible to the entire organization, and it results in a predictable pattern that plays out in terms of underperformance, misalignment, low levels of credibility, a negative Say/Do ratio and relationship dysfunctions.

Those who study and observe organizational culture and high-performance teams will tell you how constantly amazed they are by how much noise exists in the typical organization. Noise is a terrible distraction and, in the organizational context, noise amounts to toxic waste and displaced energy, a sure sign of lack of focus and underperformance. Chatter, confusion, speculation and miscommunication all contribute to a loss of value.

A culture that suffers from noise overload cannot be a focused culture. Cultures that are not focused on the right stuff cannot aspire to high performance. On the other hand, cultures that banish white noise and make crisp focus a baseline competency for all leaders tend to be cultures of reliably high performance.

35

Superstars, Studs and Starlets

There are a few things we know for certain about high-performance, talented people. Chief amongst these is that they only want to work with other talented people. Similarly, they will only work for talented leaders, and they demand an environment that allows them the freedom to do their very best. It is pretty easy to see why the culture and environment matter so much to talented people, because they will only work in conditions that maximize their abilities and release their potential.

The truly talented have options, alternatives and a level of self-confidence not enjoyed by those trapped in the more mediocre layers of the human capital structure of the typical organization. Consequently, highly talented people tend to be less loyal and much less tolerant. This means that the more you need better talent to get the job done, the more you need better leaders to build better teams in order to create the conditions that talented people demand in order to stay loyal and give their very best.

Leaders who genuinely seek to perform at the highest possible level know they need talented people, both from within their organization and from the outside. They know this because there are some special tasks and responsibilities that can only be assigned to exceptionally talented people. The more talented the people, the better they will be able to identify and scope the real issues, solve the frustrating dilemmas, break the back of the wicked problems, resolve the incongruities and overcome the barriers and obstacles.

LESSONS FROM CANADIAN BUSINESS

Below are the stories of two Canadian organizations that have approached the culture question from unique perspectives and, in both cases, the culture is a reflection of the beliefs ingrained in those organizations from the beginning by their founders.

Magna International Inc.

The story of Frank Stronach has been told many times before. A tool and die maker from Austria, he came to Canada in 1954, formed a company known as Multimatic in 1957 and subsequently made it big in the automotive parts manufacturing business. Together with two other immigrant colleagues, Fred Gingl and Fred Jaekel, the three expanded Magna's footprint aggressively through a combination of building greenfield manufacturing sites and tactical acquisitions under the Tesma, Cosma and Decoma names.

The company has grown from its humble roots to have 263 locations spread across 26 countries, and it now employs over 100,000 people. Annual sales in 2011 reached $27.8 billion, and its track record of navigating various economic downturns in the very cyclical automobile industry has been pretty good, and much better than most. Magna is a success story by any measure, and a company that knows the Canadian flag helps it internationally.

Despite what others may think of the dramatic personality and healthy ego of Stronach, the fact of the matter is, Magna's success has come from just the opposite, a decentralized operating model with lots of authority delegated down into the body of the organization. In the Magna world, General Managers at individual plant sites are encouraged to be mini-entrepreneurs, often going so far as to bid against each other to win contracts to help keep their plants operating at full capacity.

These manufacturing sites are more often than not led by very young managers who have come up from the front lines, not the front office or the hallowed halls of academia. The Magna model is to keep close to its entrepreneurial roots and, in Stronach's mind, the ideal size for a manufacturing facility is 100 employees, which encourages committed performance from local management teams who treat their plant like their own company.

In 1971 Stronach formalized his long-held business beliefs into what is known as the Governing Constitution. It details the manner in which profits are shared between employees, management, investors and society. An Employee Charter was added in 1988, which spells out the roles, rights and responsibilities of all employees. It would be fair to say the Magna "magic" flows from the artful balance they have been able to instill between performance accountability at the individual and business-unit level and the adherence to an enterprise-wide set of values, behaviours and expectations. While not easy to implement or maintain, this is exactly the type of leadership framework that would serve any organization well in the current climate and the evolving future.

WestJet Airlines Ltd.

The airline industry is one of the most brutally competitive in the world. The capital costs of new airplanes, the exorbitant cost of gate fees at major airports, erratic and unpredictable movements in the price of jet fuel, not to mention the vagaries of Canadian weather, make this industry one not suited to the faint of heart.

Despite this, Clive Beddoe formed Calgary-based WestJet in 1996 to go head-to-head against Air Canada, believing a leaner, more fleet-of-foot and customer-friendly organization could cut the Goliath down to size. As extra insurance for achieving success, he also believed that 8,000 employees who were owners would act very differently than 8,000 who were members of a union. WestJet is union free and is not a member of any airline alliance.

(continued)

The heart of WestJet's success is its culture, presented nicely on its corporate website, which summarizes its many accomplishments, including:

- earned top spot in Waterstones' study of Canada's 10 Most Admired Corporate Cultures for four years straight
- designated as a J.D. Power Customer Service Champion in 2011 (one of only two Canadian companies and the only airline to make the list)
- ranked third on Aon Hewitt's "Best Employers in Canada" list
- chosen as the Canadian airline with the best flight attendants by www.flightnetwork.com

WestJet's success can also be measured in at least two ways. First, by its financial performance, with revenue having grown from $2.1 billion to $3.0 billion from 2007 to 2011, a period plagued by the worst economic downturn in 70 years. By way of comparison, its annual sales were $863 million in 2003. Second, the WestJet culture is unique in Canada. As their television ads constantly remind us, "owners" act differently than employees and WestJet shows it is possible to blend the two together for the purpose of creating a customer-centric, empowered, accountability-based environment. Perhaps even more impressive is the fact that WestJet has done this in one of the most difficult and metaphorically turbulent industries in the world.

Corporate Culture and Performance

The reason culture matters, and the reason the environment a leader creates within the organization is so important, is not to win an award or have satisfied employees. The real reason is to drive business results, achieve superior organizational performance and secure the necessary resources to implement the programs, create the tools and develop the talent that allows high performance to be sustained. As a result, when it comes to talent, high-performance cultures know how to attract the best, retain the best, bring out the best, showcase the best and reward the best.

Cultures can be distinctive, and the best ones usually are. The reliably high-performance cultures choose to codify their "magic" by describing it in vivid terms in their value propositions and competency models. The difference between them and others is they actually believe in the power of words and are relentless, if not religious, in holding the organization and its leaders accountable, by measuring the health of the culture on a regular basis.

People work for reasons that go well beyond their paycheque. They work to contribute to something meaningful from which they can draw personal pride and self-esteem. People work for organizations big and small to get a sense of purpose in their professional lives that aligns with their personal lifestyles and aspirations. The very best people only want to work for the very best organizations. If a culture can be created that allows individuals to excel and reach their own potential, the organization will be the beneficiary, just as much as the individual.

One element of culture that leaders will need to build into the DNA of their organizations is the ability to live with ever-increasing levels of uncertainty and ambiguity. The high-performance culture of the future will require individuals who have this capacity and who can thrive in the world of not knowing everything about everything all the time. This will be a huge shift and one that suggests leaders will in fact, as Jim Collins has suggested, need to be much more humble than in the past.

STRAIGHT TALK NEXT STEPS: CRITICAL COMPETENCY

Ambiguity Intelligence (AQ)

Grey is very likely to be the colour of the future, with at least 50 different shades in play. The successful leader of the future is going to have to become very good at living in a world of uncertainty and helping others to do likewise.

Let us assume, for a moment, any organization worth its salt wants to achieve superior results, and wants to do so for as long as it possibly can. If so, the leaders will have to develop a culture geared toward embracing the benefits and advantages of life in the midst of the whitewater conditions necessary to keep the organization in a permanently heightened sense of readiness. This means leaders need to develop an ability to cope comfortably with chaos, turbulence and ambiguity. It's about constantly moving your feet, staying on your toes and remaining in perpetual motion while not knowing exactly how things will play out.

Leaders need to understand that extrinsic motivation will only take you so far. The more powerful enabler is intrinsic volition, and that can only emerge within a culture that understands how much the external context has changed and in which the internal contract has been rewritten to the point where discontent with the status quo is actually worshipped. The inevitable result of allowing chronic discontent and dissatisfaction to surface is a higher level of ambiguity that is generated from within rather than as a reaction to some sort of external stimulation.

High performance is achieved when

- inner restlessness is high and is constructively directed;
- intolerance for stupidity and unnecessary bureaucracy is high;
- impatience to get results and drive improvement is high; and
- intensity is high, the focus crisp and the resolve exceptional.

At the end of the day, organizational strategy is not implemented in a vacuum. The success of a particular strategy is dependent upon the talent that is available and the environment within which it is set. In organizational life, that environment is the culture.

The leaders of tomorrow must have strength of character that is quite different than in the past. They need to understand that the command and control methods, models and structures bred out of the postwar management theories and practices will not work in the new theatre of modern global business warfare.

Our leaders need to become the chief agitators for change in their businesses, the inevitable result of which will be even more ambiguity. They cannot be the generals positioned a long way back from the heat of battle and demanding compliance. Instead, they must be the ones who question, challenge and break the rules in order to release their organizations from the tight grip of convention.

Step 1: Identify the Gap

There is absolutely no point avoiding bad news. Ignorance of reality and denial of circumstance are no excuses. If you are going to be serious about building a better, healthier culture, then you'd better find out what's broken or not working well and begin to address it head-on.

The role of the leader is to identify the dangerous terrain that could very well expose the organization to failure. As a result, leaders need to embark on a search for the cracks, fissures and

(continued)

gaps that spell risk and need to be dealt with. Leaders need to embrace a level of candour and straight talk many have avoided in the past. If need be, they may have to issue immunity passports to people, allowing them to come forward without fear of recrimination for speaking the truth.

The leader needs to ask tough questions, such as:

- What unresolved bad trade-offs are we making time and time again?
- What are the incongruities we have allowed ourselves to become immune to?
- What are the "maybe" answers that we have to begin to say "yes" or "no" to?

Step 2: Think Fast Forward

Most of us get some comfort from thinking about the past and embracing the warm memories that can wrap us so nicely in the blanket of nostalgia, providing some temporary relief from the stresses and strains of the day. However, when it comes to transforming an organizational culture and helping it adopt new competencies, such as comfort with ambiguity and chaos, the key is not to offer the troops pablum to soothe their distress. Rather, it is to aim high at an ambitious moving target, way off in the future. It's not about creating comfort with today, but rather discomfort about how quickly we can get to tomorrow. It's not good enough to reflect on yesterday, or even just build for today. You have to predict the future.

To do so, the leader needs to rev up the metabolism of the entire organization and create energy in pursuit of the future. It is hard to manage in the moment and also think in the future, but treading water is not likely to produce success. We are all victims of the tug of war between the urgent and the important. Leaders have to find a way to separate the two parts and give both equal attention.

A transformational leader needs to think in bold ways that, while creating anxiety in the short term, will also awaken the spirits of those who are anxious to join the leader on a journey to the future. It's about recreating the confidence in our modern leaders that so many new immigrant Canadians had in the past when they decided it was better to break from the past, and adventure boldly into a new and unfamiliar place, rather than remain in a place that no longer offered enough opportunity for improvement.

People are not afraid of change; they are afraid of uncertainty and afraid of change imposed by others. They want change to be their choice, and so the leader must paint a vivid, appealing picture of the new place that allows others to choose with their hearts.

Step 3: Make Hard Choices

There is always more than one choice when you come to a fork in any road. Typically, there is the tried, tested and comfortable path, and then there is the other one. As the poet Robert Frost told us, the road less travelled is often the better choice, albeit less defined and more uncertain.

In the case of organizational culture, it's almost always better to make the tough choice, rather than take the easy path. When we look back from the future, we often note it is choosing the road less travelled that made all the difference. Leaders need to take responsibility for carving the new path and offering others the freedom and the thrill of joining the journey.

Final Thoughts

The leaders of the future will be a special breed. They will be focused on transforming not just their own businesses, but also the world at large. They will have the same pioneering spirit as those who carved Canada from the wilderness, and they will be relentless in their pursuit of opportunity, no matter where it is to be found.

PART V

Strategic Thinking vs. Strategic Planning

We have allowed our business leaders to perpetuate a myth that the only way to showcase and judge leadership superiority is in terms of how well leaders can plan for the future and how well they implement processes and policies to ensure that their organizations stick to the plan. The problem is that premise assumes the leader has some sort of special genius in terms of his or her ability to accurately predict the future. Moreover, it suggests that rigid conformity and total adherence to a set plan is the best answer to performance excellence. While conceding that in the slower-moving, more certain days of the past that formula may have worked some of the time, the deep changes in the environment suggest its odds of success are diminishing as we go into the future.

In Part V, we set forth an alternative premise built around a new definition of strategic leadership, one that speaks to the superiority of the thinking that goes into a strategic plan rather than the plan itself. We reference some Canadian organizations that have done a good job of upgrading their strategic thinking, and we note how it has given them a breadth of strategic opportunity that others should not only marvel at but also quickly copy.

37

Peripheral Vision as a
Competitive Advantage

The ability to develop an inspiring, coherent, game-changing strategy to frame an organization's direction has long been considered one of the key responsibilities of any senior leadership team. Unfortunately, most organizations would not receive top grades for their business strategies in terms of inspiration, coherence or game-changing impact, let alone all three! The truth of the matter is, there are very few Apples, IKEAs or Sonys anywhere in the world, let alone in Canada.

On the other hand, there are some pretty basic reasons why the rest of us fail to achieve even a fraction of the dominance or brand recognition of these and other global market leaders. The fact is, most strategies are adequate enough to allow an organization to get by, but they are simply not creative nor challenging enough to allow for true differentiation. They fail the test of ambition required to set a new standard, to change the entire direction of an industry or to dominate the space. As a result, they are surely not distinctive enough to create new opportunity out of thin air. In other words, they are not strategies at all, but rather a collection of tactical goals and objectives, conveniently clustered together under a banner that the leaders have chosen to call a strategy but which, in reality, is not.

The leaders we have produced since the end of WWII have all had a belief and a grounding in the principles of incrementalism and process efficiency. They grew up as managers and proved themselves as leaders by invoking the tightly constraining economic principles of control, zero defects and narrow tolerances. As a result, they emphasized the science of management and believed that good strategic planning would produce good recurring results. Their narrow perspective and intellectual naïveté, albeit understandably bred out of a simpler time, suggested that wise men could gather to create a strategic plan that would be created scientifically on a foundation of facts and precedents, and that their superior technically proficient plans or blueprints need only then be executed.

The trouble is, whether intentionally or not, they denied an equally rightful place be given to the "art" of strategic thinking and were not even open to the possibility that it was the quality of the thinking that went into the plan that ultimately determined the quality of the plan, not just the quality of the planning per se. Strategic thinking is about new possibilities, new combinations, new answers and, more than anything else, the competitive advantages flowing from disruption, disintermediation and dissonance. These are the three horsemen of the apocalypse that break free from the constraints of a plan and in so doing create new space and new strategies.

At the national level, the same could be said of Canada. We do not have a national economic or business strategy that guides our thinking, focuses our efforts, leverages our strengths or creates distinctive value within the domestic context, let alone globally. In Canada, our complacent, branch-plant mentality and our ultra cautious and deeply conventional way of thinking mean we have allowed ourselves to become not only risk averse, but also intellectually lazy when it comes to strategy development.

Our national inferiority complex, at least in the presence of Americans, has meant we are afraid to take a bold strategic position and wave our own flag in the face of the stars and stripes. In Canada, economic patriotism is seen as somehow awkward and un-Canadian, while in the United States it has long been part of their national spirit and core DNA to think big and think bold. The predisposition on the part of Canadian business leaders to shy away from thinking strategically, combined with our general lack of assertiveness, has resulted in our tentative willingness to pursue new markets and new opportunities. This has already led to serious consequences, and there will be more down the road. These self-limiting behaviours and deferential personality traits limit our national economic flexibility and threaten our standard of life. Canadian business leaders need to find a way to think more progressively and take bolder, more confident and more strategic decisions about the future.

38

Digging the Puck Out of the Corner

Naturally, there are some exceptions, some bright, shining examples of Canadian businesses doing things in exciting, new and original ways. However, the fundamental issue lies in the fact that we simply do not have enough truly game-changing examples across a broad enough range of industries, segments and geographies to allow us to claim anything like the global competitiveness we need. Unlike hockey, where we are comfortable and excel in terms of confidence, skill and assertiveness, it seems it is just not part of our national character to chase the puck when it comes to business. Instead, we shy away from going hard into the corner with our elbows up when we see others fighting for possession of a market, a segment or a service.

It is as though rather than playing the game of business the way we play the game of hockey, hard, fast and determined, we pull out a musty copy of the 19th century Marquess of Queensberry rules and allow outdated definitions of good sportsmanship to guide our action. We then sit back with smug civility and allow someone else to gain possession of the puck, apparently failing to understand the basic rules of the game and the fact you miss 100% of the shots you do not take.

The focus of opportunity-creating and value-building business strategy should be on identifying unique solutions to wicked problems, and combining that with energy, determination and grit. It requires a bold declaration of intent and a commitment to tackle those problems in a focused and determined manner, no matter what it takes. It begins with the identification of a chronic, worrisome problem, a curious anomaly, a puzzling paradox or a troubling trade-off that demands to be resolved. It ends with an all-out effort to deploy the available resources in a creative manner in order to execute the strategy with full force and effect, gaining strength along the way and leaving others puzzled by the secret of your success.

Business strategy should be a deliberate, provocative argument, a bold if not brazen point of view. It should attract attention, criticism and maybe even ridicule. It should destroy old ideas, alter rusty paradigms and debunk dusty beliefs. In order to craft a strategy of this type, there has to be a vibrant exchange of wild ideas and a ferocious debate amongst those charged with bringing the strategy to conclusion. The objective must be to craft a distinctive strategy, not a cheap imitation of what others are doing already. Leaders must fuel the planning exercise with abundant honesty, positive purposeful energy and total intellectual curiosity, and they must demand it of others.

39

The Importance of Total Candour

Love him or hate him, there is very little doubt Jack Welch was a great success during his time as CEO of General Electric. In 1999, *Fortune* magazine named Welch the "Manager of the Century." During his tenure, revenues grew from $26.8 billion in 1980 to $130 billion in 2000 while market value went from $14 billion to more than $410 billion. By the end of 2004, GE was the most valuable company in the world.

Today, Jack Welch is perhaps even better known for his views on business leadership. One of the most compelling and passionate declarations he has made about the failure of business leadership focuses on the lack of candour he has observed in most organizations, what he calls *superficial congeniality*. In his many books and speeches on this subject, he talks about the serious, hidden harm done when organizations, their leaders and their people fail to be brutally honest with themselves and each other.

Strategy is serious business. It deserves nothing less than honest dialogue and total candour. Candour must be encouraged, developed, modelled and rewarded by the leaders at the very top of the organization. Unfortunately, there are simply not enough organizations where this is a deeply embedded cultural reality. Indeed, there may be less candour today than just a few years ago, as people have become more concerned about holding on to what they have, rather than reaching out for something new or better.

Authors James Allen and Chris Zook, in their best-selling book *Repeatability*, talk about "strategy as reinvention vs. strategy as prevention" and how the leader must "create a sense of disorder or discontent in order to fuel strategic urgency." Unfortunately, quite often when you hear a leader talking about the need to create the proverbial burning platform to help ignite a dramatic change in organizational strategy and culture, it probably means it is already long overdue. The smoke has very likely been thick for quite a while before the fire has been declared.

Going into the third period, down by three goals and with your backup goalie in the net is not exactly the set of conditions that are ideal for pulling out a win. Impassioned ranting by the coach in the locker room cannot change the position the team finds itself in, nor does it eliminate the inevitable heavy lifting it will have to do after allowing itself to get so far behind. It is almost as though Canadian business is playing a casual game of shinny on a frozen sunlit pond while others realize it's a hard-edged, winner-take-all game, which is already well into overtime.

40

Avoiding Conflict Is a Mistake

Inferior, let alone outright lousy strategy can generally be traced back to a lack of willingness on the part of senior leaders to be honest about the fundamental challenges they face. There are far too many cases that support this particular argument. Whether it is the loss of the dominant market position once held by Nortel, the squandering of a huge lead on the part of RIM, the slow, painful death of an iconic national retail brand at Eaton's or the dismal failure of Royal Bank to execute its U.S. strategy, Canadian companies have lost too many important business games, including those in which we once had the lead.

Canada suffers from a serious and debilitating conflict-avoidance tendency when it comes to business, and far too many business leaders have adopted it as their natural default position. This mentality appears to be deeply woven into the Canadian business psyche and has become part of our self-effacing national personality disorder.

This could prove deadly in the world we now face because it is based on a misguided belief in the virtue of pumping up the positive news and tamping down the truth. It speaks to a strong predisposition to focus only on the good news and our past strengths, rather than admitting our flaws and acknowledging our future limitations. All this good news hyperbole is rooted in a false premise and, to quote prolific author Dr. Marshall Goldsmith, it signifies the basic failure to understand "what got us here, won't get us there." It's time for Canadian business to sober up and get real. There is no shame in taking Goldsmith's advice, especially since he was recognized as the number one leadership thinker in the world at the 2012 Thinkers 50 ceremony, sponsored by the *Harvard Business Review*.

This particular deficit in our thinking, and the fatal flaw it reveals in our business logic, has prevented many organizations from acknowledging the fundamental fallacy of the strategies they are currently pursuing. It results in the inability, or unwillingness, to call out the primary challenge, identify the primary obstacle and ask good people to rally around to help solve the core problem. All too often, the tendency is to strive for a beautifully concocted, watered down, consensus-driven strategy, which may feel good at the moment, but which does not produce superior results or competitive advantage in the long term.

No matter how painful it may be, when it comes to crafting a competitive business strategy, it all begins with absolute honesty and unabashed candour.

41

Acting when Pivot Points Emerge

Military, political and business history is full of rich examples in which a leader, often against great odds, used a certain set of bold strategies to outmanoeuvre the opposition. In almost all of these cases, victory came because the leader made a critical decision that, in retrospect, became the eventual turning point. These deciding moments become the pivot points that spur definitive action and serve to shift the momentum and set the course for eventual victory. They are the game-changing decisions that mark the dividing line between the successful breakthroughs of some and the disappointing failures of many.

These decision pivot points are not accidental or random events. They are deliberate, defining moments of unique and disproportionate strategic advantage. They arise because a decision was made to direct the full effort of the organization, with extraordinary force and effect, toward a specific, clear, bold outcome. This ruthless focus and unwavering commitment is what provides the necessary energy to tip the scales.

In business, we are not particularly good at the kind of singular focus required to take full advantage of these pivot points. It often seems we feel the need to mitigate absolutely all of the natural risks associated with a big decision. As a result, we never quite make the commitment necessary to take full advantage of the situation. Instead, we carefully hedge our bets, rather than aggressively pursuing our options and, in the process, we limit the full scope of the opportunity we have.

Another way to understand the leadership competencies and strategic mindset required to exercise this kind of bold, pivot-point thinking is to view it from the vantage point of monitoring the "vigilance gap" in our business or marketplace. In their book *Peripheral Vision*, authors George Day and Paul Schoemaker explain that most business failures occur because the leaders were not vigilant enough in identifying the gaps between the way things really are and the way they would like them to be. Leaders not only fail to see the gaps that can become giant chasms, but they also ignore the signals that would have told them change is inevitable.

This early warning system is akin to skating with your head up, which is something young boys and girls are taught to do from the time they begin to play hockey. It's too bad this same competency is not carried over into the business world, because some of the most important game-changing moments, some of the most violent hits and career-ending business injuries, occur when your head is down and you get sideswiped by someone or something your peripheral vision did not pick up.

LESSONS FROM CANADIAN BUSINESS

We have several sterling examples of this strategic leadership and peripheral vision capability in Canada. Some of our leaders are very much aware of and totally attuned to the importance of managing the vigilance gap. While the two leaders that follow both happen to come from the rough-and-tumble world of retail, they serve as excellent case studies others can learn from and apply in their own way.

The Hudson's Bay Company

Bonnie Brooks is President of the Hudson's Bay Company, a company taken private in 2008 by the American investment wizard Richard Baker and his company NRDC. As most Canadians know, the historical roots of the Hudson's Bay Company date back to 1670. Today, they have been combined with U.S. retail giant Lord & Taylor to provide Brooks with a North American–wide platform in the very competitive and ever-changing retail space.

Prior to assuming this combined responsibility, Brooks had been President and CEO of The Bay chain of department stores since returning to Canada in 2008, having been President of the Lane Crawford Joyce Group in Hong Kong from 1997 to 2008. Brooks's pedigree in fashion retailing is strong, having held senior positions at Holt Renfrew as well as having served as

Editor-in-Chief for *Flare* magazine. She was named one of the world's 100 Most Creative People in Business by *Fast Company*.

The keys to the very successful turnaround of The Bay, which she has orchestrated in a few short years, were her international experience, her commitment to putting the customer first and the radical brand makeover she launched. Brooks had the peripheral vision to see and understand what was happening around *The Globe* and bring it all together with a Canadian spin. She has taken an iconic brand and successfully meshed it with some exciting new and modern concepts. Amongst these is the micro-retailing concept that incorporates smaller, more fashion-forward boutiques, such as Topshop and Mexx, within the much larger general merchandise stores.

She has risked putting her own image and personality forward as the new face of The Bay, including using her distinctive voice in radio advertising. In so doing, she has not just changed the brand image and the in-store experience, but she has also made The Bay a place where fashion and service come together for the average Canadian. Within the organization itself, Brooks has rejuvenated morale and raised the sense of pride and engagement amongst employees and executives at all levels. The thing that Brooks understands very well is that people want to strive for success and are not afraid to go on a journey of change or transformation. When a leader paints a vivid, aspirational picture of what is possible and then removes all of the extraneous noise and distractions that may get in the way of achieving it, she discovers that people rally to the cause and can get great things done. It's about the leader putting the emphasis on authenticity, clarity, focus and resolve, all of which Brooks has role modelled for the entire organization.

Lululemon Athletica

Christine Day has been Chief Executive Officer of lululemon athletica, a specialized Vancouver-based fashion retailer, since June 2008. She earned her BA from Central Washington

(*continued*)

University and is also a graduate of Harvard Business School's Advanced Management program. She has done such an outstanding job that she was named CEO of the Year in 2011 by *The Globe and Mail*'s "Report on Business." The company was originally founded in 1998 by Dennis Wilson, a force in the specialized Canadian retail market for many years. He currently continues as the Chairman, and *Forbes* magazine lists Wilson as one of the 10 wealthiest Canadians.

Day joined lululemon in January 2008 as Executive VP, Retail Operations, having spent 20 years at Starbucks in a variety of senior positions. Blending her experience from the world of gourmet coffee retailing with her own experiences as a professional working woman, she was able to cross industry lines and build on what Wilson started, bringing new experiences to a totally unrelated industry.

Day and Wilson have essentially created a new, high-growth market out of thin air. Their peripheral vision allowed them to see a trend that was emerging amongst women who were looking for trendy workout wear. Similar to Steve Jobs at Apple, they saw two trends that presented an opportunity, if they could be successfully joined in a meaningful way. The first trend was an increase in the number of women, young and old, who were putting their health first and joining gyms or yoga classes to stay fit. The second was those same women's desire to look good while they were working out and wishing to present themselves in unique and colourful ways, rather than limiting themselves to traditional shorts and tank tops. Today, lululemon operates in not just Canada, but also the United States, Australia and New Zealand.

Similar to Bonnie Brooks, Day understands that providing consumers with new choices is a way to build a loyal following and, today, it is virtually impossible to go anywhere without seeing the lululemon logo attached to some piece of trendy activewear. In fact, the product now transcends its roots in the yoga studio, and is seen as totally acceptable fashion at the grocery store and, yes, the local Starbucks.

Lululemon's management practices and culture are unusual by any standard, let alone those practised by other companies in Canada. They are progressive, if not avant-garde, and are based on a strong belief in getting a committed group of employees working toward a common goal. The company has a strong, well-defined culture and hires talent based on a rigorous assessment of fit. The company places a strong emphasis on training new employees and encouraging teamwork amongst them, and they are committed to the belief that all good, high-performance cultures begin with the right people focused on the right things and motivated by the right values. The defining ethic that Day uses so well to guide her leadership is based on a belief in the power of people and teams and the chemistry that must exist, at all levels, in order to produce a truly high-performance organization. She understands that if leaders allow a gap of any size to be created between what they say and what they do (or allow others to do) then their own credibility is diminished. At lululemon, the culture is founded on trust at all levels, between all people and with customers. It is for this reason the entire recruitment, talent-management and promotion processes have been refined to almost perfection and have become the very basis on which they perpetuate excellence, enable accountability at all levels and fulfill their customer-centric promise.

In both of these cases, the leaders knew they had to redefine the very way in which the game was played. They both knew the traditional strengths, standard approaches and conventional wisdom of retailing were becoming obstacles to future success, profitability and a great customer experience. These two organizations, and their leaders, had to take the risk of abandoning what had once worked, acknowledging it was no longer appropriate and then totally redefining the mindset and approach it would take to execute their chosen strategy in the market. They embody the very best in world-class strategic thinking, but sadly, they are the Canadian exception rather than the rule, even though their models, frameworks and approaches can be applied to any business, in any sector, in any part of the country.

42

Thinking in the Future Tense

It is time to question why Canada does not have more strategically oriented leaders of the type personified by Bonnie Brooks and Christine Day. One reason is, perhaps, the confusion that exists in many quarters about the definition of what strategy is, what it involves and how you go about developing it.

It is simply not possible to devise a great strategy when the predisposition of the senior leadership team is to slow the thinking process down, scale back the sense of adventure and laboriously force the organization to grind through reams of empirical data to find ways to support "smart" risk taking. More often than not, this results in the endless wringing of hands and the never-ending search for the perfect way to balance all the variables before stoking up the courage to act. While this may be an appropriate course to follow if you want total safety and comfortable mediocrity, it is not the way in which an organization comes to dominate its space or change the course of history.

Strategy should be a choice—a clear, crisp, bold and deliberate choice that you commit to with your full effort and all of your available resources. To be truly effective, the entire organization must have a laser-beam focus on a specific, clear objective, even if it's difficult to fully comprehend the rationale for and implications of the strategy.

There is a huge and important difference between strategy as we are talking about it here and the collection of goals, objectives and tactics seen in most strategic plans. But the difference is not very well understood and, as a result, we can easily find ourselves seduced into calling something a strategy when it is not. Strategy formulation requires the courage to acknowledge a problem, shine the bright light of attention on it and make it the centre of everything the organization does.

There are many reasons why this does not occur, including:

- It requires a proactive, candour-seeking, transformational leader to help the organization take the initial step of acknowledging the need for change. In many cases, this first step never occurs, because the senior leaders, and the organization, are afraid to identify and acknowledge the weak spots.
- To many leaders, ignorance is bliss. As a result, many executive teams are simply not willing to have the necessary, sometimes painful, exploratory discussions to find the deeply hidden secrets. They hope by avoiding discussions or pretending there are no secrets to be found, they will simply just go away.
- Many leaders don't have the ruthless, deliberate focus and energy necessary to take full advantage of the pivot point (which is only an advantage if you find it in the first place). When you do, you have to be willing to act on it and devote everything you have to executing the strategy quickly and boldly.

The very best strategic discussions are often about how to help the organization get unstuck. Author and business guru Keith Yamashita talks in detail about this process in his book of the same name, *Unstuck*. Yamashita has won accolades for his work with companies that include Apple, IBM, Nike and Gap Inc. Canadian business leaders could take a valuable lesson from Yamashita and force themselves and their organizations to shed the heavy burden of caution and conformity, which weighs them down, and focus instead on releasing capacity by removing what does not work even before they think of adding on new things that might work. In short, practising the special math of addition through subtraction!

43

Opportunity Sensing

There is a distinct emotion that accompanies the arrival of a great business opportunity. It is part adrenaline, part fear and part excitement. It is the same emotional high that comes with being close to inevitable victory in a season-ending hockey game. It is the point at which everything around you slows down, your vision becomes crystal clear and things seem to be effortless, because you can taste victory.

In business, moments like these are all too rare. They may be found, from time to time, in the thrill of concluding an acquisition, the inauguration of a new manufacturing plant or the opening of a new store, but seldom are they part of an organization's day-to-day experience. Amongst the many challenges for today's business leaders is finding a way to create these highs on a more frequent basis and to make them part of everyday business life. This can only occur by channelling the intentional energy of the organization toward a clear, passionate common cause, rather than just another set of dry metrics. Just as athletes practise visualization to help put them in a winning headspace, this appeal to passion serves to increase the level of anticipation and heighten the emotions of employees.

Most unique, groundbreaking and genuinely worthy opportunities lie at the very edge of our comprehension, and they tend to present themselves at inconvenient moments. As a result, it is often easier to pass on those opportunities, rather than pursue them with the vigour they deserve. Good leaders and great strategy ensure that never happens. These pivot points are critical to creating a disproportionate advantage. They represent unique opportunities that allow an organization to dominate a certain space and to shape it accordingly.

This kind of strategic opportunism is very seldom logical. There is usually no precedent to rely upon, and it always embodies unknown risks. This is exactly why it is so important for the opportunity to be converted quickly into a clear, focused strategy, so you can act boldly when the moment arises.

Opportunity sensing is about taking advantage of the discontinuities when they appear. Opportunity sensing is about staking a claim on an unknown piece of land. Opportunity sensing is knowing, deep in your bones, that what you are about to do just feels right. The leader who can get comfortable with this new way of thinking is the one who will be able to take maximum advantage of the opportunities resident in the state of disequilibrium in which we find ourselves today.

44

The Narrative of Intentional Choice

Leading an organization is never easy, let alone in times of uncertainty and chaos. The only way to help ease the mental pressure and the emotional stress of the ambiguity created as you accelerate is to ensure each stage of the journey adds layers of additional coherence to the uncertain situation you face. In order to provide coherence and confidence, the leader must dramatically turn down the noise level in the organization, eliminate any unnecessary distractions that inevitably get in the way of execution, and banish the fear of uncertainty. This is best accomplished by committing to a narrow, sharp set of aligned strategic imperatives, rather than making things overwhelmingly complex. Things will be complex enough without adding more to the mix. In other words, the leader must jettison all of the extraneous activities, pet projects and non-essential activities that might exist, in order to help focus the organization on a singular set of interrelated objectives.

In order to get your organization properly coordinated, you need to hone the focus such that no matter how far into the future you look, the picture is still clear and unclouded by the frivolous or the unimportant. It is amazing the lack of clear-headedness you can find in some leaders. It is shocking how often organizations allow themselves to become trapped by adding unnecessary layers of complexity on top of far too many priorities, and then mixing them together with countless trivial diversions. It's a sure recipe for underachievement.

Strategy is a choice. By definition, it means choosing one thing over another, not hedging your bets or sitting on the fence. The problem is, this deliberate process of making an intentional choice and accepting the inevitable trade-offs is often forgotten. Clarity of choice should be the quid pro quo for developing a strategy in the first place. When it is not, the strategic decision takes too long to make and, when it is finally made, it is second-guessed and has no institutional stickiness. The buried mole of cynicism eventually raises its head, and the organization loses focus by continuing to allow the mole to roam the halls at will, spouting its negative, fatalistic mantra to everyone and anyone who will listen.

Curious, isn't it, how so many tough-minded, hard-charging, chest-thumping executives can have trouble saying "No"? This is especially perplexing since the ability to say "No" is amongst the most important requirements necessary to develop good strategy, and it is essential to ensuring the strategy is executed in the manner intended. Strategy, by its very nature, involves the imposition of clear criteria to guide actions, frame decisions and force the organization to maintain focus.

Good strategy requires the leader to have the ability to say "No" to those things that get in the way of total focus. The ability to say "No"—to call off wasteful, energy-draining initiatives, to abandon those activities peripheral to the mission—is a critical discipline and a key competency of the transformational leader. Good strategy involves choosing one course of action over another. It's when we allow the lines to blur or overlap that we get into trouble. We send mixed signals, we misallocate resources and we add fuel to the silo mentality of turf protection.

45

Focused Ambition

Strategy is about amplifying the efforts of the organization to pursue an ambitious objective. In order to do so, we have to make the hard black and white decisions that clear the path for total commitment. In far too many organizations, there is a belief that by somehow dividing or spreading our efforts, we are reducing our risks. It is just the opposite.

Allowing too many priorities to flourish, allowing too many executives or departments to put their agendas first, is precisely what starves the "mission critical" priorities of the oxygen they need to thrive and survive. As a result, the diffusion of effort and focus increases the risk of failure or suboptimal performance, because the full force and weight of effort is not totally committed to those things that really matter.

All too often, leaders feel the need to nail a fancy slogan above their strategic plan. It's as though they believe it is necessary to reduce the strategy to a few simplistic, motivating words to help galvanize the organization and ensure the strategy is more easily understood. It makes you wonder why they don't just make the strategy easy to understand in the first place. Great strategy is not a syrupy slogan, it's a bold intention. Nothing should get in the way of making that crystal clear to everyone.

The quality of a strategy should not be judged by the complexity of the arguments that support it, or the way in which they are beautifully packaged into a dense PowerPoint presentation, delivered by eloquent spokespeople. All too often, this is nothing more than a fancy masquerade, an attempt to demonstrate a level of intellectual superiority and expertise, which, by virtue of its very complexity, reveals its false promise. There is no place for fluff and illusion in the crafting of a good competitive strategy.

Leaders need to overcome the temptation to embroider the strategy. Instead, they must reduce the level of complexity by forcing the organization to concentrate on what Jim Barksdale, the former CEO of Netscape Communications (now part of AOL) once called the "main thing." They must help the organization focus on the one thing that sits at the very core, the necessary essential, the thing that really matters and the thing that will make the biggest difference.

Ron Ashkenas, in his book *Simply Effective*, reminds us there is great beauty, and one may even say elegance, hidden in simplicity. Simplicity is a means to help drive performance. Simplicity can make our ungovernable, unwieldy organizations more effective. Ashkenas goes on to call complexity "quicksand" or "crabgrass," and warns that it can easily consume an organization, unless there is a strategy to combat it. Simplicity adds strength to any strategic plan and allows the people charged with executing the plan to achieve the outcome in the most efficient manner possible.

Leaders have to be alert to the diversionary strategic propositions that can be put forward; these are usually based on the most flimsy evidence and wrapped in elaborately concocted arguments. It is about focus, relentless focus. This can only occur when the leader and the organizational culture prove willing to aggressively jettison lightweight propositions promoted as important strategy.

STRAIGHT TALK NEXT STEPS: CRITICAL COMPETENCY

Strategic Intelligence (SQ)

The ability to manage the "vigilance gap" is a critical competency for the transformational leader and encompasses a trio of capabilities that define strategic intelligence, including

- deep insight into the core issues;
- clear foresight as to how things will play out; and
- an acutely honed and hypersensitive peripheral vision capacity.

Peripheral vision is what helps a leader avoid the threat of being sideswiped or bypassed by a faster moving, more nimble

(continued)

and opportunistic competitor. What better time than right now to declare war on the things that keep us busy but don't really matter, and instead focus on those things that do.

Instead, too many leaders and their organizations are pursuing a strategy of hunkering down, cutting costs, reducing headcount and crossing their fingers in the hope Adam Smith's invisible hand will somehow swoop down and safely return them to the halcyon good old days of the past. In reality, all these leaders have done is lash themselves to the mast in an apparent strategy of riding out the storm, rather than rising appropriately to the challenge at hand.

It is as though the greater the uncertainty and instability in the external market, the less willing many leaders are to stare down the devils within their own organizations and deal with the things holding them back or getting in the way. This is not the time to be anything less than candid in identifying and tackling the issues that make the real difference.

Strategy has always been about developing a radically new point of view, a new way of looking at the world and a new way of defining success. Opportunity arises as these viewpoints shift, and it affords a great leader a moment to destabilize and disorient the competition. This strategy is what Richard D'Aveni of the Tuck School of Business at Dartmouth College calls "hypercompetition."

Today's leaders will ultimately be judged, as they always have been, by those who come after, and they will be judged harshly based on the strategic choices and decisions they make today. The jurors of the future will look back with the obvious benefit of 20:20 hindsight and ask why the leaders of today did not deal with the fundamental flaws, the obvious inconsistencies and the challenging paradoxes of the times.

This fate can be avoided if leaders wake up to the need to develop strategies that do not simply perpetuate the past, but instead break free and create the opportunities of tomorrow. Strategic intelligence is not a mysterious potion cooked up in some dark hidden kitchen; it is a competency that demands to be seen more often in the fresh air and sunlight of the executive suite.

Today's leaders are not helpless, and they are certainly not alone. There are things they can and should do, but they will require abandoning some anchors that have been holding them back. One way to kick-start the strategic rejuvenation process is as follows.

Step 1: Dig Deeper. Much Deeper

If your resolve is to get straight answers to the wicked problems hidden beneath the surface, the search will depend on how willing you are to do the heavy lifting necessary to find them. Begin by making sure you have selected the right people to help you think, probe and discover, and then provide them with the necessary air cover and support they need and deserve.

Mining for the hidden issues, unresolved dilemmas and confusing incongruities lurking in your organization will require far more penetrating questions than have been asked before. The questions need to be questions of exploration, focused on the unknown territories, and you must be prepared to follow the line of investigation, no matter where it takes you.

Step 2: Call It Out Loud

Organizations tend, over time, to take on the characteristics of their leaders. If there is a meaningful shift to be made in the way strategy is conceived, then the leaders will have to model the new behaviours. This very likely means an intentional, visible commitment to calling out the superficial arguments that do not hold water and putting an end to the twisted logic and timid, evasive responses to the tougher questions. Raise the bar. Increase the standards. Demand better.

In this new world of hypercompetition, you will also need to change how you analyze the external conditions. This means

(continued)

examining the data you have in new and more interesting ways. Then, just to add yet another level of tension, you will need to seek out new information from new places and in new combinations.

It is a flaw of human nature that we can very easily allow ourselves to become distracted and, in the process, allow our minds to wander. At the organizational level, this is multiplied several times and, very soon, we can find a complex maze of conflicting opinions, priorities and messages masking the underlying reality or truth.

The trick is to eliminate the excuses people use to divert their energy and attention. Sharpen up the messaging. Simplify the strategy.

Step 3: Go Big or Go Home

Business is about balancing shareholder risk and return with market need and customer opportunity. Unfortunately, it appears as though many leaders have been forced back onto their heels by recent economic circumstances while others still have tried to lessen risk by narrowing their field of vision and going small in an effort to weather the storm. Some strategically impaired leaders have justified a "defend and protect" strategy by promoting it as the safest thing to do.

Strategy is an offensive weapon, so leaders need to get out of their bunkers and into the game. The opportunity landscape is richer than ever before, but can tempt delusional leaders and their organizations into thinking they are relevant when, in fact, they may simply be getting better at the wrong game. How many buggy whip producers, or other organizations, were doing quite well just before they became irrelevant?

The authors of the book *Stall Points*, Matthew Olson and Derek van Bever, have produced an excellent study into a phenomenon that should serve as a warning to others. They point out how the majority of big companies in the United States that have failed since the 1950s actually accelerated dramatically just prior to the point at which they stalled. In other words, they allowed themselves to believe they were doing better than they really were and, when the end came, it came swiftly and without warning.

Being good at something that no longer matters is essentially the ultimate definition of being bad at strategic thinking.

Final Thoughts

There are moments when the job of leading can be deadly boring and, once you have been at it for a while, it can even become monotonous. Inventing the future is just the opposite. It has the potential to make a huge difference to customers, employees and shareholders, not to mention the opportunity to leave an important legacy.

The strategic-thinking ability of any organization can be improved. It is an organizational leadership muscle that must be flexed, especially when market uncertainty rises. Around today's leadership table, a premium has to be placed on those leaders who can break free of the mental models that trap originality and limit opportunity. Canada needs transformational leaders with the strategic intelligence necessary to help us occupy a front-row seat in the arena of global business battle.

PART VI

The Importance of
Human Capital Management

How many times have you heard a business leader convincingly tell you, "Our people are our most important asset"? While the statement has a nice ring to it and evokes honourable sentiments of caring and appreciation, it is hardly ever backed up with meaningful actions to prove its validity in practice. The fact of the matter is this: the world has progressed further and faster than most business leaders understand when it comes to leading people and managing human capital. The gap that already existed has widened even further since the recession of 2007–2012 and has been fed by a whole series of actions that leaders have taken in a vain attempt to roll back the clock on progress or, at a minimum, erect a wall to hold the forces of change at bay.

In Part VI, we begin to change this stale thinking and suggest new and important ways for leaders to better understand the importance of human capital and introduce modern tools and techniques to turn it into a distinct competitive advantage. The leaders of the future simply will not be able to lead successfully without a deep, visceral appreciation of people and an emotional intelligence that allows them to create organizations where great people are allowed to do great things as a result of their differences rather than their rigid compliance to a single behavioural template.

46

Building Bench Strength for the Future

In the face of pressing day-to-day business challenges and continuing economic uncertainty, it may seem totally unreasonable to expect senior executives to push back from their desks and invest some quality time in thinking about the future of their human capital balance sheets. However, in a world of uncertainty and instability, one of the few things we know for sure is the future is coming, whether we are ready or not. As a result, we should all be concerned about the changing nature of the employment contract and the fundamental reshaping of the human capital market.

It is only reasonable to predict that the type of talent required on the other side of the current economic doldrums will be very different from what we see today. The changing economic context, increased globalization, continuing demographic shifts, unrelenting invasion of technology and the networking phenomenon of social media will all combine to create an environment quite unlike anything we have ever seen.

We have witnessed consumer behaviour change significantly in recent years as shoppers became more green-sensitive, more value conscious and more brand aware. This has caused them to become more thoughtful, more demanding and less loyal. The same types of fundamental changes have already begun to take place in the talent market as well. The likely result will be a continuing shift in the employment power base, with talented employees, at all levels, becoming far more discriminating, considerably more judicious and far more demanding when it comes to what they consider to be the choice jobs. This will especially be the case in the value-added sectors of the economy, the so-called knowledge jobs and those in which author and academic Richard Florida, of the University of Toronto, has called the "creative class."

As Florida and others have been warning for some time, we can expect the talent market will splinter, and we will see the divide between the haves and the have-nots widen. In other words, those who have developed their creative side, their distinctive and varied experience repertoire and their unique personal brand and value proposition will have a huge advantage over those who are skill dependent rather than competency rich.

As if this were not enough to worry about, there will be a continuation of other trends we have seen for the past 10 years. This will include less employee loyalty and less permanence on one hand, exactly the trend Daniel Pink spoke of in his book *Free Agent Nation*. On the other hand, there will also be much higher expectations from employees, and a premium will be placed by them on the quality of the employment experience and not just the paycheque or pension plan.

All of this will leave senior executives with yet another serious conundrum to resolve. They will be challenged with finding ways to position their organization to compete for an intake of new talent while also facing an increase in the number of long-serving employees who will be flowing out of the organization.

47

Decline of the Dream

The nature of work inside the modern organization has altered in recent years, and most experts agree it will continue to do so. The changing global marketplace, the silver tsunami of aging baby boomers and ongoing economic discontinuity are all part of the puzzle, but they are only the obvious and most visible changes. There is, in fact, something even more profound taking place just beneath the surface that is significantly affecting the world of employment. It can be seen in the shifting relationship between employers and employees. It can be seen in the changing attitudes toward the pursuit of professional careers in large organizations versus the advantages of choosing a more independent, entrepreneurial path. We can see it in the professional services markets amongst young lawyers and accountants, as well as dentists and doctors. We can see it in the manufacturing sector amongst young engineers, technicians and quality control specialists. We can see it in the retail sector amongst buyers, store managers and marketing professionals. We can see it in the young journalists, reporters and bloggers in the increasingly digitally oriented mediascape.

No matter where it is, it is the same basic phenomenon. The professional pathway forward, in every sector of the economy today, is just not the same as it was even 20 years ago. The fundamentals have changed and so, too, must our response.

There are a number of overlapping forces that have conspired to drive the change, including:

- the significant de-layering and hollowing out of the middle management ranks, which means there are just not the same number of introductory management level jobs available to aspiring professionals in which they can gradually hone their professional skills

- the number of reliable stepping-stone positions leading to regular progression and upward mobility have been reduced, and the flow through the professional pipeline from the junior ranks up has been significantly slowed
- the first rung on the ladder to a promising professional career is much higher off the ground than ever before, and many people are just not able to reach that first step

These are fundamental, long-term structural changes that alter the opportunity landscape for young professionals. As a result, they present real challenges, both economic and social, for our businesses, our communities and our country. While current high unemployment levels seem to attract the majority of attention from educated observers (and represent a legitimate concern in the short term), the more concerning problem runs much deeper and has an even greater long-term impact, both social and economic. While the problem has many tentacles, which reach into many different corners of society and the business world, the underlying problems are the deterioration of the trust we place in our business and political leaders and the decline in hope we see in the more disadvantaged parts of society, including the whole spectrum of youth employment opportunities.

48

Paradise Postponed

The speed of professional development, growth and promotion through the ranks of most organizations has slowed when compared to the 1970–1990 period, and the trajectory has flattened out. Paradoxically, we also find ourselves with a better educated, more confident and more worldly pool of young professionals than we have ever seen before. They believed, not so unreasonably, they were entitled to enjoy a seat on the same comfortable professional gravy train their parents enjoyed.

Instead, they find themselves seriously disappointed and severely disillusioned, and they have every right to ask the tough questions about why this has happened, who is responsible and what it means for them going forward.

The prospects for the next generation are not great, in either the short or the medium term, and for a couple of very specific reasons. First, the number of those crucially important and valuable entry- and middle-level jobs has shrunk considerably. Second, those roles, or at least large portions of them, are now being handled by aging middle managers, working down a level from their proficiency as they desperately try to hold on until retirement.

The extreme pressure being applied from both ends of the employment market vise creates a deeply worrying dilemma. The traditional apprenticeship pool has been so compressed that we will have a talent and experience vacuum well out into the future. In turn, this presents a variety of other hidden risks and challenges, which most organizations are simply not prepared for. These range from a simple shortage of talent to a much deeper concern about the cost of attracting that talent. To make matters worse, there is a very good chance that even when supply and demand come back into balance, the pool of fully apprenticed individuals will simply not be there to draw upon.

This talent deficit will be more acute in the Western economies of Europe and the United States than it will be in India, China and South America due, in part, to the older age demographic in those parts of the world and the comparatively larger percentage of unemployable middle-aged people. In Canada, it will be even worse still because of our size and the fact we do not have enough of the "creative class" workers that Richard Florida has spoken about. We need to hedge our future position now by taking action in anticipation of the inevitable, or we risk being at a serious competitive disadvantage when it comes to qualified management talent in the years to come.

Having presented one side of the case, it is only fair to present the other. It is the one most often talked about inside organizations: the need for a generational attitude adjustment. One way or another, every organization has had to come to grips, in recent years, with the phenomenon of learning how to adapt to the Generation X and Y cohorts. They represent a generation popularly labelled as being more entitled, less hardworking and more easily distracted than those coming before. This caricature of the carefree, spoiled and indulgent brat is widely broadcast and even worshipped through the colourful personas of today's music stars, actors and sports heroes.

OMG—They Are Back!

Over and over again, all across Canada, you can find 50- to 60-year-old parents wincing as their 25-year-old children shamelessly display their hyper inflated expectations and high standards. This embarrassed reaction undoubtedly comes from the fact the baby boomer parents are the same ones who produced a lifestyle and provided an upbringing where these expectations and standards were made possible.

Most parents born in the 1950s assumed their children would follow the same predictable, upwardly mobile path built on good jobs and relative security. Instead, they see that their adult children have acquired a taste for gourmet burgers, expensive craft beers and addictive electronic devices that they might not be able to afford if it weren't for parental economic assistance (42.3% of young adults between the ages of 20–29 are now living at home, up from only 26.9% as recently as 1981). These numbers from Human Resources and Skills Development Canada are based on the 2011 Census and are just one part of some new data that should be of concern to all Canadians who have a stake in the health of the employment market of the future.

We have spawned a generation who have enjoyed the benefits of the final destination, but who have no sense of the journey itself and the sacrifice it entails. The result is a generation of young men and women who logically assumed there would be an active, vibrant, willing market for their services. Unfortunately, that market has simply not materialized as they had expected it would once they graduated from university or trade school and were seeking the kind of well-paying middle management jobs they need to keep them in the lifestyle to which they have become very, very accustomed.

Generations X, Y and Z?

Generation X is a term widely used to describe the generation born after the post–World War II baby boom, with birthdates ranging from the early 1960s to the early 1980s. The term was popularized in Douglas Coupland's novel *Generation X: Tales for an Accelerated Culture*.

Coupland, and others, generally use terms such as individualistic, technologically adept and flexible to describe this group. They then quickly add that this cohort has a preference to "work to live, rather than live to work."

Those in Generation Y, also known as Millennials, have birthdates ranging from the early 1980s to the early 2000s. The term first appeared in an August 1993 *Ad Age* editorial and was used to differentiate them from Generation X. Sometimes referred to as the "Echo Boomers," due to the significant increase in birth rates during the 1980s and into the 1990s, they are mostly the young adult offspring of the now aging baby boomers.

Some common traits that define Generation Y include tech-savvy, attention craving, family centric (which includes a willingness to trade high pay for more flexible schedules and a better work/life balance) and achievement oriented. They typically have high expectations of their employers, value teamwork and seek the input and affirmation of others. They want to be included, involved and informed, specifically with regard to feedback and guidance. They appreciate being kept in the loop and look for frequent praise and reassurance. They seek mentors and benefit greatly from relationships based on accelerated personal development.

If the natural rhythm of history is our guide, we can certainly expect that the next generation will have different needs, wants, fears and dispositions still, and very shortly, we will have to begin to cope with the rise of what we shall call here Generation Z. We can gain an initial perspective on how this may play out by examining work that has been done by several people in trying to understand the long cyclical sweep of history.

William Strauss and Neil Howe, who wrote *Generations: The History of America's Future, 1584–2069*, see a recurring phenomenon they define as a "four-stage cycle of social eras," which they believe typically happens over the course of a 20-year period and moves through predictable phases.

The essential premise behind their work and echoed by others, such as Warren Bennis, is that we are all products of the generation in which we are born. Their theory suggests we all grow up looking at the world very differently depending on the events that shape and define the era in which we are raised and turn into adults. Their study, which has been updated in their more recent books, *The Fourth Turning* and *Millennials Rising*, presents an interesting lens through which to think about the leaders we need and how they are motivated and called into action.

Using their terminology and definitions, we would define the current cycle as the *Crisis*, a time in which our societal frameworks and institutions have failed us and are therefore challenged by the community at large. As a result, we can expect that the mindsets, attitudes and beliefs held by the next generation of leaders will be shaped by the events of this particular period. If the authors are right and the pattern, which has recurred over centuries, holds true, we are about to enter the next period, during which confidence rebuilds, and so we will have a natural societal tension to cope with as people from different periods come into conflict based upon the broader events of the times in which they were born and matured.

Of particular interest to us should be the way in which each period tends to produce a certain type of leader. We can use their framework to help us determine how to best build leaders for the particular times in which we live and take a proactive stance to accelerate their positive impact and limit the negative. In short, Canada would be well advised to accelerate out of this period and use the knowledge we have about the broad cycles of history to catapult us into an even stronger position on the global economic stage.

51

Shifting Values, New Challenges

Alongside the rational economic explanation of pure supply and demand in the employment market, we have a more perplexing shift taking place in values, attitudes and behaviours. No doubt every generation has felt the one coming behind is less hard working and committed, but that would be far too superficial and too generalized a label to place on this current generation of young wannabe professionals. However, if we take a somewhat more objective and broader perspective, we can perhaps begin to better understand what lies beneath the visible symptoms we all see on the surface. In short, we have a generation that, generally speaking, is

- more broadly aware and better informed than previous generations;
- more networked across a much broader universe of friends than anyone could have imagined;
- more cynical, more suspicious and less trusting of the establishment than the generation before; and
- more intolerant of perceived injustices and unfairness, regardless of whether they are from the right or the left.

At the same time, these same young adults are also

- less gullible and far less likely to be manipulated by either the media or their elders;
- less inclined to want to be seen as clones of each other and far more individualistic in many ways;
- less driven to keep up with the Joneses in terms of physical and traditional material possessions; and
- less interested in gaining experience within a confining silo, instead wanting lots of variety and exposure.

The future gainful employment of this next generation of Canadians should be a concern not just for them, but for all of us, especially those in the business sector. It is vital for our continuing economic welfare that we have reliable, affordable and ready access to a rich reservoir of human capital, in the same way businesses need to have access to financial capital.

Today we have perhaps the most diversified and well-educated pool of talent in the history of the world at our disposal. As a society, we need to figure out how to develop that raw talent and channel its energy and ambition so it can meet the needs of business at the junction where the hope and opportunity of employees meet the needs of business and commerce. This is a responsibility we all share, regardless of whether we are working in governments, unions, communities, educational institutions or businesses.

However, the unprecedented transformation of the global economy and the impact it has had on economic and social welfare suggests that business should shoulder the heaviest load. As both the creators of employment and the stewards of prosperity, business leaders need to elevate their role, revise their view and assume responsibility for talent development to the national level rather than restricting it to the narrow enterprise level. The quality of our talent will determine our future ability to compete, and business should champion a national talent-development plan because they will directly benefit from it. It's time to step up to the plate and ask business to do more, think more broadly and take a longer-term strategic view.

52

The Experience Economy

As we navigate this period of change, we should remain cognizant of the long sweep of economic history, as Joseph Pine and James Gilmore have written about in their book *The Experience Economy*.

As the co-authors point out, if we stand far enough back, we can trace wave after wave of shifts in the economy and track how they have impacted society and business. We can see the shift from the Agricultural Era to the Industrial Era and how it put unique adaptive strains on the human capital market of the times. During this shift, we saw men go from being largely self-employed farmers and labourers to becoming indentured workers toiling for someone else in very strict and rigid factory settings.

We then saw the subsequent shift from the Industrial Era to the Service Era and how it put new and different pressures on both employers and employees. Work during this shift became less about individual craft and narrow skill sets, and more about collaboration and interpersonal relations.

Then, very quickly on the heels of that seismic shift, and overlapping to some extent, came the arrival of the Information Era. We are still in this period, where workers have become valuable not for what they do, but for what they know and their ability to access new knowledge.

Today, the latest shift has already begun into what Richard Florida has called the Creative Era (others have referred to it as the Conceptual Era). In this period, the value of human capital is defined not by what you did or what you knew yesterday, but rather by what you do with what you know in terms of creating the future.

The hidden talent that must be released here is all about the cognitive and design thinking power of people, the ability to weave together diverse components and insights to create products, services, relationships and experiences that feed the emotional needs of others.

Organizations can provide experiences that allow people to feel good, be connected and be treated as unique individuals within an otherwise commoditized environment where mass production gives way to mass customization with the accent on choice and specifically the choice of experience.

This presents employers, in all sectors of the economy, with a huge challenge. In the same way consumers are increasingly willing to exchange their historical loyalties or bypass conventional channels to find products and solutions they perceive to provide higher value, better utility and a more satisfying experience, so too are employees. In this environment, employers need to create new and exciting ways to engage their workforces and create the developmental opportunities that will, in turn, create the type of talent needed to serve the customers and markets of the future. If they do not, we will continue to have a gap between the needs of the market and the ability of organizations to deliver to their external customers and internal workforce. It's a holistic solution we need, so leaders need to stop seeing the external and internal worlds as separate parts of some mysterious phenomenon from which they are somehow disconnected.

Redefining Work

In 2001, Daniel Pink wrote a best-selling book, titled *Free Agent Nation*, in which he articulated the likely consequences of a permanent trend toward a far more flexible, less loyal and more entitled employment market. It paints a vivid picture of a market in which the non-traditional employers of the future will begin competing for talent with the conventional employers of the past. Whoever wins that tug of war will set the overall tone for the future.

Pink suggests a rising proportion of the more highly sought-after and valued jobs in the future will be in three non-traditional spheres.

- **The Soloists**—people who hang out an individual shingle in order to give themselves freedom of choice and flexibility of lifestyle.
- **The Temps**—who will simply refuse to commit to a full-time gig with any one employer, but instead will move from job to job as it suits them.
- **The Microbusinesses**—offering a smaller, more flexible and less formal alternative work environment within small businesses of fewer than 10 people.

At the end of the day, the inevitable result will be the need for the larger, more traditional employers to differentiate themselves even more than they already do. It is their only hope if they wish to compete with the more flexible and enticing options these forms of alternative employment offer younger workers.

The War for Talent, Version 3.0

Increasingly, it would seem the situation that McKinsey & Company forecasted in 1997 has come true. The attraction of human capital and true talent has become one, if not the major, source of competitive advantage. According to the survey they conducted and then released at the time of the book *War for Talent* in 2001, companies that excelled in talent management achieved a total return to shareholders that was 22% better than the average in their industry.

It seems McKinsey accurately forecasted the future, which is now the present, back many years ago when it very accurately pointed to the five talent management imperatives that organizations in all sectors need to adjust to. They were prescient back then and remain critical today and include:

1. Instilling a talent mindset at all levels of the organization, not just within the human resources department.
2. Creating a winning employee value proposition (EVP) that brings talent through the door and keeps it.
3. Recruiting great talent continuously and seizing the opportunity to build the bench whenever you can, not just when you need to.
4. Growing great leaders who can, in turn, grow other great leaders.
5. Differentiating and affirming talent, understanding that fair does not mean equal in the world of human capital.

The creation of a relevant employment brand and employee experience will allow those who master it to thrive in the ongoing search for talent. Those who don't will be left to pick up the pieces.

Today, one in four jobs is already found in the so-called non-traditional sectors and, as the numbers increase, conventional employers will be pressured to find competitive talent solutions. In the case of Canada, we have a diverse and well-educated workforce to build on that would be the envy of most other nations. However, we need businesses to create the opportunities for young, talented Canadians to begin their careers before they become so bitter and alienated from the business world that it will be too late to convince them that getting into business is good for a future professional career.

LESSONS FROM CANADIAN BUSINESS

Below we discuss two Canadian organizations that have adopted fresh approaches to human capital management. They have not waited for the market to tell them what to do; they have gone out and found a way to do it today.

The Bank of Nova Scotia

The Bank of Nova Scotia, or Scotiabank as it is known to most of us, is Canada's most internationally oriented bank, with overseas roots dating back to 1889 and a presence in countries like Jamaica, Belize and the Dominican Republic. Today, it operates in almost 50 countries, including Mexico, where it has over 13,000 employees operating under the red and white Scotiabank logo.

In recent years, Scotiabank has had a series of outstanding CEOs, ranging from Cedric Ritchie to Peter Godsoe to Rick Waugh. Waugh is a Winnipeg native who is just as comfortable now in New York, Washington or Bogota as he is at the corner of Portage and Main. Waugh has built Scotiabank into an internationally diversified global enterprise, following a path quite different from his domestic competitors. He understands the power of the Canadian brand in the world at large, and he has been able to ensure his organization is well received and able to integrate comfortably in local communities all around the world. While at one time Scotiabank would have seen Royal Bank and CIBC as its competition based on a domestic Canadian definition, Waugh has set his sights higher and now looks at HSBC as the type of institution he wishes to be benchmarked against using a much broader definition of his competition.

Waugh has succeeded with two senior deputies riding shotgun. The first is Sabi Marwah who, as Chief Operating Officer, rules over the day-to-day business and financial management of the bank. Marwah was born in Asansol, a small town near Calcutta. He graduated from the University of California with an honours degree in Economics and an MBA to go along with his Master's degree in Economics from the University of Delhi.

The other loyal deputy is Sylvia Chrominska, former Global Head of Human Resources and Communications. Her very challenging role was to watch over the human capital needs of what has become an increasingly multicultural, multinational organization with offices spread far and wide. Her job was to mix multiple cultures that had very little in common, whether it was differences in language or customs, and to ensure they all served the overarching strategy of the bank.

Chrominska joined Scotiabank in 1979 as a credit analyst, having graduated from the University of Western Ontario with a degree in Business Administration. Within 10 years she was Senior Vice President of Corporate Credit and then, in 1994, made a huge functional switch to the human resources area, becoming Executive Vice President. In 2004, her position was expanded, yet again, to include Public, Corporate and Government affairs.

It's difficult to imagine a more demanding executive role than the one she occupied. It is not just a matter of keeping control of the day-to-day transactional elements of the human resources function, it is much more. Chrominska was responsible for ensuring that the Scotiabank culture was embedded around *The Globe* and that the various functional areas, retail, commercial, investment banking and wealth management, collaborated to ensure that the bank realized its full potential in each and every market.

(continued)

The key to its success at merging cultural perspectives from around *The Globe* into one Scotiabank culture has been to promote and build confidently upon the very best of historical Canadian business values and competencies and then allow management in local subsidiaries to find the best way of integrating them into the local context. The emphasis has been on communication, collaboration between units and people of exemplary character, all of which transcend individual cultures and represent what is seen as vital to high performance no matter where you live or work.

Holt Renfrew

Chances are not too many Canadians have ever met or even heard of Mark Derbyshire, the current President of Holt Renfrew, even though he was named one of Canada's Top 40 Under 40 in 2009. One reason may be that prior to assuming his current role, he was in the human resources function, not the traditional place from which most large organizations draw their top leaders. Derbyshire was Chief Talent Officer for the Wittington Fashion Retail Group, owned by the Weston family. The company oversees Selfridges in the UK, Brown Thomas in Ireland and Holt Renfrew in Canada. He was charged with keeping tabs on first-rate talent in the global retail sector.

Holts is now based in Toronto, but was founded in 1837 in Quebec City. It has nine high-end luxury retail stores across Canada, over which Derbyshire now presides. Since taking over at Holts, he has shifted the organization onto a new trajectory of growth and customer appeal that is unprecedented in the Canadian market. One of the reasons he has been able to do this is that he sees his competition not as other retailers in Canada, but rather every retailer anywhere in the world.

As he explains it, his customers are the global trendsetters—those who tend to travel frequently and, therefore, shop in the very best stores in Hong Kong, London and New York. They have been exposed to the standards and selections of Harrods in

London and Saks in New York and are looking for the same high standards in Montreal, Vancouver or Edmonton.

Derbyshire's challenge is to ensure they are not disappointed when they walk into a Holts store and, beyond the merchandise, the best way to do that is through the people who work there. Using the knowledge gained from his PhD in organizational behaviour from the University of San Jose, Derbyshire is focused on ensuring that his people "stage" the very best experience in the world for Holts' shoppers.

In his view, the skills of presence, human touch and emotional connection that actors use in staging a great performance are the same ones needed to create a great customer experience. He knows the expert, well-heeled, high-end global shopper and the neighbourhood soccer mom are both equally interested in, and entitled to, a quality shopping experience, and this requires that they be met by employees who are themselves a reflection of the brand they represent. This talent is rare and, as a result, Holts has had to develop a recruiting process that ensures it attracts the best of the best and people naturally oriented to delivering on the brand promise.

This sophisticated, modern understanding of the critically important intersection between employee and consumer is what distinguishes Derbyshire and his company. He has infused it into not just his executive team but also into employees at store level, which has set Holts on an exciting path. The key to the continuing success of Holts is taking that global appreciation of fine taste and strengthening the talent base even further, from an already high level, in order to leapfrog the domestic competition and allow Holts to compete with the best of the best. Derbyshire knows that people matter, whether they be employees or customers, and honing that people touch will be the key to winning the hearts and wallets of consumers.

55

Role of Academia

Several years ago, noted McGill University professor and author Henry Mintzberg wrote a very controversial book titled *Managers not MBAs*. The premise of his book was to suggest the traditional MBA degree has served its purpose and, going forward, it should not be used as the de facto proxy for determining who gets access to the hallowed halls of business. Indeed, he suggests a more well-rounded background might be more desirable in a world in which practical skills, creativity and insight will be in greater demand than the standardized processes, formalized theories and deep wells of statistical information on which the MBA is founded.

Mintzberg could very well have been reading a crystal ball, as the boomerang generation heads back home with their newly minted degrees under their arms and no quality job prospects on the horizon. Whereas the MBA was once seen as a primary filter through which organizations could effectively vet the available up-and-coming talent, thereby reducing their employment risks, today the skill sets have changed so dramatically the old filter has a significantly reduced relevance and is not the test of baseline competence it once was.

In the emerging workplace of the future, the leading business schools will need to dramatically rethink their roles, and we could see a re-emergence of the technical schools that teach young people a practical craft, rather than a theoretical set of principles. In fact, this trend is already underway and more undergraduates are taking continuing education in the college world, rather than in Master's programs.

Regardless of the nature of their curriculum, it can only be a matter of time before there is a new kind of partnership required between the academic and the business worlds. This will create a value chain that runs seamlessly from front to back in an integrated manner, helping to maximize the effectiveness of our national human capital. In this regard, the natural solution might be to expand and even reinvent the current co-op program model, boosting it in order to create the kind of real-world experiences and internships that were previously part of the junior manager ranks in larger corporations.

56

Role of Governments

In the old industrial economy of mass-production-based blue-collar employment, governments were expected to play an important role in funding major national infrastructure projects. Their role was to ensure businesses across the country had the benefit of the modern means necessary to conduct their business and compete effectively and efficiently. In recent years, it has become popular to suggest that less government involvement in business and the economy is a necessary part of the free market ethos even when it comes to the more strategic, long-term investments required to underpin an attractive investment climate.

While that may be true in those areas where private industry can realistically fill the void, it needs to be totally rethought in the context of the modern human capital and technology infrastructure needed to be competitive today. The heavy investments that nations and their governments once made in the roads, airports and sea terminals of yesterday have today been replaced by the infrastructure investments required to build the electronic superhighways and virtual workspaces of the future, which have become the new baseline needs for a competitive national economy. We need to embark on building the modern equivalent of the great Canadian railway—one that not only transports knowledge, talent and creativity across our vast land but also builds it in areas directly tied to our national economic plan.

Maslow taught us something about the hierarchy of needs and how our needs change as we mature along the sophistication and satisfaction continuum. Once our basic needs have been attended to, we begin to seek different satisfactions and strive toward self-actualization. So it is in business and the economy in general. Now that we have our basic, traditional infrastructure needs attended to, it is only natural we should aspire to lift the bar higher and focus on the next challenge, which is securing the social and human capital infrastructure of the future.

Workforce planning is a major part of that evolution and is the responsibility of any good management team. Setting aside, for a moment, whether business does a good or a bad job, any government that wants its country to be competitive on the global stage must still address the macro-level, long-term national planning requirements. It is only logical that governments, at all levels, have to do more than provide job assistance or bare-bones basic training. Our societal needs have increased along with our sophistication, and there needs to be a long-term plan to develop our national human capital base so we can sustain our social and economic well-being into the future.

STRAIGHT TALK NEXT STEPS: CRITICAL COMPETENCY

Emotional Intelligence (EQ)

Since 1995, when Daniel Goleman popularized the phrase "emotional intelligence," which was initially coined by Wayne Payne, there has been an increased awareness of the need for our business leaders to have a better appreciation of human nature, human behaviour and, therefore, human capital in the organizational context.

Despite the hard work of Goleman and others, it is still all too common to hear executives whisper under their breath about wasting their time on the "soft stuff." They can be found talking about human resources in terms you know are just slightly demeaning when compared to the "hard stuff" they like to believe makes them successful.

In today's world, and certainly going forward, the deeper appreciation of people, emotions and relationships that comes with mastering EQ in the business context is going to mark the difference between leaders who succeed and those who struggle. It is inconceivable that a leader who fails to understand EQ can be the leader of an organization that puts talent spotting, talent development, collaboration and innovation very high on the list of executive responsibilities.

(continued)

To the extent EQ provides someone with the ability to understand the emotional tone and motivations of others, it is crucial to managing relationships within the social environment of an organization. The makeup of the workforce from a diversity point of view, when combined with the complexities of demographic change, make understanding people and their fears, motivations and aspirations central to achieving performance excellence.

It is hard to imagine that any leader who wishes to genuinely break down silos, increase collaboration and improve creativity will be able to do so without first having this as part of his or her own skill set and then having the ability to instill this master competency deep into the organizational tissue through leaders at all levels. It is important that leaders don't just take a superficial interest in EQ; they must make it an important, if not core, part of their leadership code and expectations.

While conditions in the employment market are difficult in the short term, they are not impossible to overcome in the long term, if business leaders take the kind of progressive steps necessary. The leaders who will best enable their organizations to succeed will be those who adjust their approach and focus on improving organizational climate and culture so that the work environment is conducive to the changing requirements of the modern employee.

This more enlightened approach must include a willingness to invest in deepening the talent pool in the broader communities in which we live by building stronger bridges to the world of education and training.

It is not good enough to just rely on shopping for talent in the external market. It also requires taking steps to build and nourish the internal market, so that when you need to access it, it has the right people who can perform today, and also unleash their potential tomorrow.

Step 1: Invest in a Resiliency Buffer

Headcount management is always a big, recurring issue around the executive table, and headcount is a number everyone focuses on as a crude proxy for cost control. Maybe it's time to take a slightly longer-term, bigger-picture view of things and to consider creating a talent pool "buffer" that is outside of the traditional headcount number and comes under the direct control and management of the CEO.

This could be populated by the younger, first-time hires and high-potential employees the company will need in the future, and managed as an investment fund, rather than a line item of cost. There are no doubt sons and daughters of your good employees who are currently looking for work after finishing their undergraduate degrees, and who could be hired as part of an expanded definition of your employee benefits program. Our guess is they would come to work with the right attitude and their working parents would see this as a positive reinforcement of their own commitment to the organization.

Step 2: Create Meaningful Apprenticeships

It was not so long ago that organizations understood the benefits of having apprentices as part of the labour pool. A small group of individuals who could learn on the job and, along the way, provide an extra set of hands to support the more experienced workers. It may be time to create a modern form of this practice in not just its blue-collar form, but in a white-collar one as well. Some professions, like law and accounting, still find this a useful process, and perhaps others can as well.

University students, and those from colleges and trade schools, are finding it more and more difficult to secure meaningful and relevant co-op opportunities to augment their academic training. It seems to me that business has a societal obligation to step up its own commitment to these kinds of programs, as they are in the mutual best interests of all parties and the community at large.

Job sharing between two deserving young job seekers may be another way to provide valuable experience and training to a generation who need a leg up. It might be better for them to

(continued)

take half of a decent job, somewhat related to their personal interests, than a full-time job that does not match their skill sets or motivations.

Step 3: Develop In-House Learning Academies

At one time, some of the more advanced organizations in Canada, led by the big banks, formed In-House Learning Universities and Training Centres, where interns and experienced managers could be introduced to the workplace through further education provided by business managers.

Over time, most of these facilities were either closed, mothballed or only allowed to continue in a severely shrunken form. As organizations focused on cost cutting, they took an easy, short-term view based on the P & L statement. These cuts were made by even the most enlightened leaders so one can only imagine how easy it was for training budgets to be cut by the less committed. These cuts were easy to justify when there was no apparent consequence or downside, but the hidden cost is about to come back and hit those same organizations right between the eyes when they find themselves unable to compete for talent in the open market of the future.

Final Thoughts

It's once again time to ask leaders to commit to the future and begin to rebuild and reinforce the practical skills, training and orientation needed. Leaders have to play a much bigger role in helping the country adjust to the new realities and, since human capital is such a major part of determining business success, they should step up to the table.

The Canada of the future needs to be a place where businesses, governments and the academic world work together in ways that support the long-term aspirations of people, not just the short-term profit-reporting needs of the quarterly investment analysts meeting.

PART VII

The Critical Role of
Talent Management

Over the long sweep of history, business leaders have generally considered themselves to be good at many things. Somewhere near the top of the list is a belief they are reliably superior talent scouts with a special eye for identifying the up-and-comers and the superstars. The trouble is, no one keeps track of their success rate, and while professional baseball may consider .400 to be a good batting average for a truly great player, professional business leaders need to set the bar far higher than that in order to claim legitimate excellence.

In Part VII, we explain the leadership competency associated with true talent intelligence and provide a new model to help leaders think about the best ways to identify and groom talent for the future. The essential premise is that the game of business leadership has changed so much we need a different type of talent to succeed in the future. If so, then it is only reasonable to ask the leaders of our organizations to replace their raw talent intuition with a more sophisticated form of talent intelligence.

57

Owning the Podium

Leading up to the Vancouver 2010 Olympic Winter Games, there was a fair amount of controversy over the "Own the Podium" program. It was an umbrella funding and sponsorship program, launched in January 2005, to help prepare Canadian athletes for the 2010 Games. The program was created in response to our failure to win a single gold medal in the other two Olympic Games hosted in Canada, Montreal (1976) and Calgary (1988).

Canadians appeared to be seriously conflicted, in our own peculiar way, between privately wanting the country, and our athletes, to do well in the medal count, and yet feeling rather awkward and somehow uncomfortable with setting bold achievement targets and making them public. It just did not seem right, let alone Canadian, to be so blatantly competitive and to direct funding to the sports more likely to win medals at a cost to those in which we had no chance. It is as though, in Canada, we are still holding on to a quaint, outdated belief about fairness being defined as treating everyone the same, regardless of their performance level. Many thought it was un-Canadian to set the bar higher than it had ever been set before and to put public pressure on our athletes to meet those high expectations. It was as though some felt that accountability was a dirty word!

In the first two days of the 2010 Games, we all sat nervously in front of our televisions, fretfully waiting for the gold medals to begin rolling in. We were becoming increasingly concerned until Alexandre Bilodeau from Rosemere, Quebec, won our first gold medal on February 14, 2010. It turned out to be an exciting display of freestyle skiing, matched in emotion only by the iconic picture of his brother Frederic embracing him in celebration after the race.

This period of seemingly prolonged national anxiety provided additional fodder to those who had been saying all along the "Own the

Podium" campaign was ill considered, potentially damaging and would only serve to set us up for failure and humiliation. The good news is, even those cynics backed off when Manitoba's Jon Montgomery was seen a few days later, walking down the street in Whistler Village chugging good old Canadian beer from a pitcher, following his gold medal win. It did not really matter that his medal came in skeleton, a sport only a few dozen Canadians could truthfully admit they knew anything about, but which we were all quite happy to embrace as ours once the medal was safely in Montgomery's hand. The "Own the Podium" program had been shown to be a great success, with Canada winning more Gold Medals than any other country had ever won at the Winter Olympics and placing third in the overall medal count.

58

Striving for Mediocrity

It is almost as though we take a certain pride in our modesty as we carefully wrap it in our inferiority complex and cloak it with our strange national insecurity. In Canada, we seem more comfortable setting the bar of expectations low, and then professing to be just fine with the result when we fail to meet even that low standard, coming away with a fourth-place finish behind the Americans, the Russians and the Germans.

We see a version of this very same Canadian tendency in far too many organizations, and boardrooms, across the country. While it might not exactly have the dramatic impact of an Olympic medal count scrolling across the bottom of our TVs, there is an equivalent process of keeping score of individual performance in most organizations. We can certainly question whether or not it is properly and effectively used, but this is the role of the performance management process.

The trouble is, for the most part, the underlying process does not work very well, and it is certainly not producing the highly talented business leaders we need for the future. As a consequence, we find ourselves at a point of such performance mediocrity that we may need to consider introducing an Own the Podium program for developing high-performance business leaders. It is well past the time for us to throw away our modesty and show the world we are capable of producing talented leaders who can perform to world-class standards on the grand stage of international business.

It is perhaps a blinding statement of the obvious, but while managers and employees can and do disagree on many things, they often share the same unsatisfied and bewildered opinion when it comes to the ineffectiveness they see in the performance management processes used by most organizations. They don't like it because they think it is forced, contrived and subjective. They don't like it because they believe it is too time consuming, too bureaucratic and too superficial. They don't like it because they fail to see how it serves to improve performance or accelerate development, either their own or that of the organization for which they work. The process has become degraded and denigrated because it simply does not do the job, and it is usually executed with only half-hearted effort, lukewarm enthusiasm and rampant abuse.

On the other hand, shift the conversation and talk to a front-line employee, a shift worker on the factory floor, a mid-level manager in a cubicle or even an executive in an office about their future and, all of a sudden, you will have a much more alert conversation, and a far more engaged and relevant dialogue. Reflect for a moment on where you spend the majority of your private thinking time and what occupies the intimate conversations you have with those closest to you. Is it conversations about your current or past job performance, or is it about your future hopes and aspirations? Is it about last quarter's objectives and targets that were set for you by your boss, or is it about your professional dreams, your personal desires and how you might find the perfect job outside of the cramped confines of your current role? I think we all know the answer.

Putting so much organizational time, effort and emotion into administering, and then policing, a performance management process that is, at its best, mediocre in content and retrospective in nature, makes no sense. It is an outdated concept in a world where the conditions necessary for performance success are changing daily. Performance management is only valuable, to either party, when it is balanced by an equal or greater emphasis on what really matters. What really matters is identifying, managing and releasing the future potential of people.

To put a not so subtle point on things, most organizations are simply being negligent when it comes to the responsibility they have to capitalize on the future potential and hidden talents of their people. Performance matters, and that's not up for debate. The real problem lies with the fact there is an even more important conversation to be had, and it receives far too little emphasis. It is about the process of managing, measuring and maximizing human potential, which, if done well, provides returns that are essentially infinite and will have a long-term positive impact on organizations that embrace the thinking and apply the disciplines.

59

Intellectual Capital

Canada is now competing in a world where the intellectual capacity and knowledge of our people has become far more important to our future success than our natural resources. We live in a world where the traditional barriers to entry in most businesses, including access to capital, have either fallen or significantly weakened. The key to future success and economic value creation today, and into the future, has more to do with the originality, design, delivery and functionality of the customer experience we provide. In this world, Canada's competitive ability depends on the quality of our ideas, not the size of our balance sheet or the mineral wealth hidden in rock formations beneath our fields and oceans.

The original ideas, novel products and inspiring services we need will all come from the minds and imaginations of our people. The pendulum swung, long ago, away from bricks, mortar and machines as the fundamental contributors to economic success and wealth creation. It has shifted to the differences we can make through our people, the way they are educated, trained, managed, incented and deployed.

Reflect for a moment on how much money organizations, of all sizes, are spending each year on recruiting external talent through headhunters and/or employment agencies. Think about it. The very same organizations who have done such a poor job of identifying, developing and managing their own talent base, in a failed attempt to ensure access to a steady stream of qualified human capital, go outside and pay good money to identify able-bodied outsiders. To make matters worse, those outsiders then get added into the same talent pool that we know, by experience, is not being properly developed or managed in the first place, and so the cycle repeats itself, ad infinitum. It's lunacy!

There is nothing wrong with people making money because there is a legitimate market demand and a specific need to fill—that is fair ball. On the other hand, it is just not smart to fuel that demand by not paying enough attention to the alternatives and doing a better job of nurturing the talent within.

The argument is really pretty simple. Talent matters more now than it ever has before. Talent identification and management can and must be improved. The future potential of a talent base is harder to determine and judge than past performance. Past performance is not an accurate predictor of future ability or future performance. The traditional economic return on investment formula has shifted, and it will continue to do so, because the terms of competitive reference around the world have changed dramatically. As a result, the much more relevant metric should be the return on human capital, and we have hardly even begun to understand what that would look like.

The fact of the matter is the future competitive success of any organization will have more to do with the ability to identify, manage and release the latent, hidden potential that resides within its people than it will in managing current performance or reducing costs. We simply need to wake up to the fact the entire equation has changed, and adjust accordingly. In this regard, Canada is, with very few exceptions, at the same starting position as everyone else. The countries that may have an edge in the harnessing of their human capital include Singapore and the Nordic countries, which have smaller populations, off-the-chart literacy and tier-one education at the highest levels. If we are smart and motivated, and if we can create some urgency, then we will have as good a chance as anyone in taking home the "gold."

60

Human Capital Planning

In organizational life, we have typically tended to emphasize and praise the benefits of learning on the job and then, with practice, slowly getting better over time. It is, perhaps, still reasonable to follow that approach when it comes to the more manual or rote tasks that continue to exist, to some extent, in all organizations. However, when it comes to human capital management, it's time to change that view and develop a level of sophistication that better fits the times. Ask yourself some simple questions:

- How many hours of talent and human capital management training does your typical supervisor, mid-level manager or junior executive have before they are "licensed" to manage people?
- How do you test those individuals to ensure you have your best people managers managing your best people?
- How do you ensure accountability for maximizing the economic return on the human capital with which they are entrusted?

It would be hard to estimate the cost of mismanagement and the waste of human potential most organizations have experienced over time because of poor people management and inadequate human capital skills. This is attributable to a lack of rigour, a shamefully basic awareness of the skills needed and an incomplete understanding of the importance and value of properly managing human potential. We could gain an immediate incremental economic benefit if we were simply willing to invest the same amount of time in managing the future potential of people as we currently do in trying to manage their past performance.

The contradictions in business are too numerous to list. In most organizations, the annual business planning and budgeting process takes hundreds of hours, countless mind-numbing meetings and the time of dozens and dozens of people. It uses complex spreadsheets, detailed analysis and sophisticated forecasts to identify and justify the various investment options and capital allocation alternatives for the future. Those same organizations then commit even further time, money and resources to developing rigorously detailed trickle-down budgets for each business unit and, finally, they allocate the capital accordingly.

Contrast that, if you will, against the time spent on the annual human capital plan for the very same organization, not the board-mandated formal succession plan for the select few senior "C-Suite" jobs at the very top, but rather the evaluation of succession potential through the entire organization. Let's just charitably suggest the ratio of time, money and attention spent is not 1:1.

In fact, chances are most of the time that leaders currently spend on the various elements of the human capital portfolio is being split between grinding out performance reviews that add little value and the more urgent firefighting that comes with managing people. This would especially be the emergencies caused by those last-minute panic drills resulting from the need to fill holes in sales or operations, now that Sally or Sam has chosen to leave without providing you with the courtesy of two years advance notice so you can conveniently get your ducks in a row.

It is almost a guaranteed bet the talent management process gets shortchanged, year after year, and yet no one tracks the cost and consequence with the kind of rigour and discipline it deserves.

61

Tears and Disappointment

In eastern Canada, hockey fans have been accustomed to the chronic underperformance of the Ottawa Senators and the Toronto Maple Leafs. Even the more traditionally successful Montreal Canadiens franchise has provided its own fans with a fair share of heartbreak and grief in recent years. It seems as though the General Managers of those organizations just can't seem to find and develop the right internal talent upon which to build a winner. To make matters worse, they are similarly unable to source the right free agents to augment the talent they have, and the net result is year after year of underperformance.

At the same time, the most talented players only want to play for the right coach with the right system and the right winning culture. In return, frustrated sports fans question whether the loyalty of the players lies with the name on the back of the jersey or the logo on the front. In the future, this same free agent attitude and approach will increasingly be found in the business workplace, where the vast majority of us toil and where the same essential psychology is at play.

In baseball, there has been a great deal of interest generated by the unconventional General Manager of the Oakland Athletics, Billy Beane, and his use of Sabermetrics, as portrayed in the popular movie *Moneyball*. This novel approach to talent management was initiated so the A's, a perennial low-budget team, could compete with the bigger budget teams, like those in Los Angeles and New York. The talent selection system is based on a rigorous objective assessment of player statistics, through the application of a range of seemingly unconventional measures, to help locate that very special talented individual with just the right stuff who might be otherwise hidden.

While such an approach might seem odd to some, the idea of adding improved rigour, better science and greater objectivity into the talent identification process is anything but crazy.

In fact, it is quite the opposite if you consider

- how little quality, focused and disciplined time you currently spend on forecasting your future people needs;
- the lack of rigour surrounding your analysis of changing conditions and market context; and
- whether or not your evaluation process is based on objective science or outdated subjectivity.

Stepping back for a moment, you should use the same logic and rationale in the realm of talent management that you would use in any other part of good business management practice. We know that accurate foresight and knowledgeable anticipation can give you a huge competitive edge when it comes to building a talented organization. On the other hand, the cost of poor human capital management is real, in terms of the actual cash outlay for headhunter fees, etc., and in terms of the hidden cost of opportunities lost and the waste of untapped human potential. In general, these costs are out of control, and they would not be allowed to continue unchecked in any other part of an organization.

The lack of rigorous systems and objective scientific processes in the talent management sphere is only one reason for this deficiency. The other, perhaps even more important, reason is the lack of understanding, poor judgment and the subjective biases that impact our perceptions when it comes to talent spotting and talent management. We all think we are better than we really are when it comes to our people sense.

Our frailty, in this respect, includes breakdowns related to our sense of:

Sight—in other words, our failure to look far enough forward, to anticipate what tomorrow's broad talent needs will be and to acknowledge and accept they will likely be radically different from today. As a result, we don't change the formula as often or as much as we should.

Smell—this would include our repeated failure to trust our instinct and intuition on those occasions when we sense a singular act of brilliance or potential on the part of a specific employee. All too often we fail to fully appreciate the scent of their future potential. On the other hand, we are not always sensitive enough to the toxic odour of those with limited potential.

Hearing—we can be incredibly tone deaf when we choose to be. We are prone to only hearing what we want to hear and are, therefore, not open to the full range of possible alternatives. We get stuck in a sound groove where the only possible, credible answers lie in what we have heard before, not in the new or different.

Taste—failure to understand that our own preferences may be quite different from those of others. Some like it hot. Some don't. Some like salad. Some like steak. We are extremely vulnerable to allowing our own preferences to distort our view of other people and, more importantly, our view of their future potential.

Touch—this reveals itself as a fundamental failure to comprehend and then accept that leadership, no matter how much we would like it to be otherwise, is not all logic and proven science. As Henry Mintzberg has said, leadership is "equal parts art, science and craft." The artist in most of us has been suppressed over the years and, yet, it is the artist who appreciates the subtleties that flow from a fine touch, especially when it comes to people.

62

People, Practice and Perspiration

The crisp, cool air of autumn signals a time of great promise and excitement in Canada, marking the beginning of yet another hockey season for young Canadians from coast to coast. In some cases, they will be taking to the ice for the very first time as House League players in local community leagues, while for others, who play at a more advanced level, it will be tryouts for the Select and A-level travelling teams. In each case, they will be met by an eager set of volunteer coaches who willingly give up their Saturday mornings or Thursday nights to hang out in cold arenas, eating hot dogs and drinking bad coffee, and teaching their willing students the skills they need to enjoy our national pastime.

These coaches, along with club managers, timekeepers and referees, make this commitment not for the money or fame, but for the love of the game. Whether factory worker or desk jockey, whether blue-collar labourer or white-collar executive, these volunteers are all motivated by the same intrinsic need to teach, share and contribute. They come together at the rink as equals, stripped of their stations in life and fuelled by a common desire to pass along what they know to another generation of budding, hopeful stars.

They all know those eager young faces will, for the most part, only ever be good enough to tell their children about the time they won the Peewee Championship in Antigonish, Nova Scotia, or Brandon, Manitoba. No one will dash their dreams and remind them not even 1% of them will ever have the chance to make the NHL (obviously much less if they are young girls). Instead, these coaches and the others allow their teams to think about the simple joy of scoring a goal, the special camaraderie in the dressing room or the excitement of riding on the team bus to a tournament in another city.

All these kids want, all any of us want in any part of our lives, is a chance to play the game to the best of our ability and not be relegated to the end of the bench where we will sit until we get cut, choose to retire early or are forced out in a manner not of our own choosing.

63

Cost of Benign Neglect

In business, we don't devote a fraction of the time these young kids get to the necessary training, coaching and development of our next generation of leaders—the future stars who will be asked to guide our businesses forward. It is as though the practice time we ask our young players to invest so they can master the game of hockey is somehow seen as unnecessary when they graduate to the junior ranks of organizational life and the game of business.

Sure, some organizations have orientation programs in place, and others may even have a Training and Development Department. Some may offer to pay a portion of an employee's tuition to support an Executive MBA, but that is not what is required to develop talented leaders. As in hockey, it's more ice time that is needed. It is the business equivalent of skating figure eights around cones. It's about taking endless shots at the net. It's about suicide drills and passing drills and skating drills.

Even more, it's about those moments when you are not playing. It's about the moments when you find yourself standing alongside the boards catching your breath or sitting on the bench with your buddies when the coach comes along behind you and taps your shoulder. It's about the coach whispering in your ear and telling you what to do next time the opposing forward comes up the centre of the ice with the puck.

In hockey, practice certainly helps, but the real learning comes when you actually get to play the game. It is during the game that young players begin to see how a team works together, how linemates have to complement and compensate for each other and how good plays can be spoiled when someone on the ice fails to do their job.

Business is arguably an even rougher, tougher, faster sport than hockey. Unfortunately, when you come off the ice at the end of your shift in business, it is highly unlikely you will be met by an experienced coach who loves teaching the game and who whispers in your ear and tells you to keep your stick on the ice and your head up. It is only when the coach cares enough about the development process that he or she will take the time to help ensure you learn from both your successes and your mistakes.

64

Investing in Development

If we do not invest at a much higher rate, and in a more significant and focused manner, in the coaching and development of our emerging talent, we will simply not be able to compete at the high level of skill necessary, let alone have an opportunity to reach the business playoffs. All too often, we send our business players off to compete without the tools and training they need to be successful, and we certainly do not coach them after every shift.

It seems as though the barrier for most businesses is justifying the time and money it takes to create and manage the equivalent of a developmental league for up-and-coming players. Beyond that, there is a lack of commitment to upgrading the process needed for the scouting of talent from both within the organization and outside. As a result, we do not identify a sufficient pool of young, talented players at an early enough stage. Inside most organizations there is, at best, a half-hearted talent identification process and almost no time whatsoever spent on developing the coaching skills necessary to help players master the game and mature as professionals.

According to the Canadian Society for Training and Development (CSTD), Canadian business has traditionally invested approximately $1,100 per annum per employee in training of all kinds, most of which is technical in nature. This is insignificant if we wish to have a major impact on the effective performance of an employee or the organization overall. In other countries, we see a level of investment that far exceeds what we provide in Canada, and this does not take into account what might be the more important issue of where the money is spent and how it is targeted to achieve maximum impact.

Canada has a serious human capital investment deficit at all levels, and we do not have a strategy to focus and channel our slim financial commitments in a way that generates a maximum impact over time. We have not done an adequate job of looking at ourselves or holding ourselves accountable for our own failure to think forward and plan accordingly when it comes to human capital and talent.

As Richard Rumelt explains in his book *Good Strategy Bad Strategy*, the job of the leader is to create the conditions that make the effort both worthwhile and effective, but "in many large organizations, the challenge is often diagnosed as internal." So it is in Canada. We have become our own worst enemy and the fault lies within our business organizations, which have not taken the bold steps necessary to equip themselves for the future.

Societal Change in High Gear

The exciting world of tomorrow, and the very fortunate people who will get the chance to inhabit it, will be nothing like that of today. In order to survive, the progress of civilized society has always required a constant evolution in thinking, combined with an ability to adapt to changes of circumstance in response to the signals the future emits. These are the critical pivot points that we need to better understand and master. From an organizational point of view, they require us to have an informed view of the qualities, attributes and competencies that will be necessary to achieve success in the emerging environment. If leaders do not take the time today to identify these qualities and attributes for the future, no one will know what to look for as we refurbish, retool and repurpose the talent base.

The implication is clear. Leaders must spend much more time than they have to date fully understanding the underlying changes in the human capital universe and how those changes will impact their business models and future talent requirements. If not, they will find themselves at a serious disadvantage when the buzzer sounds to signal the end of the period and the beginning of overtime in the winner-takes-all game of competitive relevance and economic prosperity in the future.

As we look forward to the next 20 years and beyond, with all of the societal, technological and demographic challenges we will face, we can predict with certainty that great talent will matter even more than it does today, and it will be in shorter supply. Consequently, accurately identifying and finding new and creative ways to release that talent will become an even greater leadership imperative, and it will be central to how you succeed and win in the marketplace.

The Cost of Incompetence

In most organizations, the role of practical skill development and real-time coaching is left to managers and executives who are not necessarily the best teachers or coaches. Even worse, they do not really see this role as central to their mandate or their own future success. They are being asked to coach, counsel and develop employees, but that usually means nothing more than completing an annual performance review that is the equivalent of providing a player with feedback after the final game of the season. It's just not good enough if we are serious about being competitive at the highest levels of performance excellence.

The answer lies not in improving the form we use to provide the feedback, or even the process we use to evaluate performance. It is not even in upgrading or expanding the programs we sponsor for training and development. The answer is in improving the practical coaching skills of front-line managers and executives. We are leaving far too many promising employees with good potential in the hands of far too many incompetent managers, who have neither the personal interest nor the professional skills necessary to coach and develop others.

Furthermore, while those managers may be competent enough in the baseline skill sets of the job at hand, they are not necessarily world class when it comes to knowing how to transfer their knowledge to the next generation. Many of these managers have reached their current position as a result of tenure, and the fact they have a body of experience and knowledge in the specific tasks that are required does not mean they are good at packaging and delivering that knowledge.

In the new world of business, the development of talent has to be seen as part of a much broader and more complex knowledge transfer process. Instead, most organizations see training and development as a non-essential line item cost that can be very easily cut from the annual financial plan, if and when it is needed. This occurs regularly, not only because it is easy to justify in the short term and has a direct and immediate positive impact on the bottom line, but also because the typical custodian of the training budget is the head of human resources. The sad reality of our current situation is that the person who occupies the HR role very seldom has the same muscle, influence and gravitas as other executive-level sponsors in the sales, operations and R & D sides of the business.

The net result, more often than not, is the training and development budget is starved to death, forced to survive on the scraps left over from the big table. It has become far too easy and convenient to bury the future hidden cost of the decision to scrimp on development. At a bare minimum, we certainly don't conduct the rigorous analysis necessary to assess the impact of underinvestment on future performance. We simply cut the budget to conserve cash and then fail to appreciate the extra cost incurred every day as a result of poor execution, mismatched skills and simple incompetence. It's an accounting convenience, but a costly flaw in judgment.

The answer to this dilemma is complex and difficult because it involves changing some very deeply ingrained beliefs and overcoming some extremely bad habits. There is no effective public dialogue about our national talent management and development crisis. There is no national accounting standard against which to measure and compare the rate of investment in organizational talent. There are no public disclosure rules that might require an executive team to be held accountable for the annual investment it makes in people.

Even worse, we don't have the same internal disciplines for measuring the return on investment in the human capital area that we see for investments made in fixed capital, IT and other hard-cost line items. It is as though we do not want to shine the bright light of concern on anything to do with the fiduciary responsibility a leadership team has for the effective stewardship and deployment of the human capital with which they are entrusted.

67

Knowledge Architecture

Ask any CEO to describe, in detail, the knowledge transfer process within their organization. Ask them to explain the metrics they have in place to ensure that the process is effective and how those metrics have trended in recent years. Ask that same CEO who is responsible and accountable for the knowledge transfer process. Ask them what rate of return they are achieving on their human capital. Finally, ask them how much they invest every year in the knowledge transfer and development process, and how they determine whether or not they are receiving good value in return.

It is not just the CEO who is to blame here, it is the whole system and the lackadaisical, short-term, amateurish approach we take to human capital management in general. Imagine how quickly things would change if we were to introduce the equivalent of the Corporate Social Responsibility (CSR) reporting requirements that most organizations now follow. Think about how we could take something like the ISO quality accreditation standards used in manufacturing and make them as important and as transparent on the human capital development side of the business. Imagine how much more time and attention would be spent on investments in people and knowledge transfer if the CEO was required to add his or her personal signature to a public disclosure document reporting on human capital and knowledge transfer.

The point here is not to suggest yet another hidden bureaucratic tax be applied on business, or to promote an additional layer of compliance bureaucracy to those that are already choking many businesses today, especially small businesses. The point is simply to suggest it is time to develop a business case to help senior leaders fully appreciate that investing in people, in people's development and especially in improving front-line coaching is a good, smart business decision with a real bottom-line impact that can directly influence shareholder return in a positive manner.

LESSONS FROM CANADIAN BUSINESS

In Canada, we have some very well led organizations that already understand the value and importance of this issue and that have been making human capital development a priority for some time. They are the early adopters and have gone about their work quietly, without fanfare or publicity.

They have experimented and introduced programs, initiatives and processes to help ensure they differentiate themselves, not just by what they do, but by how they do it.

Export Development Canada (EDC)

Unless your organization is one of the 8,000 or so Canadian businesses who use the services of EDC to support the export of Canadian goods and services to foreign markets, it is unlikely you are even aware of their mandate, let alone their story. Recently appointed Governor of the Bank of Canada Steve Poloz has been the President and CEO since January 2011. He is the latest in a series of forward-thinking, change-oriented leaders at EDC, having served his predecessor, Eric Siegel, in a number of different positions including Chief Economist and Senior Vice President of Financing. Upon assuming the CEO role, Poloz became one of only a very few corporate leaders in Canada who have grown up professionally as an economist. Prior to joining EDC, Poloz worked for BCA Research and spent 14 years at the Bank of Canada. He has a PhD in economics from the University of Western Ontario, and is one of the most engaging, personable and pragmatic economists you will ever meet. He is anything but a stuffed shirt or a numbers nerd. He is a progressive leader with an outstanding ability to relate to and understand people and a very clear view of the future.

Poloz has continued to build on the cultural and organizational transformation process begun by Siegel, but he has accelerated it and taken it in several new directions. As the arm of the Canadian government responsible for assisting and supporting Canadian exporters with financing and insurance tools, EDC has over 65 years of global market knowledge and experience deeply embedded in its organizational tissue. Nowhere in Canada will you find a group of 1,300 people who have a better knowledge base and a more accurate finger on the pulse of international business.

Despite his grounding in what some would consider the dry, fact-based, rational world of economics, Poloz has chosen to make his leadership mark on the people side of EDC, where things are just a little more unpredictable and complicated. He has taken a novel approach to talent development that breaks many of the conventional rules of business, but is totally in keeping with the modern view of how a high-performance organization should be run.

He has dramatically reshuffled the responsibilities of his direct reports, giving virtually every executive a new role outside of their traditional area of expertise and comfort zone. He has cascaded the same approach down the organization, and he will continue to do so. In addition, he has challenged his executives to spend more "thinking time" and to consider it a vital part of their job. One technique that has worked brilliantly is to give his vice presidents research assignments that require them to explore topics of strategic importance to the corporation and to then present their findings as white papers in a type of peer review process.

These papers are shared with the entire executive leadership cohort and are meant to shift thinking, raise awareness and stimulate dialogue. This happens both informally and in quarterly Leader's Summit meetings of the entire executive team, where the dialogue is converted into action steps. At its very core, what Poloz and his Executive Vice President of Human Resources, Susanne Laperle, are doing is building a new cultural foundation to ensure EDC remains relevant and responsive in the changing marketplace.

Perhaps the fact that both Poloz and Laperle come from outside of the traditional Ottawa mandarin society and from outside the financial services industry (Laperle spent many years at Dylex,

(continued)

the owners of Tip Top Tailors amongst other brands), is part of the reason they have fresh eyes and a bold, forward-looking perspective.

Suncor Energy Inc.

Canadians, especially those in Calgary where Suncor is based, have taken considerable pride in the success the company has had over many years. While their acquisition of Petro-Canada from the federal government put an end to the Sunoco brand that many of us grew up with, it significantly reinforced their national presence and breathed fresh life into the Petro-Canada name.

The acquisition not only cut the ties with Sunoco Inc. in the United States, but it brought Great Canadian Oil Sands (a majority-owned subsidiary) and its oil and gas interests under one Canadian roof. Today, Suncor develops and produces oil and natural gas in western Canada and engages in drilling in eastern Canada. Its international efforts include offshore developments in the North Sea and conventional, land-based efforts in Libya and Syria, as well as Trinidad and Tobago.

Much of this success was achieved under Rick George, who was the CEO for 21 years. In the process, George became the face of an industry having to come to grips with public concerns over the environmental and other practices of the big energy companies. While it was not always easy to make the case to the public, George created a company that, from its Canadian roots, was recognized globally as an ethical powerhouse in a difficult, dangerous industry. In recognition of his contribution, the prestigious Richard Ivey School of Business at Western University named George Canada's "Business Man of the Year" in 2012.

One reason for Suncor's success has been its commitment to people. The company became a pioneer in terms of its people practices. Its in-house Suncor University has provided generations of employees with the hard skills and soft leadership competencies necessary to succeed in the rough-and-tumble global world of exploration and production.

This forward-thinking approach has allowed the company to attract world-class talent at every level. In addition, it has thought ahead to the future and, in the process, has become a much younger organization. Today, the average age of its 13,000 employees is 40, and Suncor was chosen as one of Canada's Top Employers for Young People in 2012. Suncor has long understood that no matter how well skilled and educated its employee base may be at the moment, the best investment an organization can make is in developing talent from within and ensuring it is equipped for the changes and challenges of the future. Suncor has a commitment to excellence in human capital development that is rare. If Suncor can do it in an arena where global talent is in very high demand, others should be able to do it in the not-so-cutthroat industries the majority of us work in.

68

Playing the Modern Game

There is too much downside in blindly continuing to pursue the current approach, and far too much waste that occurs on a daily basis. This happens in quiet, invisible ways every day, when front-line managers and executives do not know how to effectively coach and develop their people and their teams. The problem becomes even more complex when we look at the structural challenges and accountability gaps that result from the current fixation organizations have with matrix management.

This fad-induced approach to corporate governance blurs reporting lines and, in so doing, pretty much ensures no one executive has the clout needed to advance a progressive agenda when it comes to people and talent. The tight, intuitive and perfectly understood organization charts of the 1960s and 1970s have been changed almost beyond imagination since 2000. This has taken place at the same time organizations are struggling to find the right sized, lean and efficient management machine required to generate maximum profitability from the lowest possible investment in organizational structure and people. Matrix management is the latest incarnation of the same hidden agenda process for downsizing that we saw in the 1980s under the banner of "re-engineering," which, in time, came to be seen for what it really was.

One of the hidden, unintended consequences of this entire move to lean restructuring and shared accountability has been to allow even bigger cracks to open up when it comes to human capital management and talent development. Ironically, these cracks have weakened our capability at exactly the wrong moment. The more complexity we face, the faster the speed of change and the greater the amount of competitive pressure we feel, the more we need clearer lines of accountability. In addition, we need better line managers and executives equipped to guide our teams and business units. Instead, we find ourselves weakened on several different fronts, and our exposure has, therefore, increased at a most inopportune time.

It's as though we have taken a bunch of kids who have never played hockey before, do not know the rules of the game, have old, ill-fitting equipment and no decent coaching or practice, and have thrown them on the ice and asked them to just get out there and not complain. It is hardly a winning formula. We put all of the other investments we have made in technology, products, research, etc. into the hands of amateurs, and then we wonder why we are not getting the results we thought we would.

STRAIGHT TALK NEXT STEPS: CRITICAL COMPETENCY

Talent Intelligence (TQ)

Talent management and human capital development are often areas in which organizations and their leaders like to believe they are already doing a sufficient job. The underlying problem is that too much emphasis is being placed on managing current employee performance, and too little is placed on managing future talent potential. While we religiously monitor a wide variety of performance and productivity ratios in the managing of our financial capital, we have not yet developed a similarly sophisticated awareness of how to monitor our ROP (return on potential).

The problem needs a solution, and the solution begins with a heightened level of awareness, understanding and enlightenment on the part of CEOs, owners and boards of directors. At the individual level, it begins with improving the talent intelligence of our people leaders.

Talent intelligence is the competency required by leaders to identify, develop and support the talent base they have been asked to guide. While one of the essential building blocks of managing people is emotional intelligence, TQ is the skill you might find in a movie director, or an orchestra leader, or a hockey coach who

(continued)

---

has the ability to watch raw talent perform in front of them and recognize, in an instant, if they have what it takes to excel. It is the intuitive judgment to see past the rough edges to the core talent lying just beneath the surface.

Ask a talent scout in any discipline to explain how they do it, how they know and how they can be sure. If you are a left-brained, fact-based senior executive, you will not like what they tell you. They will say it is something they just sense, something they feel about how people carry themselves, how they project, how they flow and how they do it all so effortlessly.

Those answers will not sit very well with typical hardened executives until you ask them what process they use to judge talent. The inevitable answer may shock you, but once they finish talking about the person's depth of experience, drive and can-do attitude, they will also tell you "they just know."

TQ can perhaps best be thought of in the way Liz Wiseman and Greg McKeown explain it in their book, *Multipliers*. It is the bundle of skills found in a modern, progressive leader that enables them to

- accurately and dependably identify raw talent at a very early stage;
- determine which innate attributes can be developed quickly in the individual to ensure excellence;
- sense the inner resolve and motivation of the individual to do the work necessary to exploit his or her own skill;
- pinpoint the series of developmental hurdles and experiences needed to fully maximize the talent; and
- have total confidence in a developmental plan that can be successfully executed.

Wiseman and McKeown expand on this point and drive it home with a very simple explanation of the math of multiplication by telling us:

- Most people in organizations are underutilized and/or not in the right positions in which to excel.

- All capability can be leveraged with the right kind of leadership.
- Intelligence and capability can be multiplied without requiring a bigger investment, but rather a smarter approach to the whole talent equation.

Wiseman and McKeown sum up their findings by listing the five key attributes of a talent multiplier, suggesting they have the ability to act as:

1. **The Talent Magnet**, attracting talented people and using them at their highest point of contribution.
2. **The Liberator**, creating an intense environment that requires people's best thinking and work.
3. **The Challenger**, defining an opportunity that causes people to stretch.
4. **The Debate Maker**, driving sound decisions through rigorous debate.
5. **The Investor**, providing people with the opportunity to learn, grow and develop.

In a world of perceived scarcity, talented people can be a valuable, renewable resource, but as with any other resource, we have to be good stewards in order to ensure future generations can have the same or better benefits than we have today. As a result, we have to think in a much different and more long-term way about the talent pool we have at our disposal and what we can do to strengthen it, modernize it and ensure it can be deployed in effective ways at the right time.

We need to change both our thinking and our language when it comes to human capital. People are not "our most important asset," as we used to believe. In fact, it is quite a derogatory term to use when you think about it, and it should be banished. People inside organizations are not assets that we own and that can only depreciate over time. People need to be treated more like investors. They have to be courted, convinced, enticed and allowed to see for

(continued)

themselves the benefits of making an even greater discretionary investment in themselves and their organization with their sweat and intellect. The role of the leader is to create an environment where those investments will be made out of the free choice of self-motivated people.

There are a number of steps that can be taken, by small and large organizations alike, to begin the shift necessary to ensure our human capital wealth is managed the way it deserves to be. This is a long-term project and the progress will certainly be uneven, especially in the early years, but the journey must begin.

Executives will need to view this like any other long-term investment initiative they might make in the regular course of business. It has to be treated in a similar manner to an acquisition, a large capital investment in new plant and equipment or large-scale R & D in search of a breakthrough product. It will entail a heavy upfront cost, a risk component and the promise of a future economic return, but not an immediate improvement in cash flow. As a result, it should be treated and supported in the same way and with the same rigour as any other material investment project.

Step 1: Reporting Guidelines and Process

Most leaders have come to understand the importance of documented, measured and improvable processes in most parts of their business operations. It is highly unlikely they do not currently have a warehouse management and logistics process, a sales and business development process and even a performance management process. Why should the human capital and knowledge transfer processes be any different?

The same process rigour and continuous improvement should be applied to the knowledge transfer and human capital processes. It will need to go well beyond the writing and storage of manuals and operating procedures, and include the means necessary to transfer intelligence from one generation of workers to another.

Step 2: Certification

It's hard to imagine any amateur hockey coach who has not had to go through some sort of rigorous, objective, third-party certification program before he or she is handed a group of kids to train. In business, we seem to feel this type of baseline criteria for skill sets is not necessary. We do not feel some basic licensing protocols might make sense before we hand over a chunk of our human capital to a manager, or even an executive, who has no understanding of how to coach and develop people or how to manage the complex interpersonal dynamics that occur when we ask people to work in teams.

Surely it makes sense to require some form of training certification for those people who, through their management and coaching of others, will either succeed or fail in helping the business to perform.

It's time to refresh our views, improve our understanding and revisit our priorities. Organizations are going to have to shift their focus forward and place more time, care and attention on the issue of identifying potential, not just managing performance.

Living in the moment will not work during a period when both the rate of change and the level of complexity are on the rise. It's time to pause, project forward and imagine how the universe will unfold for your organization, and how that will impact your talent needs. It's time to decide where you want your people managers to spend their time and what you want them to do with that time. It's time to refocus attention on the potential side of the human capital equation and to make our people leaders responsible for identifying future talent and, in the process, introduce some hard metrics of accountability.

Step 3: Prospecting

There is no point going blindly into the business of prospecting for talent, so leaders will have to face the fact that they need better discipline and have to learn how to make some hard calls in

(continued)

terms of where to look for talent and drill the first test holes. We all do it. We all get lazy. We all look for shortcuts, but we can't keep doing this when it comes to the talent game. We need to put hard talent identification disciplines in place and make talent management an organizational priority.

The quality of conversation and deliberation about talent management issues in general is pretty poor. The senior leadership team needs to lead in this regard by ensuring the dialogue about talent is as rich and deliberate as it can be.

Final Thoughts

It seems that all too often the best intentions of the leadership team are not fulfilled and, consequently, the promise of talent evaporates into thin air. All too often, this is because the escape hatches were left wide open and, when it was convenient, some people found it too tempting to avoid accountability for talent management.

In order to be a globally focused, high-performance organizations, it is essential the leaders take the talent agenda under their own control. It is too important to be outsourced to anyone else, given the link between talent and culture. The ownership and accountability for human capital has to begin at the very top of the organization.

PART VIII

Building the Collaborative Organization of the Future

At the heart of healthy organizational life and sustainable performance success is people's ability to communicate and collaborate for the common good. As organizations have become more complex and the parts more interdependent, we have responded by creating a more cumbersome, complex and dynamic organizational maze. This often masquerades as a matrix reporting structure, which, more often than not, works against the objectives we claim to have.

In Part VIII, we debunk the myth that surrounds the common view of collaboration, and we suggest that leaders have not done enough to equip themselves or their organizations with the essential competencies to lead in a truly modern collaborative environment. We have failed ourselves by building a highly sophisticated theoretical model of working together on top of an archaic set of skills and competencies. We then stand back and wonder why the magical benefits of silo-busting behaviour have not been fully realized. The conclusion will shake many leaders who have come to settle for the half benefits of compromise and consensus when they could have the full benefits of collaboration. The successful leaders of the future will not only know the difference, but will also build their organizations to establish competitive superiority through superior collaboration.

69

Compromise: The Enemy of Success

If you have ever had a bad back or neck, you know how much a nagging pain caused by misalignment can wear you down over time, without you really noticing. You also know how easy it can be to live with the pain for a considerable period before the discomfort becomes so bad you are finally forced to seek out the help of a professional. It's only when the doctor takes an X-ray and tells you your spine is misaligned and the nerves are pinched that you wake up to the need to finally find a permanent solution. You are forced to face the reality that continuing to pop Tylenol morning, noon and night is only masking a much more serious underlying condition.

It's the same in business. There are some well-known but all too easily ignored or dismissed signs of organizational pain, discomfort and misalignment. In almost all cases, the pain is a direct result of an undiagnosed organizational pathology or an approach to leadership that is warped, seriously flawed or simply out of date. One sure way to prolong organizational pain, and the mediocre level of performance that comes from it, is to carry on under the mistaken belief that decisions should be made with the objective of reaching compromise or achieving consensus.

Unfortunately, many leaders who are "conflict avoiders" at their core have perpetuated this rather popular organizational myth. They are the kind of leaders who would rather live with the day-to-day pain of misalignment than do the hard work necessary to help their organizations address the chronic problems that led to the pain in the first place.

Gaps and misalignments, and the subconscious pain that comes from them, are the enemy of a high-performance organization and leadership team. Typically, there are known sets of common misalignments, which any good leader should be able to spot from 10 feet away, but which go unattended for a variety of reasons. This continues, even though the low-level background pain tells them something is fundamentally out of whack and needs fixing. These misalignments include:

- **Misalignments of the cerebral cortex**. These are gaps resulting from fundamentally flawed logic and poor cognitive processing capacity. They are gaps in the strategic thinking and insight ability of leaders. They are the gaps that signify a lack of contextual intelligence and understanding, and they diminish the ability of leaders to accurately gauge where and when real change needs to take place.
- **Misalignments of the lower spine**. These are gaps in the backbone and core structure of the organization—gaps in terms of the competence, character and capability of leaders within the organization. These undermine the whole organizational structure, causing it to become brittle and stiffen up, and they prevent the organization from responding with flexibility and resilience.
- **Misalignments of the upper body, shoulders and arms**. These can best be thought of as gaps in personal accountability—gaps in the collective willingness and ability of the organization, its leaders and its people to get their arms around what really matters. These are gaps in the overall heavy-lifting ability and overall fitness level of the organization and its leaders—gaps that result in holes or even chasms in the responsibility framework of individuals and teams.
- **Misalignments of the lower body and feet**. These include gaps in decision making, follow through and execution. These gaps can indicate a worrying disconnect between what the organization commits to achieving and the results it gets at the end of the day, and include gaps between what is said and promised and the development of the agility, speed and risk appetite to actually seize the opportunity.

Since the sudden collapse of Lehman Brothers and the tumultuous events and aftershocks that followed, cascading ripples have been felt from Wall Street to Main Street, from Montreal to Moscow, from the financial services sector to health care and education. They are the result of serious institutional misalignments and preventable gaps in the business and financial markets in general, and the regulatory framework in particular. They are also the result of gaps that were easily exploited by business leaders looking for shortcuts, financial institutions looking for a quick and easy buck and consumers trying to game the financial system to pad their own wallets.

Whatever their origin and regardless of the motives, these compromises and the pain they have caused should signal the need for landmark changes in the way business is conducted and organizations are led, both domestically and globally. If nothing else, the resulting pain should have taken away any illusion we might have had about what it takes to be competitive and remain relevant in uncertain and changing times.

This is not the time to shy away from facing the truth. This is not the time to cheat the system on one hand or sugar-coat the brutal reality on the other. We all need to face up to the imperfections that lie just beneath the scarred surface of the global economic landscape. This is the time for bold action, not cheap compromise or lazy consensus. This is the time to confront the issues, not avoid the conflict.

70

Carpe Diem

As a country that has weathered the global economic crisis in much better shape than most, Canada now needs to seize the mantle of global leadership and respond aggressively and proactively on the world business stage. We need to initiate a bold, direct response to the changing environment. We need to seize the day. We simply cannot allow change to be dictated by others, who may not share our views, our enviable fiscal position, our high moral standards or our open, tolerant and embracing national nature. We need to be more assertive and ensure we have a stronger position of influence in the world of business, and we have to lead from a position of confidence, character and civility, not compromise, consensus and complacency.

This is our time to lead, and we should not be slow to respond, timid in our approach, self-effacing about our own abilities, lethargic and safe in our actions or naïve and narrow in our thinking. It's time to let the world know that the word "Can" is part of what Canada stands for and believes in. Canada can, if it puts its heart into it. It is not acceptable for us to settle for second best, or second tier, when we should be competing at a level that impresses our trading partners and competitors. The only thing standing in the way is our resolve to achieve it.

Author Jim Collins believes "good is the enemy of great." In this environment, second best is not good enough for Canada. In this environment, settling for the lowest common denominator solution to any issue, whether domestic or global, is not good enough. Compromise and its ugly twin sister, consensus, are the enemy in this battle for economic relevance and global leadership in a changing world where the rules are being rewritten as we speak. Genuine, full-bodied collaboration must be our goal, and we cannot be willing to settle for anything less.

Compromise, by definition, will never be better than second best. Compromise dominated the mindsets, rules and standards of the old game, and the evidence is pretty clear it will not be the way to achieve success in the future. The reason is quite simple: the premise behind compromise and consensus is fatally flawed. It has slowly allowed our standards and expectations to depreciate and has allowed others to play by a different set of rules of their own choosing. Canada has to do better, we have to lead from a position of strength and conviction, not allow others to seize opportunity from our grasp because we are afraid to confront what is wrong or unjust or nonsensical.

Our American cousins cannot be the only ones who get to wave their flag and assert to everyone within shouting distance they are the best nation on the face of the earth. Canada has to overcome its modesty and insecurity and show the world a better way to collaborate, at all levels, rather than settle for the inevitable results of flawed compromises and weak-kneed consensus.

71

Collaboration Recast

In recent years, the rules that historically defined and determined the way we think about and conduct business have been sorely tested. In many cases, the rules have been seriously wanting. Many of the old rules have shown themselves to be far from perfectly suited to the modern world. Others are misguided, misconceived, misappropriated or simply misapplied. The concept of collaboration is just one of these. Collaboration is not only measured by the level of co-operativeness shown but also by the level of assertiveness that individuals are prepared to show as they strive for optimal outcomes.

As referenced earlier, Canadians have a terrible tendency to believe we should be artificially kind and modestly self-effacing when it comes to confronting harsh realities, long-held misconceptions and serious misalignments. We do so in the misguided belief that the truth might cause pain and someone's feelings might be hurt in the process. This perspective results in a fundamentally flawed and unhealthy preference amongst many Canadian business leaders for conflict avoidance, rather than determined conflict resolution. It is based on the ill-conceived premise that, somehow, we can create high-performance organizations and build high-performance leaders by placing the values of harmony and tranquility higher on the scale of importance than straight talk and truthfulness.

This is an odd and twisted form of logic that might have worked well enough when our competitors were half asleep, the economy was booming and higher rates of inflation conveniently covered the cost of some of our business sins, but it is not good practice when the stakes are as high as they are now. This is when it really matters, when the going gets tough and the game gets ugly. Canadian hockey players in the mould of Maurice Richard, Ted Lindsay, Bobby Baun and Serge Savard have always know what this means—you need to play the game to win, not settle for second best.

In the interests of performance, efficiency and sustainable value creation, Canadian business leaders must improve their game. They have to become relentless, and even ruthless, in pursuit of the truth, and should not shy away from approaching it through the front door. We have to be more assertive. We cannot be afraid to go into the corner with our elbows up for fear we might get hurt or someone may take a retaliatory swing at us. Canada is a pragmatic country, and we know the shortest distance between any two points is a straight line. As a result, we have to stop avoiding the harsh truth and simply begin to call things the way they are. There is no time to waste by taking the long, winding road to the inevitable answer when a direct path would get us there sooner.

Given the brutal facts and flaws that have been exposed by the current economic situation and the opportunity it presents, there is simply no time to waste. There is no point dawdling in our search for the best, most well-considered and most impactful solutions we can find to help drive our economic performance for the future. We just need to jump over the boards and go get the puck. We somehow have to overcome our misguided belief that criticism, fierce debate and dissenting points of view are bad things. They are not. In fact, quite the opposite is true!

Constructive tension and fierce dialogue are essential ingredients of collaboration, and they are essential to the process of building a sustainable, high-performance organization or high-performance nation. Implicit in this belief and approach is an absolute intolerance for things that do not make sense, that do not work the way they should and that do not meet the highest standards of excellence or honesty.

In short, there has to be an abiding intolerance for things that are misaligned, misguided and untrue. We need a committed refusal to be held hostage to a passive-aggressive, conflict avoidance mentality if we hope to drive sustainable high performance. It is just not smart for us to continue to ignore the big things we know are wrong, or broken, or that simply no longer work the way they should. It is illogical to dismiss the little inconveniences and pains that can become huge problems and major headaches, and not take steps to address them. It does not make sense to avoid doing what is right just because it might hurt or be inconvenient. It is not in our best interests to choose second best when we can do better.

72

Reputation Management

Reputation matters—and it matters a lot! It can be measured in different ways, but at the end of the day, it is the net result of the choices we make and the things we choose to do, or not to do. Our portfolio of choices results in a certain value being placed on our brand, at the organizational level, as well as the personal and national levels. The value equates to our reputational capital as determined by others in the open market of comparative economics. Our reputational capital tells us how much goodwill there is for us to call upon when we need it. At the end of the day, it's an issue of credibility, both personal and organizational.

A damaged reputation, a dissonant brand or poor credibility have costs attached to them, some obvious and some hidden. On the other hand, a credible reputation and a resonant brand have numerous benefits that can be leveraged, as long as you choose to spend the goodwill wisely.

In the case of Canada, our business leaders have not taken full advantage of the brand called Canada and the goodwill attached to it—something that we have around the world and that makes us excellent business partners in every corner of the globe. We have not thought hard enough about the intangible value of our national brand and how we can use it to drive business opportunities, create employment and drive wealth creation at all levels of the economy.

The math is so obvious, and the economic benefits so worthwhile, you would think business leaders would pay more attention to the whole issue of reputation management and brand value. However, that does not seem to be the case. The evidence for this lies in the many incongruities observed in our business organizations and the failures of our leaders to act. These are most often, and most visibly, highlighted by the misalignments that are allowed to persist and the gaps they reveal in the foundation of far too many businesses.

The long list of common misalignments includes:

- **Misalignments of expectation.** Leaders often fail to set the bar of expectations high enough, or they allow expectations amongst their various executives and managers to be unclear, misunderstood or simply not woven together into a coherent whole.
- **Misalignments of capability.** This is often revealed when leaders commit to a certain course of action, but do not take steps to ensure sufficient talent or resources. To make matters worse, this can happen even when they know there is a misalignment and proceed anyway.
- **Misalignments of responsibility.** In many cases, this is as simple and as obvious as allowing part of the organization to march off in one direction with one set of objectives while another is pulling in the equal and opposite direction.
- **Misalignments of accountability.** Sadly, it is common to see a leader ignore that a certain part of the organization is not being held to the same high standards as others. This can either be due to favouritism, blindness or personal bias.
- **Misalignment of goals and objectives.** Quite often, the problem here is the result of multiple conflicting metrics that have not been fully thought through in terms of their impact, cost or consequence. It can be made much worse when the collective leadership team does not see the whole picture or understand the interdependencies.

Allowing these and other forms of avoidable misalignment to remain unaddressed is unacceptable, and is a form of reckless neglect by any leader. Unfortunately, reckless neglect is a much more common source of organizational dysfunction and underperformance than most people appreciate, or are willing to admit.

The reckless neglect of gaps and a tolerance for misalignments have probably contributed to more harm and unnecessary pain than most other forms of organizational dysfunction. It can be defined as a predisposition to disregard the telltale signs of misalignment. It is almost always rooted in conflict avoidance and the tendency to settle for half-baked compromises designed to buy temporary peace and avoid firm long-term action.

Like all passive-aggressive behaviour, it amounts to an intentional choice to avoid the obvious facts and continue on, with the cost to reputational capital largely denied, or totally ignored. It is the organizational equivalent of misreading the size of the iceberg that appears in front of you, and failing to appreciate that the majority of the risk lies below the surface of the water. Leaders have to be held accountable for dealing with the ugly reality. We know that when a brand loses its lustre and finally deteriorates, the signs and signals were there for others to see long before the demise. People move on to new and more beneficial places and away from bad brands when it suits them to do so, and they do not usually give advance notice. An organization therefore needs to listen to the soft footsteps that mark the early warning signs of a loss of reputation, credibility and brand value.

73

Misguided Focus and Human Nature

A common and often fatal flaw we can fall victim to is the tendency to focus on the immediate rather than the important. This is especially true when it comes to the really big things and the truly difficult problems in our lives or businesses. Unfortunately, the hidden costs and consequences of misalignment really are like the iceberg referred to above. They can be ignored or underestimated for a short period of time, but if they aren't dealt with, the risks will inevitably appear as if out of nowhere and overwhelm even the hardest working, most charismatic and most determined leader.

In organizational life, leaders of huge multinationals and leaders of small independent businesses have the same set of responsibilities to their customers, employees and community. A major responsibility is to face up to, and deal directly with, the misalignments and gaps that conspire against the ability of the organization to perform at the highest level.

Leaders must make it their absolute priority to constantly be on the lookout for the discordant signs and troubling signals that reveal things are not exactly as they should be. This requires a strong inner resolve, confidence and a balanced emotional temperament to run toward those situations with a solution in hand, not away from them in an effort to avoid conflict.

Some cynics may choose to see this as a glass-half-empty approach—a pessimistic or negative predisposition that is poisonous and demoralizing to employees. The truth is the opposite. Indeed, organizations would be well served to create cultures within which chronic discontent and perpetual dissatisfaction are seen as an important, mobilizing, performance-enabling competency, no matter how inconvenient the truth or how painful the evidence may be to acknowledge.

In modern organizations, the leader must play the active role of chief disorganizer or chief agitator, rather than the passive role of chief organizer. If the top leader is not modelling this type of behaviour, it will not be seen as an essential responsibility of the leaders and employees below. Leaders, at all levels, must be encouraged to seek the truth, identify the gaps, call out the misalignments and propel themselves forward with the help of a burning, urgent dissatisfaction with the status quo.

74

Truth, Lies and Mediocrity

We have all been caught, at one time or another, in the grip of our own self-righteous and self-serving behaviour. It's part of the human condition. We can forgive mild forms of occasional bravado and a temporarily exaggerated ego when the outcome or circumstance is not all that important and the behaviour is infrequent. Ego can even occasionally be a virtue if it allows us to gain the courage to break out of a rut or a bad situation. However, in the case of transformational leadership, recidivist behaviour of this type can be fatal and cannot be tolerated.

No organization, or leader, can allow exaggerated claims of comparative peer group excellence, superior operating performance or absolute product or service proficiency to remain unchallenged when there is available evidence to the contrary.

There is no amount of hyperbole or exaggeration that can forever conceal the cracks in an organization's foundation. It is essential that leaders at the top of an organization set a clear, steadfast and uncompromising tone by passionately embracing a fact-based approach in all parts of their business. It is disingenuous to demand high standards and levels of compliance when it comes to financial reporting, yet not demand the same degree of rigour for the various measures of organizational effectiveness. Examples of this lack of rigour include:

- employee engagement and satisfaction surveys that are overstated and manipulated to pump up egos and feed the need for self-congratulation
- customer satisfaction scores that are "gamed" by anxious front-line managers, coerced from customers and/or manipulated from above to hide the facts

- performance reviews that are simply not objective or accurate and are padded to avoid the type of crucial conversations the process is meant to facilitate
- top talent reviews and/or succession plans that are cloaked in mystery by senior executives who meet in private to talk about the flaws and imperfections of their subordinates, yet take no action to help their employees get on track, let alone honestly tell them where they stand

At the end of the day, we have to ask ourselves why we accept so much spin, deception and denial when it comes to measuring the so-called softer elements of organizational effectiveness when we would not accept it in any other part of the business. There is a very good reason why published statistics and line scores have always played such an important role in measuring excellence in sports. It's because they help us objectively distinguish between the good, the great and the underperforming, and they allow us to make better, more informed decisions.

Sure, we can all feel bad for the team that ends up losing the play-off series in overtime. We can all readily sympathize with the athlete crossing the finish line only a few seconds behind the winner. It is painful for all of us to see the fourth-place finisher be shut out of the medal count or the ballplayer whose slumping batting average is posted daily for the whole world to see. It can be uncomfortable to see some-one lose, but it is worse to avoid the truth or hide the facts.

75

Fresh Air and Brilliant Sunlight

Over and over again, organizations shy away from measuring themselves objectively. Too many fear the bright light of transparency and have convinced themselves that gentle kindness, half truths and a sheltering mentality are somehow better for morale and performance than the fresh air of truth. It is impossible to create truly high-performance organizations and leaders if we are afraid to "post the stats" and keep score. Creating and fuelling the organizational conditions where the hunger for excellence is sacrificed for harmony and mediocrity is no way to build greatness.

When an organization cheats in terms of objectively measuring competency, capability and performance, it will never excel. It will go through the motions, say the right things and then set the bar just high enough that most, or maybe all, will succeed in achieving the standard. In so doing, they effectively relegate themselves to continuing down a path of suboptimal performance.

In almost all endeavours, timing and good luck have something to do with success, at least some of the time. However, the very best leaders and organizations know when to rightfully claim true success and when to attribute the credit to the random forces of an invisible hand. They also know how important it is to be able to tell the difference between good fortune and good performance.

LESSONS FROM CANADIAN BUSINESS

Here are two examples of Canadian organizations that have been working hard to master the benefits of truly fact-based, candour-infused collaboration and that have been willing to grind it out in pursuit of achieving a sustainable, collaborative culture.

(continued)

Aimia Inc.

This Montreal-based company (formerly known as Groupe Aeroplan) is the holding company of the Aeroplan loyalty card business, having changed its name in 2011 to better reflect its growing international presence and diversified interests.

Rupert Duchesne is the Group Chief Executive of Aimia. Upon his arrival in Canada in 1996, Duchesne joined Air Canada, initially as Vice President of Marketing, then going on to become Senior Vice President International. Upon the acquisition of Canadian Airlines, he became the Chief Integration Officer. He was appointed President of Aeroplan in August of 2000 after it was spun off by the airline, and since then he has taken the company on a spirited expansion drive into new businesses and new geographic territories through a series of highly strategic international acquisitions.

The challenge for Duchesne has been taking the legacy Aeroplan business, limited in its scope and identified rather narrowly by its association with Air Canada (as a frequent flier card), and turning it into a broadly based global marketing and data intelligence business. He has done so by delinking it from its airline heritage and acquiring major non-airline loyalty businesses in the United Kingdom (Loyalty Management Group) and the United States (Carlson Marketing). He has also ambitiously entered new markets in partnership with local companies while expanding and reinvigorating the core franchise in Canada.

There are several keys to Duchesne's success at Aimia. The first is a collaborative mindset that permeates everything it does with its business partners and customers. Aimia understands that collaborative business partnerships strengthen overseas expansion. It has tweaked and adapted its model to suit the areas it wishes to grow in, such as India, Italy, the Middle East and Mexico. The second key to success has been the decentralized senior leadership team Duchesne has built, hiring outsiders who had no knowledge or experience in the loyalty business, but who had a proven pedigree in transformational leadership and human capital management. Duchesne is a big believer in the benefits of spirited dialogue and diversity of opinion, and in allowing his leaders to exchange their strong opinions, which he asks them to hold loosely. As an example of this, he asked a cross-functional team from around the world to develop a set of Core Values for the global business that would bind them together. When the Values were presented at a global management meeting, they were not only enthusiastically endorsed by executives from Dubai to Montreal but also became the guiding spirit for everyone to gauge their personal conduct. Today, those Values are so vital to the internal working of the organization they are listed on its corporate website for all to see.

Four Seasons Hotels and Resorts

The story of Four Seasons Hotels and Resorts is already well known to most Canadians, and it will be forever closely entwined with its founder Isadore Sharp. Sharp is responsible for creating an iconic chain of luxury hotel and resort properties, located in some of the most interesting and exotic places you can imagine. Visitors to Four Seasons properties around the world may not know the company has its roots and head office in Canada; however, Four Seasons represents Canada proudly around the world, and it is a shining example of how Canadian businesses can partner and collaborate with anyone, anywhere, at any time.

It would be impossible for the company to own or operate properties in 80 locations while at the same time building 50 new ones, if it did not have a culture that embraced collaborative partnerships. Four Seasons understands that brand leverage comes from using your strengths to full advantage and sharing them with others who have different strengths. It's the old math of one plus one equalling three.

The Four Seasons' empire is a diverse one, and it demonstrates the potential for other Canadian businesses that see global partnerships as a recipe for growth, diversification and ultimate

(continued)

231

success. In 2007, Four Seasons agreed to a $3.8 billion buyout by Microsoft Chairman Bill Gates and Prince Al-Waleed bin Talal of Saudi Arabia. The pair now own 95% of the company, in equal shares, while Sharp retains the rest, maintaining the Canadian connection. The key to their success is understanding, in a very deep way, how the essence of creating a memorable customer experience is invaluable whether it is in the cozy bar at their property in Prague or at the ski concierge at Whistler. Four Seasons understands that pampering guests is not only good for business and profits but it is also the key to creating the kind of word-of-mouth social media publicity that any amount of good traditional advertising cannot buy.

Shared Pain, Shared Gain

Canadians naturally embrace collaborative partnerships as part of every-day life in our communities, towns and businesses, where diversity is seen as a strength, not a threat. We don't offend, ignore or abuse others simply because they are different or foreign. We can use this tolerant, embracing national character to become a force for international business expansion in a way that benefits us and those we partner with.

Having said that, as Canadians we have to learn how to keep a sharp edge on our collaborative spirit and avoid watering down our choices to the point where they become so bland and inoffensive they have no teeth with which to grip the big issues. The more we are prepared to engage in fierce dialogue with each other across the various divides, rather than avoid them, the better off we will be individually and as a nation. Canadians have sometimes been just too polite and we have allowed what needs to be said to go unsaid so that we do not offend.

STRAIGHT TALK NEXT STEPS: CRITICAL COMPETENCY

Collaborative Intelligence (COQ)

Collaboration is about tapping into the diversity of thought and experience necessary to remain nimble and relevant in a changing world. When we begin to weave increasingly unconventional net-works of diverse people together, we will naturally generate some potential tension and awkward dialogue, but we need to see those as the necessary fuel for generating breakthrough solutions.

Collaboration occurs when you bring starkly different people and conflicting points of view together and throw them into the

(continued)

---

blender. The objective is to arrive at a superior, optimal, break-through decision, rather than a watered-down compromise or a decision based on a watered-down consensus of opinion.

Improving the organizational decision-making process, and the quality of the decisions and outcomes that come from it, does not have to be complicated. It simply requires a consistent methodology combined with a willingness to carefully dissect and then learn from experiences—both good and bad.

Collaborative intelligence (COQ) combines a series of abilities that come together to help achieve reliably superior decision outcomes.

These include the ability to:

- build a whole-brained team made up of diverse people who complement and bring out the best in each other
- create an environment where fierce debate and the merits of an idea are more important than the rank of the people who are advocating for one side or the other
- facilitate the highest possible intensity and richness of dialogue and dissent, without creating personal tensions, frictions and jealousies
- draw out passions and bold opinions from a wide variety of people and have them welcomed and understood, rather than denigrated or diminished
- insist on a high level of co-operation and assertiveness, at the same time and in equal proportion
- listen to others while seeking to understand and suspend judgment
- ask deep, penetrating questions without causing others to raise defensive shields

The pursuit of genuine collaboration has much more to do with a person's willingness to be humble than it does with the demonstration of superior intelligence. The landscape is littered with organizations and leaders who were once considered brilliant, but who fell from grace rather quickly and dramatically when their egos outgrew their competence. Those who excel at collaboration understand and accept that they do not have to be constantly proving they are the brightest person in the room in order to make a contribution. Instead, they enter the dialogue expecting that someone else will have a better idea than they do, and they place their ego at the door in the best interests of reaching a superior outcome.

Collaboration in organizations and teams can be a very difficult thing to achieve. Patrick Lencioni frames this challenge very well in his book *Overcoming the Five Dysfunctions of a Team*, in which he lists the common contributing factors as:

1. Absence of Trust
2. Fear of Conflict
3. Lack of Commitment
4. Avoidance of Accountability
5. Inattention to Results

Candour is a way to help create value, improve performance and build a culture of collaboration. Candour is one of the many mindsets and behaviours of true collaboration. It is not always a comfortable thing, and it can certainly be inconvenient at times, but it is never optional in a truly collaborative team or organization. In far too many cases, the true power and benefits of collaboration are lost because people fear candour. Until we see candour as an act of personal respect, and practise it in every part of our organization, we will be cheating ourselves and those we claim to serve.

Candour is not a part-time, occasional thing you turn on and off. It has to be an everyday discipline. It must be a natural, reflexive response to any circumstance. It represents a sacred covenant we make with ourselves that, in turn, becomes a core element of our brand—personal, organizational or national.

(continued)

In order to create true competitive advantage, we need to hold our organizations and ourselves to much higher standards and expectations when it comes to collaboration and candour. If we want to pursue the truth, identify the misalignments and close the gaps that create inefficiencies and stand between today's performance and tomorrow's potential, we need to insist on collaboration and total candour. To play the serious game of business, leaders need to face the facts, no matter how ugly.

This means embracing the relentless pursuit of misalignments that impede success and diminish performance. It takes courage, tenacity and a genuine belief that the effort required for the pursuit of optimal is better than the resigned acceptance of the perpetually bland.

Step 1: Modernize and Tighten the Metrics

There is no room in a high-performance organization for wonky numbers or bad data that do not help drive accurate insight and lead to modified behaviour and different choices. Sure, there can be pain in the truth of harsh numbers, but that pain pales in comparison to the cost of perpetuating false claims and masking hidden weaknesses.

The key to performance success rests in creating a new set of metrics that are forward facing and predictive. We don't need any more data that simply improves the view from our rear-view mirror. It's time to embrace help from the world of data mining in order to rebuild, refresh and rebalance our business score-cards. We need better data that is more useful, and we need it in real time. We need data that can be used in the moment to provide a fact-based backdrop for the mid-course corrections and adjustments that will be necessary.

In today's world, the tools exist to help ensure you are tracking the progress of projects, promises and people. Leaders simply need to modernize their dashboards and learn how to read the gauges.

Step 2: Anchor Accountability

The current fascination with matrix management has created accountability loopholes and excuses that are simply not tolerable in any high-performance organization. If you are convinced matrix management is the only way you can operate, then the least you can do is devise tighter means to enforce accountability. Consider conducting an accountability audit to identify where the breakdowns are occurring and why. Breakdowns in accountability should not go unaddressed. Reconsider how you deal with bad behaviour and bad performance, and be willing to hold people accountable so the organization will know you are serious.

Step 3: Harmonize and Calibrate Standards

In virtually every organization, when you ask any random group of employees or managers if there are silos or fiefdoms in their organization, the answer (if they are being candid) will be the same resounding—YES!

Silos are so prevalent in our organizations today that they could easily be considered an epidemic. The hidden cost of the dysfunction and underperformance that silos create is a crime against the business. Leaders need to take this plague seriously and launch an aggressive campaign to banish silos by identifying and demolishing them wherever they exist. Don't allow laziness, blindness and a tendency to avoid conflict to get in the way of high performance. If you want your organization to get fit, you are going to have to work at it. It will take time and your muscles will hurt, but don't wait for a better day to begin the process—begin right now.

At the end of the day, it means committing to total transparency and adopting an approach to leading that ensures there are no side deals or hidden agendas. The risks and cost of transparency are far less than those resulting from the continuation of protectionism and the fortification of the thick walls on departmental, functional or regional silos.

(continued)

Final Thoughts

Business is a noble pursuit, and it does not have to be the source of continuing suspicion, disillusionment and distrust. Society is right to hold business to account, and we have not always done a good job of ensuring this is done effectively. As a result, there are large pockets of the community who see all business leaders as coming from the same mould as the Wall Street robber barons of the 1920s and 1930s and the stock speculators portrayed in movies and on television.

Canada's moral compass has traditionally had a truer setting than others'. This is a brand advantage we can leverage on the global stage, but we, too, have to maintain our standards. The way to begin is by asking business leaders to raise the bar when it comes to candour, collaboration and accountability.

Canadian business leaders must renew their pledge to the organizations they serve and take responsibility for the things they can control within their enterprises. Inevitably, this will require leaders to declare outright war on the things that diminish credibility and allow gaps and misalignments to continue. It's all about setting high standards and not being afraid to hold everyone accountable.

PART IX

Unleashing Innovation and Driving Creativity

It is very likely a conservative bet to suggest that in over 75% of organizations, someone on the senior leadership team has pointed to the late Steve Jobs as the type of creative genius needed to shift their own business onto a new growth trajectory. Perhaps those same senior leaders have even read a book or two on Jobs and marvelled to themselves and their teams about his brilliance. In an age where innovation creates value at an ever-increasing rate while fixed assets and equipment continue to depreciate at high speed, they would be right to do so.

In Part IX, we dig into the topic of innovative intelligence and suggest that there is a way to create the conditions that will unleash the leaders who, like Jobs and others, can follow a new path to creativity. In today's world, so full of both risk and opportunity, the conditions are unbelievably fertile for those who understand and can unleash the secrets contained in the "black box" of creativity. For those who decode the mystery, the equation shifts dramatically in their favour, and while not every apple will shine quite as brightly as Mr. Jobs, the chances for serial success are better on an innovative path than they are on a stale traditional one.

77

Reimagination

The value of any organization is ultimately gauged by how well it performs in anticipating and addressing market needs, filling critical value gaps and providing customers with a great product, outstanding service and a memorable experience. This is more the case today than ever before, with an even bigger premium being placed on the anticipation factor. The unprecedented breadth and magnitude of the choices consumers have has changed the way in which organizations need to differentiate themselves. The sharply honed edge of competition in every sector and the advent of technological solutions in almost every aspect of our lives make market-driven, customer-focused creativity, originality and novelty the currency by which we will ever increasingly gauge the health and success of an organization and its people.

In order to meet the new and much higher demands of a more discerning global clientele, we need to embrace a very special group of people inside our organizations. We need truly talented people like never before to help us create the products, services and experiences customers crave and will pay for.

These are not the typical hard-working, loyal employees of the past who, in exchange for a promise of job security and lifetime employment, were content to follow orders, comply with standard operating procedures and not complain about the physical and mental drudgery of their job. Instead, the people we need now are wired just a little differently. These are people who, by conventional standards and past definitions, are more than a little unusual. In fact, in the minds of some, they may even be oddballs, lunatics and heretics because they challenge convention and think in novel ways.

In these more mentally and emotionally challenging times, we simply cannot afford to rely on the tried and true, the conventional and careful, the safe and secure. In this new, more demanding climate of global change, the valuable opportunities, and our long-term prosperity and good fortune, will simply not be realized through more streamlining, downsizing or structural re-engineering, or the pursuit of formulaic efficiency processes such as Six Sigma.

When Six Sigma was originally developed by Motorola in 1986, it was conceived as a way to drive manufacturing process improvement and efficiency. It might have worked well enough at the time, when manufacturing excellence was the key market differentiator, but it was certainly not nearly enough to help Motorola cope in the accelerated world of change they would come to face. Their more formidable, fleet-of-foot and innovative competitors, who perhaps could not out-manufacture them, were able to out-think them, and therein lies a valuable lesson for everyone else.

In spite of their popularity, the common tools, fads and efficiency-driving techniques of the recent past have proven themselves to be nothing more than crude, blunt instruments used by unsophisticated leaders. They are designed for temporary efficiency gains at best and not fundamental long-term transformation. They are no more than a collection of primitive, short-term survival techniques that temporarily mask the need for much deeper and more fundamental changes and give leaders the illusion that they are doing something important.

These well-branded formulas for driving efficiency, improving profits and maximizing cash flow do not open up new markets, stimulate growth or add value to the top line. Let's not forget, it is only through the external performance measures of top-line growth that we can measure consumer appetite and interest. The customer does not care about the internal programs, processes and measures we use to gauge our operating efficiency and improve our profitability.

Unfortunately for some, we have to make hard choices today that might very well diverge from those we have been making for quite a while. Vijay Govindarajan and Chris Trimble talk about this in their book *The Other Side of Innovation*. They remind us that "modern business organizations are not built for innovation; they are built for efficiency."

Given that the context around us has changed so significantly, so too must our responses. Since value is now created through innovation rather than efficiency, we must turn the page and put our priorities in a different order. Innovation first. Efficiency second. This is perhaps a radical thought, but one that we may be forced to make involuntarily, if we don't do it on our own.

The conditions that surround us today, and which will almost certainly continue well into the foreseeable future, demand something radically different from us. In response, we need to reframe the formula for success. We need to focus on altering the way we think about and view the situation, if we want better and different commercial outputs. Mind has replaced machine as the primary engine of economic success.

Such a change in approach and philosophy begins by first defining the attributes, skills and motivations of the people we choose to help us frame the context, solve the problems and seize the opportunities our organizations face. Call them whatever you want, change agents, catalysts, reformers, provocateurs or deviants, at the end of the day, final victory and ultimate success will be determined by those people who have a decidedly different mindset than we are used to. We need people around us who approach problems in a creatively different manner. While that may make us uncomfortable, it is better than making ourselves irrelevant.

78

Abandoning Certainty

As shocking as it might be to some of the left-brained, risk-averse, old-style leaders amongst us, it is quite possible there is no such thing as absolute certainty. As a result, the pursuit of certainty is an act of folly, not to mention a costly waste of time. No matter how much we might want it, and how much it would help ease our worries and make business life more comfortable, certainty just does not exist, and that is truer today than at any other time.

The search for bulletproof certainty is essentially a fool's game, and yet so much of what we do in business is aimed at mitigating risk by removing uncertainty. We can be tricked into going on the never-ending search for more and more data in order to justify taking modest, acceptable risks, rather than pursuing the brilliant risks that make the big differences. As uncertainty increases, we often allow the risk-return calculation to be dominated by the forces in favour of ensuring only guaranteed success, in many cases to the point where not enough risk is taken. In essence, we compromise and take half a loaf of economic benefit when we could have embraced greater risk and taken the whole thing.

Dr. Robert A. Burton has done some excellent work in an effort to explain the behaviour that drives economic and business decision making. He has examined the strange, unreasoned feelings of "just knowing" that we all have from time to time, and that cannot be explained rationally. This is the kind of intuitive reasoning that Burton explains in his book *On Being Certain.*

Burton has discovered through his research that the more certain we are that we are right, the less we are willing to consider the possibility that there may be other options available to us.

As a result, Burton suggests we can easily put ourselves at risk of adopting a fixed mindset that can easily seduce us, trap us, and take us down a path to disaster and irrelevance. Burton, like Dewitt Jones, knows there is always "more than one right answer," and we should force ourselves into the discipline of finding multiple right answers instead of locking ourselves into believing there is just one perfect solution.

79

Prisoners of Our Mindsets

Professor Carol S. Dweck, PhD, a leading authority in the field of motivation, personality and human development, has performed some groundbreaking research that can help us understand human behaviour in the organizational context. Professor Dweck makes the very compelling case that, more than anything else, our success in life and business has to do with our mindset. In other words, the outlook and the views we hold. She has suggested it's not our education, it's not our social status and it's not our skill sets and experiences that matter most. Dweck, and others, are convinced it's our mindset that ultimately makes the biggest and most important difference.

As we know, mindsets represent a powerful set of beliefs, and they can easily become lifelong traps that imprison us and choke our opportunities and potential, if we are not on guard. Despite how it might feel at times, they still represent a choice we are free to make:

- a choice to be outward facing and growth oriented, or inward facing, defensive and protective
- a choice to challenge the status quo, disrupt and innovate, or simply administer someone else's policies and ensure rigid compliance

Honestly ask yourself what you believe the most realistic and appropriate mindset and response should be to the situation we face. Ask yourself:

- Is it the open, growth-oriented "exploration" mindset enjoyed by people like Steve Jobs, or is it the closed, fixed, sheltered "exploitation" mindset shown by the so-called financial market experts who triggered the current economic crisis by creating financial instruments that took advantage of their complexity to exploit market growth?

- Is it a mindset that focuses on embracing the promise of tomorrow, despite all its risks and uncertainties, or is it a mindset of nostalgia for the past, when things were simpler, slower and less stressful?

We must all fight hard to ensure we do not become prisoners of our own mindsets and, as a result, end up as victims of our own self-induced misfortune.

80

Games We Play

In 1957, the term "cognitive dissonance" was coined by Professor Leon Festinger to explain the awkward mental state in which we think one thing, yet do another. In other words, the phenomenon of how we can unconsciously allow our blind spots to control our thinking.

Festinger observed, "The more committed we are to a belief, the harder it is to relinquish, even in the face of overwhelming contradictory advice." He argues the more we attempt to prove what we know, the less likely we are to examine alternatives that may be equally valid, or even superior. Taken to its logical conclusion, this means we need to begin embracing ambiguity in all of its glory as a necessary part of the innovation process.

We need to begin growing leaders who understand and live by what is known as the Zeigarnik Effect an approach to solving problems that was developed by the Russian-born psychologist Dr. Bluma Zeigarnik of the Berlin School of Experimental Psychology. She suggests people should be rewarded and recognized not for what they know to be true, but rather for how well they are able to suspend their premature judgments in search of what they do not know.

The idea she promotes, which has been embraced more recently by others including Roger Martin, provides us with valuable clues into how we can better structure organizations and leadership teams. In the process, we can improve our collective judgment and reduce the impact of the mental games we can play and which so often cause us to take a faulty premise to an inevitably bad decision.

Human Nature Revealed

The truth is, most of us don't have a very deep, complete or accurate understanding of how the human mind is shaped, nor how it actually works. As a result, we default to the comfort of commonly held assumptions about people, personality, talent and performance, whether true or not. Luckily, there are others who have made the scientific study of the human brain their life's work, people like Dr. Edward Hallowell. Similar to Dweck, Hallowell posits that what really matters is not what you have, but what you do with what you have.

The fundamental point Hallowell makes is that our makeup and our personality are defined by our intrinsic motivation, our drive and our passion. People like Dweck and Hallowell understand how the brain works. They understand how it can be mastered, and they understand how it influences our mindsets and beliefs and, therefore, ultimately drives our behaviour.

To paraphrase Einstein, Canadian business leaders cannot fall victim to the insanity of continuing to do the same thing over and over again and expecting different results. Amongst the many things we need from our business leaders of the future is a willingness to embrace new thinking. We need to build a bridge over the divide that separates business leaders from the many other well-respected leaders in other fields, such as behavioural economics and mind science.

Leading people means understanding people and human nature and, in that realm, we have a great deal to learn. We cannot allow our egos to get in the way of acknowledging the things we simply do not know or are having trouble understanding. This is a very good time to learn new and important things, and we need the help of progressive leaders in our organizations to accelerate the learning process.

Diversity, Imagination and Originality

While some Canadians still think of our country in terms of our dual French and English dichotomy or the rich heritage of our native people, Canada is really a country shaped by countless different cultures, each with their own set of beliefs, expectations, customs and peculiarities. In today's world, this rich and diverse cultural mix offers us a unique and advantageous lens through which to look at the world beyond our shores. If we are smart about it, this can become not only a powerful economic and social engine to drive change and prosperity, but it can be the very thing that will allow us to capture unique opportunities and create imaginative solutions for the future.

In recent years, we have seen a breathtaking acceleration in the pace at which innovative new applications, breakthrough products and game-changing solutions have been introduced by a wide range of players in every industry. New ideas have always presented themselves, and they have always been the fuel that energizes and drives an economy forward.

However, it is the rapid acceleration in the rate of acceptance of these new ideas that has become a true, modern phenomenon. The time between invention and commercialization has so significantly shortened that many organizations are at risk if they cannot find a way to move at pace. This reality, more than anything else, tells us the speed of the economic value cycle, from valley to apex and back down again, is faster than ever and, therefore, far more treacherous for those who are ill prepared.

You can only ride the fast-breaking wave of invention successfully if you can free yourself from the stifling constraints of the old paradigm of caution and convention. In this environment, the very concept of *kaizen*, or continuous improvement, is flawed. It is simply not fast enough, or bold enough, to maximize the return on potential that can come from breakthrough ideas that are commercialized at breakneck speeds.

Like many of the other business models we have held to be true, the concept of continuous improvement is now nothing more than a worn and outdated philosophy. Today, we live in times that look and feel much more like a rollercoaster than a Ferris wheel. To survive, we need to adjust, and sometimes that means thanking the tools that may have helped us in the past, but waving goodbye to them as we make room for new approaches more suited to the situation we face.

83

Creating Value by Creating Opportunity

In the world of modern business, the ability to create value for share-holders at a rate and level superior to the other guy is what ultimately allows you to stay in the competitive game, and that can only come from the ideas and creativity of people. Leaders should be paying far more attention to that very basic economic principle and to innovation in all parts of their businesses. Roger Martin and Tim Brown, as well as other thinkers, such as author and media theorist Steven Johnson and journalist, author and scientist Matt Ridley, appear to have it absolutely right when they talk about the ways in which we need to approach problems and think differently. All of them have suggested, in slightly different ways, that our success as leaders in the future will be determined by how we look at the future and whether we can genuinely open our minds to the opportunities rather than shelter behind convention and the status quo.

Whether it is the concept of design thinking or integrative thinking, we know innovation does not occur in the land of the safe and the familiar. Innovation occurs in the land of chaos, confusion and uncertainty. It occurs in what Heifetz, Grashow and Linsky aptly call the "zone of productive disequilibrium" in their book *The Practice of Adaptive Leadership*. It is where the heat of disagreement sparks the fires of imagination. It is the discomfort zone. It is the zone of discontent in which transformational leaders must keep their organization. It is an approach to leadership that requires a special set of interpersonal skills and masterful cognitive competency that can only come from a willingness to explore the unknown, rather than exploit the existing.

In this brave new world of ideas, imagination and invention, leaders need to be judged not just by the old economics of how much their people produce and at what cost, but rather by the new economics, which is how well they are able to get the best out of as many people's brains and creative wealth as possible. It is an issue of the leader's responsibility to release the complex ideas of people, not just evaluate the simple math of the profit and loss statement. It is time to measure success and performance not by the crude retrospective metrics of physical outputs, but rather by the more complex and sophisticated measures of future-focused intellectual inputs. It is believing you need the latter in order to get the former, and it is no more complicated to understand intellectually than getting your head around the implications of the old expression "garbage in, garbage out." Angela Duckworth, currently an Assistant Professor of Psychology at the University of Pennsylvania, is another great thinker in this realm.

Consistent with Dweck and Hallowell, Duckworth has shown how determination trumps IQ as a predictor of both performance and potential. She reminds us the brain is an exceptional creation with a dramatic plasticity and an ability to grow and change throughout our lives. It is like a muscle in that it gets stronger with use.

As a consequence, people who are learners, people who crave experiences, people with a growth mindset, have a much better ability to make the most of what they have compared to others who allow their brains to remain rigid, and even calcify. The reason learners are able to grow their brains is they are never satisfied with what they know but, instead, are driven by what they can learn. They have an innate curiosity that never dulls.

The fact of the matter is, what we are capable of learning is much greater than the volume of what we currently know. We need more people in our organizations and in Canadian society who can go with the flow, thrive on adventure, embrace novelty and live with ambiguity. These are the people who are able to make the most of what they have and are driven to do great things with it. We need to appreciate the fact that while we are in the process of trying to resolve a problem, dissent is a powerful lubricant and can expand the creative potential, if we embrace it rather than shy away from it. Leaders need to create an environment where good ideas from a wide variety of different sources can accidently bump into other good ideas and clash from time to time, even if we are too conservative to allow these wild ideas to have sex with one another, as British Lord, author and scientist Matt Ridley suggests!

84

Brain over Brawn

We know from the study of brain science that if we do not stretch and challenge the cerebral cortex, if we do not exercise our brain and make sensible use of the knowledge we gain, the brain actually gets slow or sluggish, if not stupid. A research organization called Lumosity has been a pioneer in this regard, and its human cognition project is a groundbreaking collaboration between researchers worldwide. Training exercises designed to stimulate the brain can be found online at www.lumosity.com. The most significant step the people at Lumosity have taken is making the science widely available by taking it out of the lab and putting it into the real world of practical application and access.

We have known for some time that cultures of fear, suppression, negativity and lack of originality produce low-performing and slow-witted brains. The brain essentially becomes disabled when we allow it to slow down. It begins to metaphorically shrink, and the neural pathways that carry information and make connections begin to harden. In the process, our creativity gets hijacked, and we find ourselves with no alternative other than to default to a fixed and seriously simplified mindset, where the ability to cope with change and complexity is dramatically impaired.

In the process, we essentially allow ourselves to become hostages to those leaders who promote the continuation of the status quo, as George A. Kohlrieser, a clinical and organizational psychologist, so convincingly points out in his book *Hostage at the Table*. Permitting a hostage mentality to take hold simply cannot be a smart choice to make in times like this. We don't need more hostages; we need more liberators with the courage to break free from the constraints of convention that will choke us if we allow them to.

LESSONS FROM CANADIAN BUSINESS

Below are two Canadian organizations that have had to face the reality of the new world. They have been working diligently to open up new ways of thinking and to devise new ways to remain relevant in a rapidly changing space.

Bombardier Inc.

Bombardier of Montreal, Quebec, is one of Canada's premier exporters and global superstars. Although many Canadians have probably either ridden on Bombardier's snowmobiles, high-speed trains, city trams or subways, or even flown in their regional jets, most people, even those in the business world, would be hard pressed to name anyone on Bombardier's leadership team, past or present.

A mechanic, Joseph-Armand Bombardier, who wanted to create a vehicle that could "float on snow," founded the company in 1946. This was a reasonable idea for someone who hailed from just outside Sherbrooke, Quebec, and wished to create a recreational activity for those snowy winter days we so like as Canadians. As a result, we have the Ski-Doo, or as it was supposed to be known before an accidental spelling mistake took over, the Ski-Dog.

In 1970, the increasingly successful and growing Bombardier wanted to diversify its interests. The cost of fuel began to rise because of the Arab oil embargo, and this coincided with an opportunity to acquire the Austrian company Lohner-Rotax, a manufacturer of trams. With this acquisition, Bombardier became involved in the rail business right at the strategic inflection point when urban "light-rail transit" became popular in many parts of the world.

Its transportation sector diversification effort continued in another new direction when, in 1986, it acquired Canadair from the Canadian government. A while afterward, it bought

(*continued*)

de Havilland Canada from Boeing and, later still, the Short Brothers and Learjet executive jet operations were added. The regional jet business revolutionized the market with smaller, more economically efficient aircraft. Today Bombardier is the third largest manufacturer of civil aircraft in the world, ranking behind only Boeing and Airbus.

Still not satisfied with the status quo, Bombardier acquired Adtranz (formerly DaimlerChrysler Rail Systems), a manufacturer of trains widely used throughout Germany and Great Britain. Today, they can claim to be one of the largest manufacturers of railway rolling stock in the world. Today, the company is the only one in the world to manufacture both planes and trains, albeit not yet automobiles.

The Chairman of the company is Laurent Beaudoin, and his son Pierre has been President and CEO since 2008. Pierre has been cited by McKinsey & Company as one of the best leaders in the world, and he willingly attributes the company's success and resilience to its culture. He led a complete transformation of the Bombardier culture over much of the past decade. This transformation changed Bombardier from an engineering- and manufacturing-driven company with deep cultural divisions to one focused on customers, a fully engaged workforce and innovation.

If you stand back and try to understand the secret of Bombardier's success, you have to acknowledge that its calculated risk appetite has allowed it to venture into new fields with confidence but not arrogance and then execute with an engineer's precision. The combination of right-brained entrepreneurial joie de vivre and left-brained appreciation of detail has created a cocktail of serial successes that can only be admired and would be a good model for others to take their cue from in meeting the rich opportunities the future holds for those who grasp it.

Gamma-Dynacare Medical Laboratories

Gamma-Dynacare, of Brampton, Ontario, is one of those "hidden champion" type companies Hermann Simon wrote about in his book *Hidden Champions: Lessons from 500 of the World's Best Unknown Companies* and who you would not necessarily know by name, although there is a very good chance you have been a client. If you have ever had your blood drawn in a medical testing centre, it may well have been a Gamma lab and, even though you might not have known the company, you will have had a genuine personal interest in the quality of the tests they conducted.

Naseem Somani is the CEO of Gamma Dynacare. An effervescent native of Tanzania who came to Canada and received her Bachelor of Commerce and Finance degree from the University of Toronto, Somani's laboratory industry career began in 1987 when she became a Controller with Park-Med Laboratories. Park-Med was acquired by Dynacare Medical Laboratories. Since then, she has steadily moved up the ranks, reaching her current position in 2005.

The Gamma transformation story is a good one because it speaks to the way in which organizations have to innovate, not just in the products and services they provide, but also in terms of their internal organizational architecture and culture. The platform for change at Gamma has been that provincial health care agencies are adjusting to the new economic reality, just like everyone else. As a result, they are cutting funding to private labs like those Gamma operates, and Somani and her team have to find new sources of revenue to close the gap. In the process they have shifted to commercial revenue opportunities and have added a logistics business to help improve their end-to-end value chain. At the same time, the demands from doctors on behalf of their patients are rising with respect to both turnaround time and the quality of the tests performed. As if that was not enough, as more advances are made in disease and health science, the tests used to detect and monitor patient health have become more complicated and diverse.

Somani has had to reshape and reorganize her company, turning it from an inwardly focused medical test factory to an

(continued)

outwardly focused, customer-centric value-added service provider. As a result, she has had to inject a dose of cultural transformation into the veins of the organization to ensure it can keep pace through innovation across the whole value chain. As part of the process, she has restructured her leadership team, pushed added responsibility and accountability down to other senior executives and began upgrading middle management with the introduction of a new Leadership Competency model and the introduction of 360-degree feedback. At the very core of Somani's leadership credo are a sharp sense of what is right and just and a passion for people. Her ability to listen, consult and then act is what has allowed her to take a sleepy organization that framed itself narrowly and force open the lens to permit the organization and its people to see the way in which they could become even more relevant despite deep changes to their traditional business model.

85

Rebels on Mahogany Row

Many have pursued the study of transformation and creativity in the business world, and at least two different sources have led us to the same new and important conclusion. The first is Tim Brown, the CEO of IDEO, who has promoted the concept of Design Thinking, and the second comes from a study by Volans Ventures (an international group dedicated to entrepreneurial solutions) flowing from work done by co-founders John Elkington and Pamela Hartigan, two thinkers in the field of entrepreneurship.

In both cases, the research speaks about the courage to rebel and how it sits at the very heart of the transformation process and the innovative, exploration, discovery mindset from which it is derived.

These thinkers, along with many others, provide us with the fact-based ammunition and emotional support necessary to unabashedly declare, *We need more rebels in business today.* If we are going to break free from our self-imposed serfdom to new ways of thinking, we first have to want to break free.

These thought leaders suggest the executive suite of yesterday, with its refined sense of order and stuffy formality, needs to be retrofitted and replaced with a new, modern style. Furthermore, they suggest we need rebels now because the world in which we live is demanding new breakthrough solutions. Quite frankly, those solutions are not likely to come from the normal people, but rather the "crazy people," as David Kelley, the founder of IDEO, has called them.

This is not exactly a new thought. George Bernard Shaw (1856–1950) is perhaps better known as an Irish playwright, but he was also a co-founder of the London School of Economics. In this respect, he wrote, "The reasonable man adapts himself to the world whereas the unreasonable one persists in trying to adapt the world to himself.

Therefore, all progress depends on the unreasonable man." Once again, we find ourselves coming back to the power of mindsets.

Finally, it is helpful to quote Elkington and Hartigan, who have written, "Being unreasonable is not just a state of mind. It is also a process by which older, outdated forms of reasoning are jettisoned and new ones conceived and evolved." This is exactly what we need more of today, in every business, no matter how scary that prospect might seem to conservative and cautious Canadians. Today, we need unreasonable people with the power of their convictions and the courage to help all of us get onto a new trajectory to the future before we get sucked back to the past.

86

Expanding the Experience Repertoire

Canada finds itself caught in the throes of a serious dilemma about how best to address our future that will require us to abandon the model that has taken us this far and to adopt a new model better suited for the times. Admittedly it is a gamble, with risks attached to it, but the alternative is equally, if not more, unattractive. It too carries risk. The rigid fence that surrounds our mental model, and the invisible traps we have set for ourselves by the way we currently think and look at the world, have now become potentially debilitating constraints. As a result, they limit our ability to imagine new, better and more sustainable solutions. We need to find a way to encourage the rebels who display the characteristics and passion that can unleash the value locked in the unconventional thinking of unreasonable people.

In a world where mindsets matter, and where our own view of the world determines our relevance and, hence, our success, we need to examine just how mindsets are shaped. As the environment has changed around us, so too has the type of mindset we need from the leaders who will help guide us.

There is a considerable body of evidence to suggest that one's view of the world, and tolerance for the new and different, is directly related to the breadth, depth and diversity of our personal life experiences. The more varied your experience repertoire, the easier it is to make new connections. This is what allows the brain to form the unique new neural pathways that, in turn, allow us to connect the dots in new combinations for new solutions.

It is important to note that the definition of experience we are using here is radically different than the one used by most business leaders in the past. It is not about the number of years of professional experience in a narrowly defined role or within a certain professional skill set. Instead, it is the rich variety and diversity of multiple different personal experiences that act as stimuli for the brain. It is the varied tapestry of personal experiences that helps ensure we do not become locked into narrow channels of thinking, but instead leap across domains to collect, share and assemble new patterns of insight.

This puts the accent on improving the rate at which we accumulate new experiences, create new knowledge and combine it with an improved ability to retrieve the new information we need on a real-time basis. In this world, our processing power (i.e., the ability to access and interpret information) is more important than our storage capacity, or the depth of our accumulated knowledge bank. This concept was first outlined in the book *Flow* by Mihaly Csikszentmihalyi, a refugee from Communist Hungary who went on to be head of the Psychology Department at the University of Chicago.

In fact, Csikszentmihalyi and others argue that our stored knowledge is a potentially dangerous source of false confidence, not to mention a rapidly depreciating asset, given that the half-life of anything new is shortening every day. To differentiate yourself as a leader, work on your timely retrieval ability, rather than on your storage capacity. The more novel and different things you experience or have an interest in, the more likely your brain will be able to fill in the missing pieces and make the new connections that allow us to make sense out of apparent nonsense.

Mindset for the Future

Several experts, including Howard Gardner and Daniel Pink, have suggested there are probably five to eight key mindsets required for someone to thrive as a business leader today. Regardless of the final destination we choose for our organizations, or ourselves, we know the starting point is the same. It begins with developing a rich experience repertoire from which our attitudes and competencies can then flow. It is the complex combination of insight, intellect and practicality that together allow great leaders to not only have a superior radar system with which to detect signals, but also the ability to make rapid-fire connections. It is based on their confidence, amplified by their adaptability and fuelled by their intellectual curiosity.

Intuitive Genius Unleashed

Innovation is not developed by digging for the provable facts and empirical evidence hidden deep in the well of our retrospective data banks. It is not the deep analytical source of insight that will somehow help us make sense of the future. It is quite the opposite. Our ability to understand the future will come from the more intuitive, fluid, experimental process of looking forward, visualizing and anticipating the many changes that are just out of sight, around the corner and over the horizon.

It is the type of innovative mindset we see in people like Richard Branson and the late Steve Jobs, to whom being a prisoner of the status quo is simply not an option. In its place, we find a certain bold imagination that fuels their creative genius and combines it with a distinctive flair and a rebellious, revolutionary zeal to make something different, and to do so on their own terms. These are the types of leaders who reorder and reshape the pieces of the puzzle to arrive at solutions the rest of us hold in awe and envy. These are the leaders who violently shake the Etch A Sketch® to clear the old image and then proceed to draw a new one.

The raw material for creative insight of this type comes not from years of deepening the level of existing knowledge, but from the ability to access and connect information across a broad and diverse platform of experiences and networks. The more new and different experiences you have, the better you will be able to make sense of the future.

Tim Brown and his colleagues at IDEO have shown us the creative process begins with inspiration and imagination. They have shown us how only these can lead to the next steps of ideation and intuition, which, in turn, fuel our idea bank and lead to the originality from which new value is created.

Successful business leaders know it is not about carving up the pie or even growing the pie, it is about creating a brand new type of pie. This type of originality and opportunity only comes from combining previously unrelated pieces of insight into new combinations, which allows for the creation of products, services and even processes that essentially create value out of thin air.

Doing this effectively and with a track record of serial success requires us to look at the essential elements of the creative mindset. They can best be explained in the words of Roger Martin from his book *The Opposable Mind* as the ability to:

- withhold judgment and avoid rushing to conclusions
- hold multiple hypotheses in your mind at the same time while avoiding the temptation to jump on one conclusion over the others until all but one have been exhausted as viable alternatives

In a type-A, results-driven world, where we are easily addicted and attracted to sweat and place the doers amongst us on a pedestal, this is a very, very uncomfortable concept. However, we need to understand the more sensitive, highly attuned right-brain thinkers are the ones who create the value platforms that the others then exploit.

Competing for Relevance

In order for Canada to become more relevant in the rapidly changing and reordered world, we need to pay more attention to the mindsets we have allowed ourselves to develop as Canadians and those we foster in our business leaders at all levels. The Canadian inferiority complex and the comfortable stereotypes we have allowed to form around us need to change if we are to assert ourselves on the stage of world commerce.

While there are undoubtedly many different ways to look at this, perhaps the simplest way is, as Carol Dweck suggests in her book *Mindset*, to think about people in terms of whether they are learners or non-learners. Clearly, people with a learning mindset are going to be more comfortable with experimentation and ambiguity than non-learners. They will not only seek out challenges, but they will thrive on them.

These are the people we need as the captains and crew on the good ship of Canadian business. There are certainly more than enough challenges for us to chew on, so perhaps we should begin by doing a much better job of identifying, liberating and deploying these special people, wired with an innate learning instinct and natural curiosity.

As Peter Senge, the author of *The Fifth Discipline: The Art and Practice of the Learning Organization*, has shown, people with a learning mindset embrace an essential belief in the benefits and inevitability of change and the joy of adventure it brings.

Senge's work reminds us a learning mindset frames the way we look at the world, identify problems, interpret situations and arrive at solutions. In a world of constant change, it is much healthier to be modest and confess that there is more we do not know than we do know. Only the pursuit of new knowledge will allow us to mitigate the risks inherent in our blind spots and ignorance.

Overcoming Our National Hangover

In the case of Canada and Canadian business leaders, we have some serious sobering up to do. We have allowed ourselves to ride along all too comfortably in the wake of the American powerboat, playing the pleasant and obedient sidekick to their more forceful and domineering commercial personality. We have passively allowed our American cousins to determine the rules of the business game and to decide what general direction we should all be going in when it comes to our business methods and leadership practices.

This is not about blatant anti-Americanism or the narrow protectionism once preached by nationalists such as Mel Hurtig in *The Betrayal of Canada* and Maude Barlow in *Take Back the Nation*. In fact, while it may be based on the same underlying diagnosis of Canada's ills, it is the opposite prescription for our success. The answer is not to build walls around our own economy; it is to aggressively attack the global market with our own goods, services and intellectual property in an effort to expand our reach and leverage our brand. It is about playing to win in the offensive end of the ice, not staying back in the defensive zone and letting others do the hard work. It is pretty hard to score from our own blue line. We have to crash the net, and not be afraid to take risks in the process.

It is time for Canada, and Canadian business leaders, to graduate to the big leagues, and this will only be possible if our young entrepreneurs and explorers are encouraged and allowed to lead the way. The current generation of leaders is going to have to clear the path and open the gates of opportunity. We need to ensure that the transfer of responsibility from one generation to another is assumed by those who are currently in charge. It should become a stewardship obligation for organizations to publicly report how they intend to achieve this goal. As a society, we cannot be afraid to raise the bar on corporate social responsibility. Rather than limiting it to environmental sensitivity, we should expand its current definition to include such things as talent development.

STRAIGHT TALK NEXT STEPS: CRITICAL COMPETENCY

Innovative Intelligence (INQ)

Innovative intelligence is the mindset and outlook possessed by those who make great changes to our world through their will, determination, conviction, passion and capacity to persevere and take risks.

In so doing, they often have to face ridicule and overcome the imposing obstacles to social acceptance. Canada needs more of these people in order to become the world leader in creating an environment in which they can thrive and multiply. We need to cast off our traditional cloak as a domestically oriented, production-based, natural resources and service economy, and instead become the Mecca for creativity. We need to do this urgently and as a matter of national economic policy.

The mindset we need is very much like the one employed for thousands of years by the court jester, the individual who was given immunity by the King to poke fun at the status quo and who, much to the delight of the court, revealed the truths that others dared not speak. In business terms, this is about liberating the heretics and deviants who suggest something new or different is needed because they see the limits of a current approach or an existing product, process or service. We need Canada to be the place that allows these forces to be unleashed, to be the country that has the courage to distinguish itself on the world stage by our willingness to carve a new and bold path.

It is time to abandon what does not work and stoke up the courage to step outside of the mental models and mindsets that trap us. To carve a new path, Canadian business needs to focus on transformation and define new spaces and move to occupy them quickly.

The world evolving around us is an exciting and challenging one. It is a world in which the array of possibilities is endless and the need for novelty, imagination and originality has never been higher. The world of business has an important role to play in shaping our destiny at home and abroad.

Step 1: Identify the Deviants

The current, and future, competitive climate requires new ideas, and those ideas are likely to come from people who view the world just a little differently. Organizations will need to do a much better job of identifying these people and bringing them into the circle of influence. Wise leaders will not only find them, but will listen to them, give them a voice and, therefore, an opportunity to help shape the future.

Leaders need to think seriously about how to reshape their talent evaluation process. The individuals we need thrive on freedom of expression and passion, so we will have to let them loose. We need to find a way to tap into their core purpose and allow them to identify new areas of opportunity for their organizations. Leaders should consider creating a "Tomorrow Forum," a group of top thinkers in the organization who have a mandate to think about tomorrow and to cast their minds into identifying the emerging trends of the future.

Step 2: Provide Broad Scope

As we know from the work of behavioural economists such as Daniel Kahneman and Amos Taversky, the key to effective problem solving and decision making is in properly framing the challenge. Accordingly, we need to be open to a healthy divergent phase of investigation, and we must learn how to examine multiple scenarios in tandem. Rushing to a premature conclusion within a narrow frame is exactly the wrong formula.

(continued)

Step 3: Weave the Narrative

Humans relate best to stories and pictures, and we like metaphors as a means to understand our own challenges and dilemmas—it's a natural part of our cognitive processing ability. In an era of blogs, Facebook and other social media, there are many ways to create virtual storytelling communities that will get people involved and engaged in the crucial conversations about tomorrow. Leaders need to craft the story, share it in ways people can understand and then relate to on an emotional level to help them internalize.

The people we need to help carve the path to the future will very likely be people who stand out from the crowd and make others uncomfortable. We will need to ensure those who understand the value and purpose of creating a new mindset are not discounted or marginalized. We cannot allow the good efforts of a few new, radical thinkers to be drowned out by the practitioners of the status quo. The story has to rise above the noise and capture the audience who is desperate to receive it.

Final Thoughts

As children, we knew the simple joy of discovery and relished the ability to play and have fun in an unstructured environment. Slowly, over time, those innate abilities were suppressed and we were reprogrammed to "stay between the lines" and "paint by numbers." It's time to go back to our natural instincts. We have not lost the ability to do things in an unstructured and even rebellious manner; we have simply allowed it to be stifled by convention. It's time to liberate ourselves and go back to improvisation and imagination.

PART X

The Art and Science of Effective Decision Making

The true value of any enterprise can best be measured as the sum total of all of the decisions made by all of the people in the organization over time. The formula, when you think about it, is actually quite elegant in its simplicity. We need to understand that any organization is only as good as its ability to repeatedly make great decisions and to have those decisions executed as they were originally intended. Yet, look deep into the mind of an organization, and you will very likely detect more than one flaw in the organizational decision-making process and in the many individual moving parts that make up decision-making excellence.

In Part X, we reveal the mechanics of this key leadership competency and suggest ways in which leaders can learn from the science of behavioural economics and the light it sheds on the biases, illusions and misunderstandings found at the root of decision-making under-performance.

91

Decision Risk

Over the past number of years, the emerging field of behavioural economics has helped us gain a much better appreciation of the complex stages and integrated components of organizational decision making. As a result, we have come to better understand the entire end-to-end process that ultimately determines the nature and the quality of the decisions we make as individuals, teams and organizations.

The two basic questions that leaders should ask are:

- Does your organization make reliably good decisions quickly, or repeatedly poor decisions slowly?
- Does your organization follow a disciplined process to help frame problems and foster collaboration, or does it apply an ad hoc approach?

We are now coming to understand how all decisions, both big and small, are made with a certain combination of rational thought and emotion. This is especially true with respect to those decisions we make in business, where the dynamics are more complicated, the process involves many other people and, so often, the decisions are risk related.

Author Stephen Greenspan's book *Annals of Gullibility* reminds us "There are any number of examples of intelligent people making poor decisions with horrific consequences, as the result of cognitive mistakes." We have come to understand how our cognitive blind spots are a serious problem, made worse by the fact that, according to the Center for Decision Research at the University of Chicago, typical business decision makers allocate only 25% of their time to thinking about problems properly and learning from experience. Even more disconcerting, the experts tell us the least capable people often suffer from the biggest blind spots and the most significant gaps between what they think they are capable of doing and what they are actually able to achieve.

Everything we think is, in some way, based on an underlying premise, which we may or may not fully understand, or even recognize. In turn, the premise, whether right or wrong, whether fully realized or partially formed, shapes the assumptions we then make and the rationale we apply. Those assumptions then combine together to form the basis for our argument, and they lead directly to the conclusions we draw and, ultimately, to the actions we choose to take or not take. It's a complicated and hazardous process, full of potential for error, confusion and abuse.

Let's simply say the premise, and its associated assumptions, are the raw materials or foundation upon which decisions are built. Get the premise wrong and it is highly likely the assumptions will be faulty as well. Get the assumptions wrong, even if the premise is correct, and we will follow the incorrect path to the wrong conclusion. Unfortunately, we very rarely devote the necessary time, effort and discipline to ensuring the premise is 100% right before we search for answers, nor do we appropriately pressure test our assumptions to ensure their efficacy.

Instead, especially in teams, we get so caught up in circular discussions and mental jousting matches around the executive table that we disproportionately focus on the fringe issues and emotional trigger points, rather than the substance. We have ample evidence to suggest senior executives do not pay enough attention to the decision-making process within their organizations, yet they still wonder why so many of the decisions made by others within the enterprise are either misguided, go wrong or are simply ignored.

Often, the very same leaders who will spend millions of dollars to improve the efficiency of an outdated IT process, upgrade an inefficient manufacturing process or invest in an expensive new customer relationship management process have never thought about how to invest in improving the organizational decision-making process. It is almost as if they assume it is working to the best of its ability.

Many leaders have never considered spending any money on improving perhaps *the* most important part of their organizations' performance effectiveness plumbing, the decision-making process. They have not made it a priority to enhance its speed, accuracy and effectiveness, and yet they are depending upon the quality of decisions to drive the organization forward. This is both a curious flaw in executive logic and a very concerning omission.

92

The Fog of Business

Every day, Canadians make any number of decisions. They make decisions in all aspects of their lives, at home, in the workplace and at the hockey rink. Every time volunteer coaches at the local rink choose their lineups for the Saturday morning game, they are making a decision. Every time they put the teams together at the beginning of the season, they are making a decision. Every time an NHL General Manager makes a trade, he is making a decision. Every time Hockey Canada chooses a team of elite athletes to represent us internationally, it is making a decision.

The difference is, the decisions made by most people in the realm of their everyday lives have typically been much better than those we observe day to day in many of our business organizations. There are two reasons for this.

- Our national hockey IQ is much higher than our national business IQ.
- Results in hockey are much clearer, easier and more immediately visible.

In business, the lag effect blurs our sensibilities. In hockey, the performance results are more transparent and the accountability higher, because we track the wins and losses and they are posted for all to see. There is no place to hide, and no excuse that passes muster.

In big business, it's quite different. The end result of a decision made by a board of directors, a CEO, a mid-level executive or a cross-functional project team is much harder to see, let alone assess objectively in real time. The fog that surrounds organizational decision making is very convenient for anyone who wants to hide from their role in a bad decision. Even when quarterly results are disappointing because of a single bad decision or a series of bad decisions, the direct line of accountability is blurred by matrix reporting lines and committee decisions that serve to dilute the most sacrosanct of leadership responsibilities: accountability!

Small business, on the other hand, is much more like hockey. A small business owner can make a decision today on, say, inventory or price, and you can see the result almost immediately. He or she can then mid-course correct, without the need to worry about how that change in decision may be perceived from above. The difference is called ownership, and it makes all the difference.

Canada is fundamentally a nation of small and medium-sized businesses. While it may be easy to forget that fact when you are sitting behind your big desk in Montreal, Toronto, Calgary or Vancouver, the fact of the matter is 80% of Canadian businesses have fewer than 20 employees.

The leaders of these businesses do not have the deep wallets or bureaucracies of their much larger corporate cousins, but they do have the same responsibilities to their customers and employees. The difference is, as owners, they hold themselves more accountable, and the decisions they make cannot be hidden beneath the dark veil of corporate mystery and spin.

93

Learning from Failure

Given the high stakes, the countless number of unknowns and the vast levels of ambiguity we see in the marketplace, there is an urgent need to refine organizational decision making. The margin for error has shrunk considerably and the turbulence is much greater, which means we need to rethink the way in which we make decisions, especially those we make under pressure.

It's time to lift our game and make sure we understand, address and then perfect the decision-making process rather than allow it to continue to be one of the dirtiest little secrets of organizational ineffectiveness. Leaders have been afraid, for far too long, to face up to the fact their decision-making processes are likely failing to deliver the intended results.

There is a popular phrase we have all used, and which many CEOs from coast to coast use in an effort to encourage their employees to take risks. It is the one about how we all *learn more from our failures than our successes.* The trouble is, most front-line employees and mid-level managers do not believe their organization is really that sophisticated, tolerant or enlightened. As a result, over and over again, employees, managers and executives decide not to decide, or they make a safe decision, and they often only do so after receiving approval from someone higher up the food chain to eliminate their own accountability.

On the other hand, too many senior executives mouth the right words, but really don't believe in the positive benefits of learning from mistakes. If they did, you would have to wonder why they have not done a much better job of formalizing the means through which organizations conduct post-mortems so they can learn from mistakes and improve the decision-making process. In short, we need to revamp the very definition of organizational decision-making. It must be expanded to include not just an evaluation of the end result of the decision itself but must also include a formal mechanism to ensure we capture the learning from our mistakes and misjudgments. In short, we need to focus on both the result and the means and constantly be on the lookout for ways to improve our decision-making acumen so it strengthens over time.

We need to tighten the post-mortem loop so our understanding of the decision-making process gets refined and becomes better as we learn. The words we speak about the mistakes we all make are nice, and the sentiment is noble and reassuring, however, the stark reality for the vast majority of employees is quite different, and they are not about to naively tempt fate.

94

Upside of the Downside

Author Seth Godin has written extensively about the issue of failure in business. His premise is that in order to get better, we need to redefine what it means to fail. We need to broaden the definition of failure to capture the cost of the disappointment, disillusionment and despair created within organizations by the poor decisions and/or non-decisions our leaders make.

In other words, Godin is asking us to acknowledge there are unintended negative consequences that go beyond the ones we see on the surface of the decision itself. It is time to be accountable to the majority of employees, most of whom are not even remotely involved in the decision-making process but who are often the silent victims of the collateral damage when a leadership decision goes wrong.

Think about it for a minute, and then ask yourself if you know:

- any line worker whose plant was closed because a senior leadership team misread the market and found themselves without a healthy order book
- any mid-level manager who was downsized because the board of directors approved an ill-considered acquisition based on faulty assumptions, which went wrong and headcount costs had to be cut as a result
- any loyal 55-year-old employee with 20-plus years of experience who was put out to pasture because the CEO, and his or her team, did not make a decision yesterday to improve how the organization makes decisions today

The point about how the value of any organization can be calculated as the sum total of all the decisions made over time has already been made. As a result, it is just common sense to focus on ways to improve the decision-making process—to assign clearer decision rights or accountabilities, to manage the decision-making process from front to back and to implement robust and objective post-mortems on decisions in order to get smarter for the future.

At the same time, we also need to discover and implement better ways to avoid unnecessary failures. We need to examine failure not just through the lens of failed outcomes, or the immediate financial loss, but also in terms of failure to seize an opportunity because of the decisions we did not make, failure of trust, failure of will and failure to prioritize.

The unquantifiable lost opportunity and human costs never get the time they deserve in the decision-evaluation process. The improvements we make, the breakthroughs we have, the innovations we implement and the outcomes we achieve are all, ultimately, based on the quantity and quality of the decisions made, both large and small. There is considerable room for improvement, and a significant economic upside, if we put some energy into improving what we know is broken.

There has been an abundance of business literature on the importance of execution, which is certainly something no leader can afford to deny, diminish or ignore. On the other hand, there can be no more important attribute for defining individual or collective success than the ability of a leader to make great decisions. Unfortunately, we have not given decision-making effectiveness the same prominence in our business thinking and our organizational priority setting.

Understanding Human Frailty

While properly executing any decision is critically important, since it is ultimately where the rubber meets the road, the process used to make the decision in the first place is arguably just as important. It turns out that, amongst the many factors that go into decision making, there are two mysterious but incredibly powerful functions within the brain that are specifically designed to help us deal with complexity, ambiguity and uncertainty.

These two mental processes help us make decisions when we don't know what to decide, and they can either help or hinder.

- **Pattern recognition** is our ability to "fill in the blanks" or find the "missing pieces." This happens subconsciously because our mind knows we have seen a certain type of pattern in the past and can, therefore, recognize it again. This ability is enhanced and improved through experience: the broader the experience repertoire, the better the pattern-recognition skill is developed and encoded in the brain. The problem is, if our experience repertoire is narrow, we are more likely to be negatively influenced by misleading judgments made from within a shrunken universe of options and alternatives.
- **Emotional tagging** is our ability to arrive at a decision or make a choice that, despite all the empirical or analytical data we might have assembled, depends on a spark of human emotion in order to be activated. The problem is, our emotional tag repertoire can be influenced by inappropriate attachments and inappropriate self-interests. These are the illogical, emotionally biased beliefs we bring into the decision-making environment, and which can silently pollute our good judgment.

The Bias Trap

There is nothing more crippling to the ultimate effectiveness of the decision-making process than the slippery little mental devil called bias. Even with the best brains and the richest, most varied experience repertoire, there is still a huge risk of being sideswiped or derailed by the biases we don't even know we have. It is always fascinating to see how those who live within an organization, or are products of a certain culture and way of thinking, are simply unable to see what can be so clear and obvious to an objective outsider.

There has been a wealth of study into the many types of bias that typically infect the organizational decision-making process and lead to errors in judgment. Much of that study has been conducted by people at Overcoming Bias, whose wisdom is shared widely through its blog www.overcomingbias.com. Their thinking, and the thinking of academics such as Dr. Sondra Thiederman and Dr. Adam Goldyne, is important and can be codified and applied in any organizational setting, provided the will to do so exists.

The long and detailed list of biases fall into four broad categories:

- **Misleading experiences**—experiences from our past that are incorrect, but we either do not or are unwilling to acknowledge them as flawed.
- **Misleading prejudgments**—seriously flawed or irrelevant judgments that frame our mental mindsets and filter our thoughts.
- **Inappropriate self-interests**—hidden or overt personal interest or stake in the decision, which can cause us to draw conclusions that are too narrowly defined.
- **Inappropriate attachments**—personal beliefs that anchor our thinking in faulty ways, but which we are unable or unwilling to alter or abandon.

While it might appear to be mysterious, bias is actually a controllable force within our organizational and personal lives. However, it is the single most powerful negative factor that impairs our judgment and limits our success.

Even if it is a reality of the human condition, the fact remains, as an advanced species, we are able to mitigate the worst effects of bias if we have the willpower to do so. The knowledge and know-how exists and there are processes we can certainly put in place to limit our exposure and risk, but the question is whether we are wise enough to do so. Leaders can surround themselves with thinkers to help them view the world in different ways and who, in the process, come to the leadership table with different perspectives, thus ensuring that biases are highlighted and recognized.

Covering Our Asses

If bias is the "up front" risk in the organizational decision-making process, serving as it does to shape and distort our judgment, we also need to understand the "back end" risks associated with a range of inappropriate responses that equally jeopardize our success.

This list can also be bucketed into four broad categories:

- **Denial**—with all of the characteristics typically associated with a refusal to accept responsibility and accountability.
- **Overcompensation**—comes in the form of extreme reactions that are inappropriate and out of proportion to the actual situation.
- **Ignorance**—which includes a total lack of awareness of the negative consequences of our decisions.
- **Blame**—a very popular response that attempts to blatantly assign responsibility away from the person who should, in fact, be held accountable.

Leaders have a collective responsibility that transcends any personal agendas. As a result, they cannot allow the leaders below them to rationalize decisions or actions and hide behind any one of the inappropriate responses listed above. The leader has to constantly be on patrol for the truth and be able and willing to ask the penetrating questions that allow the team to identify flawed logic. This personality trait, which is part curiosity and part cynicism, is a necessary part of the mind of the leader. Leaders cannot be lured into complacency when it comes to their role as the stewards of common sense, good judgment and brutal honesty.

Broadening Our Portfolio of Choices

A rich and wonderful body of knowledge has revealed itself over the recent past and has added significantly to our understanding of how to make better decisions in order to innovate and drive performance. The underlying assertion put forward, in a number of different ways by a number of different experts, is actually quite profound in a common sense sort of way. It has to do with asking leaders to start making different choices on a wide variety of things, and to ensure this starts at the top.

The leaders and designers of the new organizational structures, cultures and solutions that we need must begin by making new and different choices about how they fulfill their obligations. The evidence suggests we have been limiting ourselves to too small a tapestry of choices for far too long. If we wanted to be charitable, the best we could say is that the choices we have made to date have been nothing more than simple reflexive coping mechanisms in response to rising uncertainty. In other words, all we have done is narrow our options so we would not become totally overwhelmed with the breadth of choices in front of us. It's time to stop that self-defeating practice and to begin acting more confidently.

Better decisions come from better thinking, and we have not appropriately adjusted our thinking to the changing context. If we want better choices and want to create new and different possibilities, then we will have to address some harsh facts. We need to begin with acknowledging that the traditional, linear, analytically cumbersome thinking approaches of the past are just not suited to the complex, ad hoc, fast-moving world in which we now live.

In fact, the old approach is dangerous and will only lead to an increase in the number of flawed or suboptimal decisions made in the future. As the saying goes, if every problem you see looks like a nail, then every solution needs a hammer. We need to adjust to the new reality and become more sophisticated in the way we define problems and solutions.

LESSONS FROM CANADIAN BUSINESS

Recently, several Canadian organizations have made some pretty big strategic decisions. Companies we should follow carefully to see how their decision making turns out include BlackBerry Kinross Gold Corporation, and Maple Leafs Sports and Entertainment, owners of the Toronto Maple Leafs and Toronto Raptors sports franchises.

BlackBerry

The Waterloo, Ontario–based manufacturer of the BlackBerry not only put Canada on the wireless technology map, but also literally into the hands of millions of addicted smartphone users around the world, including President Barack Obama. Founded in 1984, and initially funded with a $5-million investment from the venture capital market, RIM (now called BlackBerry) pioneered two-way paging and dominated the space against older and more established rivals like Motorola.

The company was led, more or less from the beginning, by two entrepreneurial co-leaders, Mike Lazaridis and Jim Balsillie. They were seen as geniuses of the highest order, and they were the darlings of the technology world.

The company grew well under their tutelage, with annual sales growing by double digits from $294 million in 1992 to almost $20 billion in 2011. Net income also soared to $3.4 billion in 2011, along with the egos of the two leaders and most other RIM executives, who maintained an air of arrogance and superiority in the face of competitors such as Apple and Samsung. While well-informed outsiders questioned the ability of the company to continue

(continued)

287

the serial invention needed to stay healthy in the technology sector, the company plowed ahead without regard for the product features and benefits the market was demanding.

As recently as 2008, RIM was chosen as one of Canada's Top 100 Employers, and yet, only a mere four years later, the founders and co-CEOs stepped down in disgrace after they had to acknowledge they had lost their way, or at least their magic fairy dust. So, without a qualified Canadian successor to take the helm, the new CEO, Thorsten Heins from Germany, was given the dubious pleasure of getting the company back on track. His immediate answer was to cut heads, and 2,000 RIM employees were shown the door.

RIM fell victim to poor executive decision making as the result of a combination of arrogance and an inwardly focused, compliant culture that simply refused to admit the fact the competition was introducing superior, more innovative and more attractive products, and it was about to devour their prominent market position. Time will tell whether the organization can be saved from itself or if it will become a footnote like Nortel. The key to its future success will be in improving contextual intelligence, focusing on all elements of the talent equation and, naturally, improving the leaders' decision-making ability.

Kinross Gold Corporation

Mining has long been considered one of the few industries in which Canada can be legitimately considered world-class. Within the mining sector, the gold mining companies are a very special elite and, within that segment, Kinross had been considered a promising rising star from the time it came under the leadership of Tye Burt in 2005. The problem is, by 2012, the company had gone from a virtually bankrupt bum to an international superstar and all the way back to bum again, in rather quick and startling fashion.

Burt would normally have been considered a true Canadian success story, except in the ruthless world of mining, which eventually saw him sent to the showers after several successful years of growth and building profitability. Burt dared to do a very un-Canadian thing: he risked thinking big. As a result, he took Kinross on a roller-coaster journey that ended up in Africa, with the $7.1-billion acquisition of Red Back Mining in 2010. The decision to go big or go home was not an easy one for the management team, the board of directors, the investors or the market. Burt fought long and hard to convince all of them that this was *the* game-changing deal, the one that would catapult Kinross into the same big league as Barrick and Goldcorp.

Unfortunately, things did not work out quite as Burt had hoped. Almost from the get-go, the promises and targets that had been made to help sell the Red Back Mining acquisition and the Tasiast mine development to shareholders began to be broken. The company could not seem to find a way to improve its credibility with stakeholders by improving its Say/Do ratio and showing its ability to execute on schedule without surprises. It did not take long before a scapegoat had to be found in order to help take the steam out of a severely disappointed set of stakeholders, and so the company let Burt go with a very generous severance bonus.

Kinross now has a great deal to do if it wants to recover its investment in Africa, but the final chapter is still far from written. It will take hard work, candour and much, much better decision making for the company to pull out of its nosedive and re-establish its credibility. The very simple lessons, which the current management team needs to be guided by, are the ones about the importance of humility over hyperbole and the need for leaders to keep their Say:Do ratio at 1:1.

Canadians should keep their eyes on Kinross to see if Paul Rollinson, the new CEO, can turn things around and salvage a win out of what looks like a potential disaster. If he can, we will all have reason to be proud of Canadian moxie and hard work. The key to success will be whether Rollinson and his team can

(continued)

289

establish credibility by delivering on their promises and expunging any remaining ego from their strategic thinking and planning.

Maple Leafs Sports and Entertainment

We have all been led to believe there is no more iconic national sports franchise in Canada, or in the world of hockey, than the Toronto Maple Leafs. While unbelievably successful at the box office (they are the only Canadian sports team worth over $1 billion according to *Forbes* magazine), they are also, as any Canadian knows only too well, a franchise that has not tasted champagne from the Stanley Cup since 1967, currently the longest drought in the NHL.

Currently owned by Maple Leafs Sports and Entertainment, which, in turn, is owned by the telecommunication and media giants BCE and Rogers, the Leafs have had many unusual owners since being formed in 1917. The current group of owners is, perhaps, the most promising, at least in terms of their collective business savvy, albeit not in the sports management business. In some ways, the entire business management reputation of Canada rests on the success of MLSE, and whether or not it can combine its media, entertainment and property interests into a winning formula that carries over to winning where it matters most to Canadians, on the ice. The Toronto Maple Leafs are almost the best example you can find in Canada of chronic bad decision making.

The various owners have, in turn, made a series of bad decisions on General Managers, who have then made bad decisions on coaches and, together, they have all made repeatedly bad decisions on players. It is a perfect case study on inept leadership and, until the Leafs manage to win the Stanley Cup, Toronto will have to bear the humiliation of not being good enough at our own national game. It is a fate we must avoid repeating in the real world of international business, where the jury votes much more quickly on failure and is far less patient and understanding than the long-suffering fans of the Maple Leafs. The key to their management success will very likely be measured in terms of how innovative they allow themselves to be and whether or not they can cast off complacency as the natural by-product of financial success in order to realize there is more to brand value than what the balance sheet or profit and loss statement shows at the end of the season.

99

Decisions, Decisions, Decisions

The answer to our national decision-making dilemma is certainly not convenient in terms of timing and urgency, nor will it be comfortable to execute. We need to change the way we think, and then change the way we decide.

If the desire is to generate new answers to new questions in order to create new solutions to new problems, then we need to understand what leads to the generation of new ideas. We need to place a torch under the part of the human spirit that produces inspiration and imagination. We need to improve our decisions through better originality and a clearer, sharper perspective. This can only be done through better insight, not just better information, and through better observation, not just better analysis.

STRAIGHT TALK NEXT STEPS: CRITICAL COMPETENCY

Decision-Making Intelligence (DMQ)

There is a pressing need to improve our individual and collective decision-making competence, and it can be the differentiating factor in separating the good from the great and Canada from the rest of the business world. We can become distinctive and differentiated around the world if we choose to apply our common sense and base our decisions on Canadian values, diversity and ingenuity.

The science of organizational decision making is about to take centre stage, and the early adopters will have first-mover advantage. We sit on the cusp of a new and exciting time, where the stakes have never been higher, the changes have never been more significant and the risks and opportunities have never been greater. To those who see it and feel it, it offers energy and excitement. To those who don't, it offers a one-way ticket down a very limited path to a dead end.

Here are some thoughts on how that fate can be avoided.

Step 1: Make the Decision to Improve

Like so many things in life, the first step is making a commitment to yourself to improve. In this case, the commitment has to be to acknowledging the likely existence of breakdowns in the current organizational decision-making process and doing something about them, in full knowledge it will not be an easy or quick fix.

The decisions we make going forward must be better than the ones we have made in the past. The only way to ensure the desired impact is to introduce a decision-review process that looks not only at the outcome of the decisions made, but also examines the full value chain, discovering ways to learn from experience and continuously improve.

Step 2: Identify the Gaps

It is highly likely the breakdowns will be occurring at more than one point along the value chain. It could be at any one of the most common congestion points evident in the framing stage, the divergent-thinking stage, the convergent stage or the post-mortem. You need to have the courage and tenacity to assess those gaps through a rigorous process of fact-based analysis.

Once you have identified the gaps and breakdowns in the process, you will then be able to project the benefits of going forward and in the process have a better chance of putting a hard number on the costs involved. It is equally important to identify

(continued)

293

the non-financial benefits, which will be related to improved knowledge sharing and cross-functional collaboration.

Step 3: Reprogram the DNA

Since all decisions are fuelled by human emotion, you cannot avoid the work that will have to go into changing the mindsets, attitudes and beliefs of those in the organization—at all levels. Changing the construct without changing the DNA will not produce the maximum benefit.

If the objective is to generate new answers, you need to establish a new set of references for how the organization thinks. If the desire is to move to true design thinking, defined by some as innovative thinking on steroids, then you will have to role model and stimulate originality of thought and promote lateral, rather than linear, thinking.

Final Thoughts

The role of the business leader comprises many different components, some big, some small, some strategic and some tactical, but they all have two things in common. They all require a problem to be solved and a decision to be made. If we had a way to post the goals-against statistic next to leaders' names at the end of every day, we might have a more objective way to establish who really does make better decisions.

Regrettably, things are just not that easy in business, so we will have to find a more creative mechanism to help us achieve the same objective. In the meantime, we can do a much better job of putting some disciplines in place to help ensure that the framing, the thinking, the scoping and the learning parts of the equation get the same time and attention as the executing part normally does.

In a world where the quality of the thinking—and the decisions that flow from it—may be even more important to creating value and attracting customers than the products we manufacture and the services we sell, Canada can put itself in a much stronger position. If we choose to organize it, and if we have the leaders willing to do it, we can tap into the talent of Canadian men and women from across the country and apply our full force and effect to building businesses that compete on the merits of our minds, rather than the sweat from our muscles.

PART XI

Straight Talk Conclusion

Canada needs a long-term strategic business plan, and it has to be nothing short of a radically transformational plan for Canada's future. The plan has to be built by a new generation of Canadian business leaders who are fully equipped and competent to take advantage of the opportunities that exist. While crafted by business, it must also include a new model for how to better address the social responsibility that business has to Canadians when it comes to health, education and employment.

The plan must be built by Canadians, for Canadians, and it cannot be a cheap imitation of what someone else has already built. It must be built in a way that speaks directly to who we are as a country and a people. It must accentuate our strengths, leverage our diversity and clearly differentiate us from the rest of the world. It must reinforce our national brand and allow us to use that brand to gain a disproportionate share of global business opportunities.

Canada has long been a leader in terms of tolerance in a world of discrimination; we have always been a civil nation in a world torn by conflict; we are an open-minded people in the midst of the small-minded, inwardly focused bias of some others, but Canada is far from perfect and far from reaching its potential. The question that should haunt all Canadians, and especially those business leaders and entrepreneurs who build our wealth and create our employment, is "What should the future look like for a big-hearted, geographically vast country that has become an increasingly marginalized economic force on the new world stage?"

Our traditional Canadian complacency is holding us back at the very time we should be pushing forward, driving to the net and playing our game the way it is meant to be played, with energy, grit and passion. We have had it so good for so long that we may have forgotten what we once knew about how to compete, let alone how to compete in a new game where the stakes are higher, the pace is faster and the rules have changed. Business leaders need to think about their role in the transformation of Canada and how best we can rebrand and reposition ourselves in order to remain relevant in the long term. Admittedly, it is a huge transformational challenge and many don't see the burning platform, but change is needed and we simply cannot leave it to our politicians. We must tackle this from deep in the hearts and minds of Canadian business leaders as though it is the seventh game of the Stanley Cup playoffs.

Canadians can "do" when we choose to, but today we are drifting, and while we are in better shape than most, it is still not good enough for a country deeply rooted in strong values, with a huge reservoir of goodwill around the world and a people who can collaborate and partner with anyone. We need to raise the bar on our aspirations and begin to transform from within, beginning with our mindsets, attitudes and beliefs about our future, the future of the global marketplace and the role of Canada.

100

Defining Canada's Future

Canada has been shaped by many forces over the long sweep of our history, but there are two forces in particular that have been extremely influential in defining our national character—our geography and our weather. Neither of these represents a choice we were free to make, but instead a deck of cards we were dealt and have had to master over time, learning as we went. This should put us in a much better position than most to meet the challenges of today as we can deploy the same ability to improvise that has allowed us to build this great land. However, the challenges of today are different. They are not about clearing land, planting fields and building towns. They are new challenges, the challenges of modernizing our economy in the face of hypercompetition, shifting even further away from a traditional natural resources base and into a strong, knowledge-based economy and creating the new jobs of the future that will offer future generations the career options they deserve and we are obliged to provide.

There is no one, from any part of this country, who does not marvel at the sheer beauty that geography has bestowed on Canada. Beauty as diverse as the majestic fjords of Newfoundland, the rugged terrain of the great Canadian Shield, the endless rolling prairies of Saskatchewan, all the way to the snow-capped mountains of Western Canada. The geography of our land has granted us a stunning platform on which to build a nation. This same geography has also required us, at each and every turn, to find creative ways to overcome the endless obstacles nature put in our way. In order to survive and build this country into something that works, we have had to twist and contort ourselves to accommodate the physical demands of our geography. We have been forced to continually improvise as we blast roads through the mountains, build bridges across the rivers, drill for oil deep in the frozen tundra and create ports to which our fishing boats can return with their catches.

The sheer geographic size of Canada has presented us with another set of formidable challenges. We have had to lay thousands of kilometres of railway track and asphalt to connect our coasts. In the process, we were forced to do the very hard, back-breaking, manual work necessary to find new ways to link every town and village across this country into one connected nation. Now we must rebuild our infrastructure once again, except this time it will be the technology-based infrastructure of the modern economy we must focus on. Even more importantly, it is the products, services and intellectual capital that flow from it that we must package in a uniquely Canadian way to export to the rest of the world.

The second defining feature that shapes us as a people is our weather. It has helped create that certain element of our national personality that requires all Canadians to accept change, whether they want to or not. The dramatically changing seasons we experience and the changing weather that goes along with them have forced a certain natural rhythm of change to life in Canada. We have adapted to the inevitability that we must adjust our habits and lifestyle, throughout the year, to whatever the weather puts in front of us.

The promise of spring brings with it the strange rituals and routine rites of seasonal passage. Who else but Canadians would be so anxious to see spring arrive that they shovel the remnants of snow from their lawns and garden beds to give the growing season a helpful head start? Who else but Canadians would drive to their cottages or cabins in mid-April to open them up to the fresh air and sunlight of an early spring morning when the temperature is still hovering just above zero? Who else but Canadians would be in such a hurry for the short summer to come that cafes and restaurants set up their outside patio tables as soon as the snow has gone so eager patrons can sit in their parkas and enjoy a latte or a beer?

It is a very good thing that Canadians are used to adapting to the changes in our environment since we are still in the early days of some rather significant changes in the global economy and in the world of business in general. These changes have not necessarily been of our choosing, in terms of either magnitude or timing, yet they will have an impact on us, whether we are prepared for them or not. The question is whether we approach them with the hope of a new spring or the dread of a long, cold winter.

*   *   *

Canada is simply not fully prepared to face the kind of challenges presented by the hypercompetitive business environment of the future. We are guilty of slowly allowing ourselves to be lured into a comfortable, even complacent frame of mind. We now have to wake up fast and face the harsh reality of a world racing past us at top speed, headed in a direction that we are just not familiar with, to a destination we have never been to before.

In order to join this international race for prosperity, we are going to have to take some difficult steps, which will be uncomfortable for many, unpalatable to some and non-negotiable for all. Canada can do what needs to be done. We have the essential character and toughness to compete with the best, but the game has changed so dramatically we are not necessarily attuned to the new rules or in shape to keep up with the tempo.

Canadian business leaders need to step up and play a huge role in guiding the transformation process. It must begin, as we have suggested earlier in this book, with a willingness to meet the four big leadership challenges we all face.

1. The challenge of making sense out of what is happening all around us and to our businesses, and the twin challenge of sense shaping, which involves taking that understanding and moulding it into a sensible, progressive business strategy for the future.
2. The challenge of providing clarity to the entire organization about what the business does, what it needs to do differently and why, and all the time building the leadership credibility necessary to create the willing followers that mark the sign of any successful leader.
3. The challenge of developing a deep understanding throughout the organization of what is needed to drive value creation going forward and then combining it with a shared perspective on the changing landscape and the opportunities it affords.

4. The challenge of creating the "winning conditions" necessary to embark upon a successful transformation effort in the first place.

There is no question the first couple of periods of the new global business game are going to be particularly tough. We are very likely going to take some bone-crushing hits from the more skilled players on the other teams. It is also very likely we will have to fight back from a deficit in the third period if we want to win, just as the brilliant, quintessential Canadian combination of Jarome Iginla with his roots in Nigeria and Sidney Crosby from Cole Harbour, Nova Scotia, showed us during the Olympic Winter Games in Vancouver. No matter what the odds and no matter how much work needs to be done, Canada still has to get out there and play the game, and when we do, we have to play it the very best we can.

We need to be intelligent when crafting Canada's transformational action plan and we must insist on building it with the benefit of the eight critical leadership intelligences we have highlighted in this book. They are:

Contextual Intelligence (CQ)—The ability to sense subtle shifts in the environment, to become aware of those changes before anyone else and to predict their likely implications going forward.

Strategic Intelligence (SQ)—A trio of abilities including deep insight into the issues, clear foresight as to how things will play out and an acutely sensitive peripheral vision.

Emotional Intelligence (EQ)—The ability to know yourself, manage yourself and build effective relationships with others.

Decision-making Intelligence (DMQ)—The ability to solve problems, resolve issues and come to conclusions that fully satisfy the various stakeholders.

Innovative Intelligence (INQ)—The ability to inspire, imagine and invent.

Ambiguity Intelligence (AQ)—The ability to live comfortably with uncertainty and not allow yourself to become physically frozen or mentally incapacitated with not knowing.

Talent Intelligence (TQ)—The ability to spot, develop and release the talent that resides within each person, according to their own desires and capabilities.

Collaborative Intelligence (COQ)—The ability to connect with others and work comfortably within formal and informal networks and groups of people.

The transformational plan must accentuate our strengths, leverage our diversity and clearly differentiate us from the rest of the world. It must reinforce our national brand, and allow us to use that brand to gain a disproportionate share of global business opportunities.

STRAIGHT TALK NEXT STEPS

A Framework for Canada's Transformational Action Plan

There will be some who say the crafting of a transformational plan for business will never work and is an impossible task with little chance of success. Others will say it is the role of government. Some will simply not be able to get their heads around the merits, benefits or need for such an ambitious undertaking, and there will be some who say it is nothing more than a retrogressive step backward to the planned economies and socialist central planning of the post-WWII Eastern European countries or the few socialist countries that remain.

The fact is, the CAVE people, the "citizens against virtually everything," need to understand we have no other choice. Canada needs to begin making some new and different choices, and those choices will determine our fate and shape our future. We are not powerless pawns in a game of international high finance and political intrigue. We are Canadians with hard-won rights, free choice and the free will to do what we believe is right and in our own best interests.

Those interests are best served by taking a proactive interest in shaping the future and making sure Canada counts when it comes to building the global world we will be living in and which will be built regardless of whether we are at the table.

(continued)

Canadians have never shied away from doing the hard work necessary to preserve the world we live in and make it a better place. Canada matters in the world and Canada can make a difference, but Canada needs a transformational plan to ensure the future is even better than the past.

Step 1: Raise the Awareness Level

Canadians must fully understand what is at stake and how the business environment and the economic and political geography of the new world order have changed. We must tap into Canadian hearts and minds to help build the resolve and passion necessary for us to "go to market" with a plan to make Canada more competitive in the world.

Step 2: Build the Guiding Coalition

Canada is full of talented people with diverse backgrounds, ideas and experiences. We must find a way to bring our best minds together and then ask our best leaders to assume direct responsibility for shaping the future. Business leaders will have to take a more active role in running for government and working full time in the interests of Canada Inc.

Step 3: Look at the Future through Fresh Eyes

Canadian business leaders must take a true, active and committed leadership role in helping the country learn how to "think in the future tense." We must find a wide variety of ways to engage Canadians in the collaborative process of reimagining what the future will look like, and then figuring out what that means.

Step 4: Commit to Bold Leadership

The leaders of the future will have to be cut from a new and very different piece of cloth. The next generation will have to have the leadership competencies and capabilities suited for the times in which they will be asked to lead. We will need to build those competencies on the fly while we are playing the game, as we have no time to pause, train and equip those leaders before we begin.

Step 5: Engage the Canadian People

Canada will need to put as many shoulders to the flywheel as we can possibly find. While we are not totally and hopelessly stuck in a snow-filled ditch, we have gone off the road and stalled. We will need Canadians to help push us ahead until we regain our momentum, gain confidence and get back onto the road to the future.

Step 6: Make Brave Choices

The principal competency and master skill of any great leader is the ability to choose a course, decide what needs to be done and then rally others to help execute the choice, no matter what it takes. Canada's transformational leaders of the future are going to have to make a series of brave choices, including some of the following:

1. Which new industries of the future are we going to choose to specialize in and resolve to commit our resources to, in order to become the world leader?
2. Which specific global markets are we going to attack with full force and effect and which are the ones where we can have the biggest impact and the most success?
3. How are we going to create better, more collaborative partnerships across borders, industries and into the academic world to help us build the bench strength and talent we will need for the future?
4. How are businesses going to fill the social program vacuum that has been created by the reduction of government contribution to so many of the basic services required to glue a diverse society together?

(continued)

5. What role will Canada play on the global stage when it comes to human rights, the environment and the aid necessary to help emerging countries and their people participate in the world with dignity, freedom and opportunity?

6. What role will Canada play on the diplomatic front, allowing the Canada brand to be used as it once was, for the building of bridges between nations and the maintaining of peace and prosperity around the world?

Final Thoughts

Canada has had more than a fair share of good fortune bestowed upon it, and it provides us with some natural advantages. We have a national character that has been shaped by our geography and our weather, which should make us more open to challenges and changes than most others. We have a track record of honour, peace and good relations with nations all over the world, who see us as fair, balanced and reasonable people. We have had generations of immigrants and second-generation Canadians who have taken risks, opened businesses and been allowed to succeed on the basis of their hard work and commitment to our communities.

These are strengths that Canada can certainly build on, but they will not matter if we fail in rising to the challenge at hand and don't have the courage, the resolve and the intelligence to carve a new path, in a new world, with new ideas and a new set of national priorities.

Canada "can," if we put our minds to it.

"We are still a young country, very much in our formative stages. Our national condition is still flexible enough that we can make almost anything we wish of our nation. No other country is in a better position than Canada to go ahead with the evolution of a national purpose devoted to all that is good and noble and excellent in human spirit."
—Prime Minister Lester B. Pearson, 1967

ACKNOWLEDGEMENTS

This book would not have been possible were it not for the wonderful, educational and transformational experiences I was fortunate to be able to share with my clients, who allowed me to be part of their organizations as they went through transformations of their own.

The great leaders I have been privileged to meet and work with for over 30 years in business are too many to list. However, each one has left an indelible impression on me and has somehow contributed to the thoughts shared with the readers of this book. Having said that, the specific opinions expressed are my own, and in no way do they suggest the support of others. This book has been a labour of love, and I alone accept responsibility for its content.

I must also acknowledge the support of my colleagues at The Beacon Group, as well as my family, who provided the necessary support, free time and space to complete this project. They all reinforced my passion to serve Canada in any way I could and encouraged me to make sure the random collection of thoughts and opinions that consumed our many conversations and debates were packaged so that others could assess their value.

Finally, I would like to thank Canada for providing me with the opportunity to raise a family of six children and four grandchildren in a free and open society that, despite its challenges and imperfections, still offers the world so much promise.

ABOUT THE AUTHOR

Doug Williamson (Toronto, Ontario) is Chief Executive Officer of The Beacon Group, a leadership and strategy development firm whose clients range from global Fortune 500 companies to smaller, more entrepreneurial businesses. Clients past and present include the likes of Mercedes-Benz and Sony, several large Canadian banks and insurance companies, as well as a number of other Canadian enterprises, including Export Development Corporation, *The Globe and Mail*, Martinrea International and Gamma-Dynacare Medical Laboratories. Over his varied international business career, Doug has lived and worked not only in Canada, the United States and the United Kingdom but has also supported clients in Mexico, Saudi Arabia, the Nordic countries and Australia. Prior to founding The Beacon Group, he held senior executive-level positions with the Royal Bank and with the Canadian government. Doug regularly speaks, teaches and writes about the importance of leadership, strategy and talent management.

BIBLIOGRAPHY

Introduction

Covey, Stephen R., et al. *The Nature of Leadership*. Plymouth: Franklin Covey, 1998.

Hamel, Gary and C.K. Prahalad. *Competing for the Future*. Boston: Harvard Business Press, 1996.

International Living. "2011 Quality of Life Index." 2011. <http://www1.internationalliving.com/qofl2011 >

Market Watch. "The 10 Best-Educated Countries in the World." September 12, 2012. <http://articles.marketwatch.com/2012-09-21/finance/33997818_1_higher-education-unemployment-rates-college-degree >

Reputation Institute. "Country RepTrak." 2012. <http://www.reputationinstitute.com/thought-leadership/country-reptrak >

The Central Intelligence Agency. "The World Factbook: Country Comparison, GDP—Real Growth Rate." 2013. <https://www.cia.gov/library/publications/the-world-factbook/rankorder/2003rank.html >

The Legatum Institute. "The 2012 Legatum Prosperity Index Rankings." 2012. <http://www.prosperity.com/Ranking.aspx >

The World Bank Group. "Doing Business: Economy Rankings." 2013. <http://www.doingbusiness.org/rankings >

Part I

Altman, Roger C. "The Great Crash, 2008." *Foreign Affairs*. January/February 2009. <http://www.foreignaffairs.com/articles/63714/roger-c-altman/the-great-crash-2008 >

Bloomberg. "Wall Street Firms Cut 34,000 Jobs, Most Since 2001 Dot-Com Bust." March 24, 2008. <http://www.bloomberg.com/apps/news?pid=newsarchive&sid=aTARUhP3w5xE&refer=home >

Browning, E.S. "Exorcising Ghosts of Octobers Past." *Wall Street Journal*. October 15, 2007. <http://online.wsj.com/article/SB119239926667758592.html?mod=mkts_main_news_hs_h >

Clark, Andrew. "Canwest Global Communications Files for Bankruptcy Protetction." *Guardian.* October 6, 2009. <http://www.guardian .co.uk/media/2009/oct/06/television-pressandpublishing >

"Dow Jones Industrial Average Historical Data." 2012. <http://www .davemanuel.com/dow-jones-historical-data.php >

Fasken Martineau. "Brookfield Consortium acquires O&Y Properties and O&Y REIT for $2.1 Billion." October 2005. <http://www .fasken.com/experience/detail.aspx?experience=1474 >

Economist. "CSI: Credit Crunch." October 18, 2007. <http://www. economist.com/node/9972489?story_id=9972489 >

———. "A Helping Hand to Homeowners." October 23, 2008. <http://www.economist.com/node/12470547?story_id=12470547 >

Gaither, Chris and Dawn C. Chmielewski. "Fears of Dot-Com Crash, Version 2.0." *Los Angeles Times.* July 16, 2006. <http://articles .latimes.com/2006/jul/16/business/fi-overheat16 >

Gibbon, John Murray. *Canadian Mosaic: The Making of a Northern Nation.* Toronto: McClelland & Stewart, 1938.

Joint Center for Housing Studies of Harvard University. "The State of the Nation's Housing." 2008. <http://www.jchs.harvard.edu/sites/ jchs.harvard.edu/files/son2008.pdf >

Mortgage Bankers Association. "Delinquencies Continue to Climb in Latest MBA National Delinquency Survey." November 19, 2009. <http://www.mbaa.org/NewsandMedia/PressCenter/71112.htm >

RealtyTrac. "US Foreclosure Activity Increases 75 Percent in 2007." January 30, 2008. <http://www.realtytrac.com/content/press-releases/us-foreclosure-activity-increases-75-percent-in-2007-3604?accnt=64847 >

———. "Foreclosure Activity Increases to 81 Percent in 2008." January 15, 2009. <http://www.realtytrac.com/content/press-releases/ foreclosure-activity-increases-81-percent-in-2008-4551?accnt=64847 >

Ridderstrale, Jonas and Kjell Nordstrom. *Karaoke Capitalism: Daring to be Different in a Copycat World.* Stockholm: BookHouse Publishing, 2005.

———. *Funky Business Forever: How to Enjoy Capitalism.* Stockholm: BookHouse Publishing, 2008.

Ridderstrale, Jonas and Mark Wilcox. *Re-Energizing the Corporation: How Leaders Make Change Happen.* Sussex: John Wiley & Sons Ltd, 2008.

Romer, Paul M. and Charles I. Jones. "The New Kaldor Facts: Ideas, Institutions, Population, and Human Capital." *American Economic Journal: Macroeconomics* 2.1 (2010), pp. 224–245.

Schumpeter, Joseph A. *Capitalism, Socialism, and Democracy*, 2nd Edition. Eastford: Martino Publishing, 2010.

Part II

Csikszentmihalyi, Mihaly. *Flow: The Psychology of Optimal Experience*. New York: Harper & Row, 1990.

Day, George S. and Paul J.H. Schoemaker. *Peripheral Vision: Detecting the Weak Signals That Will Make or Break Your Company*. Boston: Harvard Business School Publishing, 2006.

Hansen, Morten. *Collaboration: How Leaders Avoid the Traps, Build Common Ground, and Reap Big Results*. Boston: Harvard Business School Publishing, 2009.

Hayward, Steven F. *Churchill on Leadership: Executive Success in the Face of Adversity*. New York: Gramercy Books, 1997.

Jennings, Jason and Laurence Haughton. *It's Not the Big That Eat the Small . . . It's the Fast That Eat the Slow: How to Use Speed as a Competitive Tool in Business*. New York: HarperCollins, 2002.

Kellerman, Barbara. *Followership: How Leaders are Creating Change and Changing Leaders*. Boston: Harvard Business School Publishing, 2008.

McFarland, Janet. "New Board 'Is an Improvement by a Mile.'" *Globe Advisor*. January 12, 2005. <https://secure.globeadvisor.com/servlet/ArticleNews/story/gam/20050112/RNORTBOARD12 >

Michaels, Ed, et al. *The War for Talent*. Boston: Harvard Business School Publishing, 2001.

Part III

Bary, Andrew. "World's Best CEOs." *Barron's*. March 26, 2012. <http://online.barrons.com/article/SB50001424053111904797004577283662192414888.html >

Das, Anupreeta and Dan Fitzpatrick. "PNC Seals Deal with RBC." *Wall Street Journal.* June 20, 2011. <http://online.wsj.com/article/ SB10001424052702304887904576396063732453334.html >

Denning, Peter J. and Robert Dunham. *The Innovator's Way: Essential Practices for Successful Innovation.* Boston: Massachusetts Institute of Technology Press, 2010.

Grove, Andrew S. *Only the Paranoid Survive: How to Exploit the Crisis Points that Challenge Every Company.* New York: Random House Inc, 1996.

Leonard, Dorothy and Walter C. Swap. *Deep Smarts: How to Cultivate and Transfer Enduring Business Wisdom.* Boston: Harvard Business School Publishing, 2005.

Part IV

Aon Hewitt. "Aon Hewitt's 2012 List of the Best Employers in Canada." <https://ceplb03.hewitt.com/bestemployers/canada/ pages/currentlist2012.htm >

Canadian News Wire. "WestJet flight attendants named best in Canada." March 5, 2011. <http://www.newswire.ca/en/story/741247/westjet- flight-attendants-named-best-in-canada >

Godin, Seth. *The Dip: A Little Book that Teaches You When to Quit (and When to Stick).* New York: Penguin Group, 2007.

J.D. Power and Associates. "Inaugural Cross-Industry Report Identifies Best Practices in Customer Service Across More than 20 Industries." February 17, 2011. <http://businesscenter.jdpower .com/news/pressrelease.aspx?id=2011017 >

Kleiner, Art. *Who Really Matters: The Core Group Theory of Power, Privilege, and Success.* New York: Random House Inc, 2003.

Kotter, John P. and James L. Heskett. *Corporate Culture and Performance.* New York: Simon & Schuster Inc, 1992.

Magna International. "2011 Annual Report." <http://www.magna .com/docs/quarterly-reports/2011-annual-report.pdf?sfvrsn=2 >

Tuckman, Bruce. "Developmental Sequence in Small Groups." *Psychological Bulletin* 63.6 (1965), pp. 384–399.

Waterstone Human Capital. "Canada's 10 Most Admired Corporate Cultures, 2005–2011." <http://www.waterstonehc.com/cmac/about-canadas-10/10-most-admired-corporate-cultures-2005-2011 >

WestJet. "Expanding our Reach: WestJet Annual Report 2011." <http://www.westjet.com/guest/en//media-investors/2011-annual-report/WestJet-Annual-Report-2011.pdf >

Part V

Ashkenas, Ron. *Simply Effective: How to Cut Through Complexity in Your Organization and Get Things Done*. Boston: Harvard Business School Publishing, 2010.

D'Aveni, Richard. *Hypercompetition*. New York: Simon & Schuster, 1994.

Day, George S. and Paul J.H. Schoemaker. *Peripheral Vision: Detecting the Weak Signals That Will Make or Break Your Company*. Boston: Harvard Business School Publishing, 2006.

Fast Company. "The 100 Most Creative People in Business 2010." <http://www.fastcompany.com/most-creative-people/2010 >

Forbes. "Chip Wilson." March 2013. <http://www.forbes.com/profile/chip-wilson/ >

Goldsmith, Marshall and Mark Reiter. *What Got You Here Won't Get You There: How Successful People Become Even More Successful*. London: Profile Books Ltd, 2008.

Leung, Rebecca. "Jack Welch: 'I Fell in Love.'" *CBS News*. February 11, 2009. <http://www.cbsnews.com/stories/2005/03/24/60ii/main-682830.shtml >

Olson, Matthew S. and Derek van Bever. *Stall Points: Most Companies Stop Growing—Yours Doesn't Have To*. New Haven: Yale University Press, 2008.

Taylor, Timothy. "CEO of the Year: Christine Day of Lululemon." *Report on Business Magazine*. November 24, 2011. <http://www.theglobeandmail.com/report-on-business/rob-magazine/ceo-of-the-year-christine-day-of-lululemon/article4252293/ >

Welch, Jack and John A. Byrne. *Jack: Straight from the Gut*. New York: Warner Books Inc, 2001.

Yamashita, Keith. *Unstuck: A Tool for Yourself, Your Team, and Your World*. New York: Penguin Group Inc, 2004.

Zook, Chris and James Allen. *Repeatability: Build Enduring Businesses for a World of Constant Change*. Boston: Harvard Business School Publishing, 2012.

Part VI

Canada's Top 40 Under 40. "Canada's Top 40 Under 40: Recipients 2008." <http://www.top40award-canada.org/2008RecipientsList.pdf >

Constantine, Greg. "Tapping into Generation Y." *FirstData*. April 2010. <http://www.firstdata.com/downloads/thought-leadership/geny_wp.pdf >

Coupland, Douglas. *Generation X: Tales for an Accelerated Culture*. New York: St. Martin's Press, 1991.

Florida, Richard. *The Rise of the Creative Class: And How It's Transforming Work, Leisure, Community and Everyday Life*. New York: Perseus Books Group, 2002.

Goleman, Daniel. *Emotional Intelligence: Why It Can Matter More than IQ*. New York: Bantam Books, 1994.

Howe, Neil and William Strauss. *Generations: The History of America's Future, 1584 to 2069*. New York: William Morrow and Company, 1991.

———. *The Fourth Turning: An American Prophecy*. New York: Broadway Books, 1997.

———. *Millennials Rising: The Next Great Generation*. New York: Random House Inc, 2000.

Human Resources and Skills Development Canada. "Family Life–Young Adults Living with their Parent(s)." April 15, 2013. <http://www4.hrsdc.gc.ca/.3ndic.1t.4r@-eng.jsp?iid=77 >

Michaels, Ed, et al. *The War for Talent*. Boston: Harvard Business School Publishing, 2001.

Mintzberg, Henry. *Managers not MBAs: A Hard Look at the Soft Practice of Managing and Management Development*. San Francisco: Berrett-Koehler Publishers Inc, 2004.

Pine, B. Joseph II and James H. Gilmore. *The Experience Economy: Work Is Theater & Every Business a Stage.* Boston: Harvard Business School Press, 1999.

Pink, Daniel H. *Free Agent Nation: The Future of Working for Yourself.* New York: Warner Books Inc, 2001.

Part VII

Canada's Top 100. "Canada's Top Employers for Young People." <http://www.canadastop100.com/young_people >

Ivey Business School. "Rick George Named Ivey Business Leader of the Year." January 10, 2012. <http://www.ivey.uwo.ca/alumni/stay-connected/awards-and-recognition/business-leader-award.htm >

Lewis, Michael. *Moneyball: The Art of Winning an Unfair Game.* New York: W.W. Norton & Company, 2003.

Mintzberg, Henry. *Managers not MBAs: A Hard Look at the Soft Practice of Managing and Management Development.* San Francisco: Berrett-Koehler Publishers Inc, 2004.

Rumelt, Richard. *Good Strategy Bad Strategy: The Difference and Why It Matters.* New York: Random House Inc, 2011.

Waldie, Paul. "A Record Haul, a Nation's Triumph." *The Globe and Mail.* February 28, 2010. <http://www.theglobeandmail.com/news/national/a-record-haul-a-nations-triumph/article4308333 >

Wiseman, Liz and Greg McKeown. *Multipliers: How the Best Leaders Make Everyone Smarter.* New York: HarperCollins, 2010.

Part VIII

Collins, Jim. *Good to Great: Why Some Companies Make the Leap . . . and Others Don't.* New York: HarperCollins, 2001.

Financial Post. "Four Seasons sold to Bill Gates, Prince Alwaleed Bin Talal." <http://www.financialpost.com/story.html?id=f2b5a69c-cf08-45e8-a402-9e01f26af301&k=714 >

Lencioni, Patrick M. *Overcoming the Five Dysfunctions of a Team: A Field Guide for Leaders, Managers, and Facilitators.* San Francisco: Jossey-Bass, 2005.

Part IX

Barlow, Maude and Bruce Campbell. *Take Back the Nation*. Toronto: Key Porter Books Limited, 1991.

Burton, Robert. *On Being Certain: Believing You Are Right Even When You're Not*. New York: St. Martin's Press, 2008.

Csikszentmihalyi, Mihaly. *Flow: The Psychology of Optimal Experience*. New York: Harper & Row, 1990.

Dweck, Carol. *Mindset: The New Psychology of Success*. New York: Random House, 2006.

Elkington, John and Pamela Hartigan. *The Power of Unreasonable People: How Social Entrepreneurs Create Markets That Change the World*. Boston: Harvard Business School Publishing, 2008.

Festinger, Leon. *A Theory of Cognitive Dissonance*. Stanford: Stanford University Press, 1985.

Gardner, Howard. *Frames of Mind: The Theory of Multiple Intelligences*. New York: Perseus Books Group, 1993.

Govindarajan, Vijay and Chris Trimble. *The Other Side of Innovation: Solving the Execution Challenge*. Boston: Harvard Business School Publishing, 2010.

Heifetz, Ronald A., et al. *The Practice of Adaptive Leadership: Tools and Tactics for Changing Your Organization and the World*. Boston: Harvard Business School Publishing, 2009.

Hurtig, Mel. *The Betrayal of Canada*. Toronto: Stoddart Publishing Co., 1991.

Kahneman, Daniel and Amos Tversky. *Choices, Values, and Frames*. Cambridge: Cambridge University Press, 2000.

Kohlrieser, George. *Hostage at the Table: How Leaders Can Overcome Conflict, Influence Others, and Raise Performance*. San Francisco: Jossey-Bass, 2006.

Martin, Roger L. *The Opposable Mind: The Successful Leaders Win Through Integrative Thinking*. Boston: Harvard Business School Publishing, 2007.

Motorola University. "About Motorola University: The Inventors of Six Sigma." <http://web.archive.org/web/20051106025733/http://www.motorola.com/content/0,,3079,00.html >

Pink, Daniel H. *A Whole New Mind: Why Right-Brainers Will Rule the Future*. Toronto: Penguin Group, 2005.

Senge, Peter M. *The Fifth Discipline: The Art & Practice of the Learning Organization*. New York: Random House, 1990.

Shaw, George Bernard. *Man and Superman*. New York: Penguin Classics, 1946.

Simon, Hermann. *Hidden Champions of the Twenty-First Century: The Success Strategies of Unknown World Market Leaders*. New York: Springer Science+Business Media, 2009.

Part X

Canada's Top 100. "Canada's Top 100 Employers–2008." <http://www.canadastop100.com/national >

Cantech Letter. "My 1996 Investment in RIM; Adam Adamou remembers." March 29, 2010. <http://www.cantechletter.com/2010/03/my-1996-investment-in-rim-adam-adamou-remembers >

Greenspan, Stephen. *Annals of Gullibility: Why We Get Dumped and How to Avoid It*. Westport: Greenport Publishing Group, 2009.

Industry Canada. "Key Small Business Statistics–July 2012." August 3, 2012. <http://www.ic.gc.ca/eic/site/061.nsf/eng/02715.html >

Jordan, Pav. "Kinross takes $3.2 billion hit on African mines." *The Globe and Mail*. February 13, 2013. <http://www.theglobeandmail.com/globe-investor/kinross-takes-32-billion-hit-on-african-mines/article8645610 >

Lu, Vanessa. "RIM layoffs blamed on failure to innovate." *Toronto Star*. July 28, 2011. <http://www.thestar.com/business/2011/07/28/rim_layoffs_blamed_on_failure_to_innovate.html >

Motiwala, Adib. "Research in Motion: On its Deathbed?" *Gurufocus*. May 23, 2011. <http://www.gurufocus.com/news/134176/research-in-motion-on-its-deathbed >

Ozanian, Mike. "NHL Team Values 2012: Toronto Maple Leafs Are First Hockey Team Worth $1 Billion." *Forbes*. November 28, 2012. <http://www.forbes.com/sites/mikeozanian/2012/11/28/nhl-team-values-2012-maple-leafs-first-hockey-team-worth-1-billion >

Russo, J. Edward and Paul J.H. Schoemaker. *Winning Decisions: Getting It Right the First Time*. New York: Random House, 2002.

Thiederman, Sondra. *Making Diversity Work: 7 Steps for Defeating Bias in the Workplace*. New York: Kaplan Publishing, 2008.

FURTHER SUBJECT MATTER EXPERTS

Part I

Roger Martin serves on the boards of Thompson Reuters and BlackBerry. He is also a regular columnist for *Business Week*, the *Washington Post*'s "On Leadership" blog and the *Financial Times*' "Judgment Call" column. Martin has written four books: *The Responsibility Virus*, *The Opposable Mind*, *The Design of Business* and *Fixing the Game*.

Henry Mintzberg earned both his Master's degree and his PhD from the MIT Sloan School of Management. Professor Mintzberg has written 15 books, most notably *The Rise and Fall of Strategic Planning*; *Strategy Safari*; *Managers, Not MBAs*; and *Managing*.

Part II

George Day is a Professor of Marketing and a Co-Director of the Mack Center for Technological Innovation at the Wharton School of the University of Pennsylvania. A Canadian, he received his undergraduate degree from the University of British Columbia, his MBA from the University of Western Ontario and his PhD from Columbia University. He has authored 15 books on marketing and strategic management, including *Market Driven Strategy*, *The Market Driven Organization* and *Peripheral Vision*, which was co-authored by Paul Schoemaker.

Daniel Kahneman is Professor (emeritus) of Psychology and Public Affairs at Princeton's Woodrow Wilson School and, prior to that, was a professor at the University of California, the University of British Columbia and the Hebrew University of Jerusalem. He was awarded the Nobel Prize in Economics in 2002 for his work on prospect theory and has published many books, including *Prospect Theory*, *Judgment under*

Uncertainty; Choices, Values and Frames; and *Thinking, Fast and Slow.* Many of his books were co-written with Amos Tversky, a former Professor of Cognitive and Mathematical Psychology at Stanford University.

Daniel Ariely has been a Professor of Psychology and Behavioural Economics at Duke University since 2008. He received his MA and PhD in cognitive psychology from the University of North Carolina, as well as a second doctorate in business administration from Duke. He was a professor at MIT Sloan between 1998 and 2008 and has published three books: *Predictably Irrational, The Upside of Irrationality* and *The Honest Truth about Dishonesty.*

Roger Martin has written several books on the subject of thinking, including *The Opposable Mind*, while Tim Brown wrote a landmark book *Change by Design*, and has published other works in *Harvard Business Review, Fortune, Forbes* and *Business Week.*

Part III

Andy Grove, who was born in Budapest and would escape Communist-controlled Hungary at age 20, moved to the United States, ultimately earning his PhD from the University of California. Although not so well known today, he was named *Time* magazine's Man of the Year in 1997, and he has written or co-authored several other books, including *High Output Management, Strategy Is Destiny* and *Strategic Dynamics.*

Dorothy Leonard obtained her PhD from Stanford University and is the William J. Abernathy Professor of Business Administration at Harvard University. She joined Harvard in 1983 after teaching for three years at the Sloan School of Management at MIT. *Walter Swap* is Professor of Psychology and former Chairman of the Psychology Department at Tufts University. He also served as the Dean of the Colleges at Tufts for nine years.

Manfred Kets de Vries is currently Clinical Professor of Leadership Development at INSEAD, where he holds the Raoul de Vitry d'Avaucourt Chair of Leadership Development. He has a degree in

Economics from the University of Amsterdam, as well as an MBA and DBA from the Harvard Business School. Kets de Vries has also taught at both McGill University and the Harvard Business School. A voracious author, he has written more than 35 books, including *Organizations on the Couch*, *The Neurotic Organization*, *The Leadership Mystique* and *The Leader on the Couch*, as well as a trilogy encompassing his work on leadership: *Reflections on Character and Leadership*, *Reflections on Leadership and Career Development* and *Reflections on Groups and Organizations*. The *Financial Times* and the *Economist* have listed Kets de Vries as one of the world's top 50 leading management thinkers.

Part IV

John Kotter is a former professor at the Harvard Business School who received his undergraduate and Master's degrees from MIT and a DBA from Harvard. To date, he has written 18 books, most notably *Leading Change*, which is an international best-seller, but also *A Sense of Urgency*, *Our Iceberg Is Melting*, *The Heart of Change*, *Corporate Culture and Performance* and *A Force for Change*, amongst others. Total sales for his books exceed 2 million copies.

Seth Godin is an interesting and thought-provoking character, a truly transformational thinker. He graduated from Tufts University with a degree in Computer Science and Philosophy, and he earned his MBA from the Stanford Graduate School of Business. He launched his first company, Yoyodyne, in 1995 and sold it to Yahoo! in 1998, becoming its Vice President of Direct Marketing until 2000. In 2006, he launched another venture, Squidoo, which is a community website that allows users to create pages for various interests. It is one of the 500 most visited sites in the world.

Godin is a prolific author, having written 11 books, including *Free Prize Inside*, which was *Forbes* Business Book of the Year in 2004; *Purple Cow*; *The Dip*, which was a *Business Week* and *New York Times* best-seller; *Permission Marketing*; *Unleashing the Ideavirus*; *All Marketers are Liars*; and *Tribes*. His blog, *Seth's Blog*, is ranked number one in the *Ad Age* Power 150, which ranks the best marketing blogs.

Part V

Richard D'Aveni is Professor of Strategic Management at the Tuck School. He received his undergraduate degree from Cornell University and his PhD from Columbia University. He has written a number of books, including *Hypercompetition, Beating the Commodity Trap, Strategic Supremacy* and, most recently, *Strategic Capitalism.*

Part VI

Richard Florida is a professor and head of the Martin Prosperity Institute at the Rotman School of Management. Florida received his PhD from Columbia University and taught previously at George Mason University as well as Carnegie Mellon University's Heinz College. He has been a Senior Editor of the *Atlantic* since March 2011, and he has written several books, including *The Rise of the Creative Class, Cities and the Creative Class, The Flight of the Creative Class, Who's Your City* and, most recently, *The Great Reset.*

Several very good writers have contributed to our understanding of generations X and Y. **Jean Twenge** explains in her book *Generation Me* how they display high levels of narcissism and reject social conventions. **William A. Draves** and **Julie Coates**, authors of *Nine Shift: Work, Life, and Education in the 21st Century*, write about how the technological and economical implications of the World Wide Web have resulted in distinctly different behaviours, values and attitudes than seen in previous generations.

Joseph Pine is a noted author who has written several books on the subject of changes in economic behaviour, including *Infinite Possibility, Authenticity: What Consumers Really Want, Mass Customization* and *Markets of One.*

Daniel Goleman is an author, psychologist and journalist. He wrote for almost 12 years for the *New York Times*, specializing in psychology and brain science, after he received his PhD from Harvard University. Goleman co-founded the Collaborative for Academic, Social, and

Emotional Learning at the University of Illinois at Chicago while also co-directing the Consortium for Research on Emotional Intelligence in Organizations at Rutgers University.

Goleman's book *Emotional Intelligence* spent over a year and a half on the *New York Times* best-seller list. Since then, he has authored many other books, including *Working with Emotional Intelligence*, *Primal Leadership* and *Social Intelligence*.

Part IX

Professor Carol Dweck has been a Professor of Psychology at Stanford University since 2004, having taught previously at Columbia University, Harvard University and the University of Illinois. Dweck earned her PhD from Yale University and has written three very important books: *Self-Theories*, *Mindset: The New Psychology of Success* and, more recently, *Mindset: How You Can Fulfill Your Potential.*

Dr. Leon Festinger, who passed away in 1989, was a noted social psychologist who, over the course of his career, was a faculty member at the Massachusetts Institute of Technology, the University of Minnesota and Stanford University, amongst others. He wrote extensively about the theory of cognitive dissonance, social comparison theory and social network theory in his books, which included *Social Pressures in Informal Group*, *When Prophecy Fails* and *A Theory of Cognitive Dissonance.*

Dr. Edward M. Hallowell is a noted psychiatrist who specializes in Attention Deficit Disorder (ADD) and Attention Deficit Hyperactivity Disorder (ADHD). He is a graduate of Harvard University and Tulane University School of Medicine, and he was a member of the Harvard Medical School faculty from 1983 to 2004. He has written many books, most notably *Driven to Distraction* and *Delivered from Distraction*, both co-written with Dr. John Ratey.

Steve Johnson is an author and media theorist who has written eight books on the topics of science and technology, including *Everything Bad Is Good for You*, *Where Good Ideas Come From* and *Future Perfect: The Case for Progress in a Networked Age.*

Matt Ridley is a scientist, journalist, author and former Chairman of Northern Rock Bank in the United Kingdom. Ridley attended the University of Oxford, where he earned a DPhil degree. He worked as the science editor of the *Economist* from 1984 to 1987. He became their Washington correspondent from 1987 to 1989 and then their American editor from 1990 to 1992. He has written a number of books, including *The Origins of Virtue*, *The Agile Gene* and *The Rational Optimist*.

Angela Duckworth completed her undergraduate degree at Harvard, obtained her MSc at the University of Oxford and then earned a PhD in Psychology from the University of Pennsylvania.

John Elkington is the founder of several organizations focused on corporate responsibility and sustainable development, including Volans, SustainAbility, and Environmental Data Services. He has written or co-authored books on topics related to sustainability, including *The Shrinking Planet*, *The Green Consumer Guide*, *Cannibals with Forks* and *The Chrysalis Economy*.

Pamela Hartigan is a PhD in Human Developmental Psychology, and she is the founding Managing Director of the Schwab Foundation for Social Entrepreneurship. Prior to that, she was director of several different programs and departments in the World Health Organization. She co-authored *The Power of Unreasonable People* with John Elkington.

Howard Gardner is probably best known for his theory of multiple intelligences, outlined in his book *Frames of Mind*. A developmental psychologist and a Professor of Cognition and Education at the Harvard Graduate School of Education, he has published a number of other books, including *Multiple Intelligences: The Theory in Practice*, *Intelligence Reframed*, *Changing Minds* and *Five Minds for the Future*. He is currently the Senior Director of Harvard's Project Zero, whose mission is to understand and enhance learning, thinking and creativity. Gardner was awarded the prestigious Prince of Asturias Award in Social Sciences in 2011.

INDEX

Index

Duchesne, Rupert, 230–31
Duckworth, Angela, 253
Dunn, Frank, 56–57
Dweck, Carol S., 246, 249, 253, 266
Dylex, 203–4
dysfunctional pathologies, 109–100

Eaton's, 58–59, 131
echo boomers. *See* Gen Y
economic downturn(s), 13, 15
economic value creation equation, 26
economic value cycle, speed of, 250
efficiency, 242
effort, 13, 104, 138, 144, 236
ego, 21, 62, 109, 114, 227, 234–35, 249, 256, 289
Einstein, Albert, 249
electronic superhighways, 174
Elkington, John, 259, 260
emotional intelligence (EQ), 46–47, 175–78, 302
emotional tagging, 282
employee benefits programs, 177
Employee Charter (Magna), 115
employee engagement surveys, 227
employee engagement, 105, 135
employee satisfaction surveys, 227
employee satisfaction, 105, 117
employee value proposition (EVP), 167
employee-consumer relationship, 171
employees as entrepreneurs, 114, 116
employer-employee relationship, 155–56
employment agencies, 185
employment brand, 167
employment, alternate, 166, 167
energy, 24, 25, 26, 27, 64, 98, 111, 120, 127, 133, 139, 140, 148, 163
English Property Corporation, 21
entrepreneurship rankings, 4
entry-level jobs, 156, 157
environment, 204, 268, 306
Erickson, Arthur, 50
ethics, 34, 58, 204
euro-market phenomenon, 51

exaggeration, 227
excellence, 10, 11, 36, 52, 75, 89, 92, 101, 104, 123, 137, 176, 179, 199, 205, 208, 221, 228, 229
excuses,12, 148, 236, 237
execution, xiii, 11, 37, 142, 200, 216, 281
executive school, 57
expectations
    high, 24, 147, 154, 181, 235
    low, 92, 101
    misalignments of, 223
Experience Economy, The (Pine; Gilmore), 164
experience repertoire, 41, 63, 76, 81, 154, 251, 261–65, 282
experimentation, 264, 266
exploration mindset, 34–35, 75, 246–47
Export Development Canada (EDC), 202–4
expression, freedom of, 269
external market forces, 13
extrinsic motivation, 118

Facebook, 270
fact-based analysis, 293
factories, 164
fads, 102, 242
failed leadership, 20–21
failure, 9–10
    avoiding, 281
    definition of, 280
    negative consequences of, 280
fairness, 181
false claims, 144, 226
false confidence, 262
Fast Company magazine, 135
fear, 41, 62, 90, 120, 140, 142, 160, 176, 254
Federated Department Stores, 20
Festinger, Leon, 248
fiduciary responsibility, 200
fiefdoms, 237, 253 (*See also* silo mentality)
Fifth Discipline, The (Senge), 266
final services, 76, 77–78
financial services industry, 44, 55, 167–70
First Canada Place (Toronto), 20
fits and starts organization, 109–10

fixed mindset, 245, 246
Flare magazine, 135
flawed logic, 285, 286
flexibility 83, 87, 110, 166, 216
Florida, Richard, 153–54, 164
Flow (Csikszentmihalyi), 51, 262
focus, 133, 135, 139, 142, 143, 144–45, 148, 225–26
follower-leader relationship, 48
Followership (Kellerman), 48
Forbes, 136, 290
forced retirement, 280
foreclosures, 16
foreign capital, inflows of, 16
foresight, 42, 44, 51, 145, 190, 197, 204, 211, 252, 302
formalization, fallacy of, 74
forming, storming, norming, performing model, 90
Fortune magazine, 129
Four Seasons Hotels and Resorts, 231–32
Fourth Turning, The (Howe; Strauss), 161
Framework for Canada's Transformational Action Plan, 303–6
framing stage, 293
fraud, 57
free agent attitude, 189
Free Agent Nation (Pink), 154, 166
free markets, 18, 174
Frobisher, John, 34
Funky Business Forever (Nordstrom; Ridderstrale), 31
future mindset, 263–64, 269
future talent performance, 186, 187
future-focused intellectual inputs vs physical outputs, 253
Futurescapes, 83–84, 85–86

Gamma-Dynacare Medical Laboratories, 256–58
Gap Inc., 139
gaps, 98, 119–20, 133–35, 137, 145, 165, 206, 215, 216, 217, 222, 223, 225–26, 236, 241, 257, 274, 293–94
Gardner, Howard, 252, 263
Gates, Bill, 232
GDP rankings, 3

Index

Index

Index

Index